AFRICAN ISSUES

Undermining
Development

Sarah Michael

Research Associate
Global Equity Initiative
Harvard University

CW00969576

JAMES CURREY
Oxford

INDIANA UNIVERSITY PRESS
Bloomington & Indianapolis

James Currey
73 Botley Road
Oxford OX2 0BS

Indiana University Press
601 North Morton Street
Bloomington
Indiana 47404
(North America)

First published 2004

1 2 3 4 5 08 07 06 05 04

British Library Cataloguing in Publication Data
Michael, Sarah
Undermining development : the absence of power among local
NGOs in Africa. - (African issues)
1. Non-governmental organizations - Zimbabwe
2. Non-governmental organizations - Tanzania
3. Non-governmental organizations - Senegal 4. Sustainable
development - Zimbabwe 5. Sustainable development - Tanzania
6. Sustainable development - Senegal 7. Power (Social
sciences)
I. Title
338.9'6

ISBN 0-85255-439-7 (James Currey Paper)
ISBN 0-85255-438-9 (James Currey Cloth)

**Library of Congress Cataloging-in-Publication Data available
from the Library of Congress**

ISBN 0-253-21772-5 (Indiana Paper)

Typeset by
Long House Publishing Services, Cumbria, UK
in 9/11 Melior with Optima display
Printed and bound in Malaysia

DEDICATION

To my parents
Albert and Edna Michael

CONTENTS

ACKNOWLEDGEMENTS

This book was written over several years and continents and I would like to thank the many people who supported me throughout. I am particularly grateful to the following individuals and organisations.

Charles Elliott supervised the doctoral thesis on which this book is built and without him it would have never come to be. He was an incomparable mentor, guide and friend and I owe him a tremendous debt of gratitude.

Trinity College, Cambridge provided me with consistent and generous funding to undertake the research included in this book and I am particularly grateful to Dr Chris Morley for all of his assistance. I would also like to thank the Smuts Memorial Fund, Cambridge Commonwealth Trust and Faculty of Social and Political Sciences, University of Cambridge, for their financial support. Sam Hickey, David Brown, Deryke Belshawe and Amartya Sen provided beneficial feedback on various versions of this manuscript and I am grateful for their time and efforts. And my colleagues at The Global Equity Initiative, Harvard University provided valuable encouragement through the final stages of this process.

Across the countries in which I undertook field research for this book, NGO workers, government officials, donor representatives, academics and journalists generously sacrificed their time to talk with me. Their openness and honesty, and the trust they displayed in interviews have made this book a more complete and relevant piece of work. I would also specifically like to thank: Gus Le Breton and David Blair in Zimbabwe; Bill Mitchell and the staff and families of the Canadian High Commission, CIDA and the CIDA PSU, and Professor Suleiman Ngware in Tanzania; La famille Diouf and the staff at Africa Consultants International in Senegal and; Sevilla Leowinata and John Brown in Bangladesh.

On a personal note, Rebecca Beale, Genevieve Connors, Jennifer Davis, Greg Fried, Coulter George, Céline Hall, Lara Jamieson, Douglas McCabe, Eric Nelson, Navraj Pannu, Jim Roth, and Tracey Winton provided much-needed editing, conversation and dinners for which I thank them all. And long before I could have ever imagined writing this book, Robert Cluett helped to start me on the path towards it.

Most importantly, I would like to thank my family. My parents Albert and Edna first sparked my interest in Africa and, with Susie and Neal, have been unwavering in their support of this, and all my endeavours.

ABBREVIATIONS

ADAB	Association of Development Agencies in Bangladesh
AI	Appreciative Inquiry
AIDS	Acquired Immune Deficiency Syndrome
BAWATA	Baraza la Wanawake Tanzania (Tanzania National Women's Council)
BRAC	Bangladesh Rural Advancement Committee
CBO	Community Based Organisation
CCM	Chama cha Mapinduzi (Revolutionary Party – Tanzania)
CIDA	Canadian International Development Agency
CONGAD	Conseil des Organisations Non-Gouvernementales d'Appui au Développement (Council of Development NGOs – Senegal)
DANIDA	Danish International Development Agency
DESCO	Centro de Estudios y Promocion del Desarrollo (Peru)
DFID	Department for International Development (UK)
EU	European Union
FASE	Federaçao de Orgãoes para Assistência Social e Educacional (Brazil)
GADEC	Groupe d'Action pour la Défense de la Démocratie en Centrafrique (Action Group for the Defence of Democracy in Central Africa - Senegal)
GNP	Gross National Product
GTZ	Deutsche Gesellschaft für Technische Zusammenarbeit (German Agency for International Development Cooperation)
HIV	Human Immunodeficiency Virus
HIVOS	Humanist Institute for Co-operation with Developing Countries (The Netherlands)
IBASE	Instituto Brasileiro de Análises Sociais e Econômicas (Brazil)
IFI	International Financial Institution
INGO	International Non-Governmental Organisation
MDC	Movement for Democratic Change (Zimbabwe)
M&E	Monitoring and Evaluation

NANGO	National Association of Non-Governmental Organisations (Zimbabwe)
NCA	National Constitutional Assembly (Zimbabwe)
NGO	Non-Governmental Organisation
NGDO	Non-Governmental Development Organisation
NGOAB	NGO Affairs Bureau (Bangladesh)
NNGO	Northern Non-Governmental Organisation
NORAD	Norwegian Agency for Development Cooperation
NOVIB	De Nederlandse Organisatie voor Internationale Ontwikkelingssamenwerking (Dutch Organisation for International Development Cooperation)
ODA	Official Development Assistance
PVO	Private Voluntary Organisation
RED	Research and Education Division (BRAC)
SEWA	Self-Employed Women's Association (India)
SNGO	Southern Non-Governmental Organisation
TANGO	Tanzania Association of Non-Governmental Organisations
TANU	Tanganyika African Nationalist Union (Tanzania)
TGNP	Tanzania Gender Networking Programme
UNDP	United Nations Development Programme
USAID	United States Agency for International Development
WCED	World Commission on Environment and Development
WWF	Working Women's Forum (India)
ZANU-PF	Zimbabwe African National Union Patriotic Front
ZERO	Zimbabwe Environmental Research Organization
ZWRCN	Zimbabwe Women Resource Centre and Network

1

The Powerful & the Powerless

Understanding NGOs in Development

International aid would be more effective, equitable, just and credible if a relational power shift occurs. Relationships need to be more in favour of those frequently least able to negotiate from a position of adequate capacity and relative strength (Alan Fowler 2000a: 1).

Few people in the international development community would disagree with this statement. It points out what many of us have long known and accepted: that power structures within development are unequal; that it is most often individuals and organisations in the South which lack power; and that powerful Southern actors could benefit local develop-ment processes. This book explores one specific example of this phenomenon, exploring how the absence of power among local African NGOs – put simply, power as the ability of an NGO to set its own priorities, define its own agenda and exert influence over others to achieve its ends – has undermined development in sub-Saharan Africa. It moves beyond the common rhetoric in our field to demonstrate exactly how local NGOs have been denied power and exactly why more balanced power relations would benefit development in the South, and in Africa specifically. African NGOs offer unique benefits to local development. Their power is not only an end in itself, but also a means of improving the sustainability of development organisations, programmes and projects in their areas.

We know what a powerless local NGO looks like – one that cannot specialise in its priority areas of interest or expertise because of its dependence on overseas donors or government favour – but what does a powerful local NGO look like? For this, we must look at examples from the NGO sector in Asia and Latin America. Powerful local NGOs have become a well recognised element of local development in these regions, where they speak with authority on issues affecting the poor and marginalised, and are able to influence the highest levels of national and international policy making. The need, development and application of

1

power among these Southern NGOs, as well as the timeline and environmental factors with which it was achieved will provide a foundation for considering how African NGOs can achieve power.

Now is a particularly crucial time to consider the power and potential of African NGOs. The need for effective development actors on the continent has increased, rather than decreased, over recent decades, in the face of rising poverty, malgovernance, post-conflict reconstruction and the spread of HIV/AIDS. Of the 34 countries currently classified by the United Nations as having a low human development index (HDI), 30 are in sub-Saharan Africa (UNDP 2003). The world's highest rates of HIV/AIDS prevalence are in sub-Saharan Africa and over the last decade, the region has been the most affected by violent conflict. The urgency of the problems facing the continent demands urgent action, and local NGOs are an essential element of such action.

In addition, global issues, campaigns and financial flows of relevance to Africa, around which local NGOs can mobilise, develop a strong voice and profile, and gain power, are also emerging. These issues include human security and conflict resolution, fair trade and WTO negotiations, intellectual property, human rights and access to essential medicines, and global disease funds and HIV/AIDS. The Millennium Development Goals (MDGs) in particular, offer African NGOs a window of opportunity around which they can gain power. The MDGs are a set of eight fixed global goals on which the United Nations General Assembly committed to focus its development efforts in 2000 (United Nations General Assembly 2001). The MDGs include poverty, education, gender, health and environmental aims and are to be achieved by 2015. To accomplish the goals, a massive global effort, involving the mobilisation of vast numbers of actors and vast sums of money has been launched. All 189 UN member states have adopted the MDGs, as have donor governments and both bilateral and multilateral development agencies. This orientation of the international development community towards the goals has created a significant space for local NGOs. Achieving the MDGs will require meaningful involvement by African NGOs, which have a unique knowledge of local realities and can help to make these globally defined goals more relevant to improving the lives of families and communities at the grass-roots level.

This book pushes past traditional understandings of the weakness of local African NGOs to show why local African NGOs lack power, and how their development of power can make a significant contribution to development on the continent. It is divided into eight chapters. The first chapter introduces readers to NGO activity in sub-Saharan Africa and to the power structures that exist within African development. The second chapter develops a concept of power based on the experiences of several powerful local NGOs in South Asia and Latin America, and uses this to build a picture of what a powerful African NGO would look like. Chapters Three, Four and Five are case studies of over sixty local African

NGOs. In these chapters the power of NGOs in Zimbabwe, Tanzania and Senegal, respectively, is described and analysed. The sixth chapter examines why power matters to local NGOs, and how its absence has undermined development on the continent. Following on from this discussion, Chapter Seven develops the link between NGO power and NGO sustainability. And the final chapter outlines the range of strategies that local NGOs and interested development actors can pursue in order to help local African NGOs to gain power.

For too long, the international development community has accepted the reality of unequal power relationships between the North and the South. The current international development climate, in which urgent need in Africa is coupled with increased attention to development issues in the South, and in Africa in particular, finally makes the powerlessness of African NGOs a particularly relevant topic of conversation. There is no telling how long this climate will last, however, as geopolitical concerns change and new issues capture the global imagination. The time, then, is now to start talking about power among NGOs in Africa, and for African NGOs to capitalise on the seeds of power currently available for the taking.

Some important definitions and distinctions

The main unit of focus in this book is the non-governmental organisation, or NGO. While the meaning and use of the term NGO have been much debated, this book makes use of the most commonly accepted understanding of NGOs: as independent development actors existing apart from governments and corporations, operating on a non-profit or not-for-profit basis with an emphasis on voluntarism, and pursuing a mandate of providing development services, undertaking communal development work or advocating on development issues. This definition could be applied equally to the many community-based organisations, or CBOs, now active and essential in development, however. Indeed, one pressing definitional challenge in our field is to find an adequate way of distinguishing non-governmental organisations from community-based ones.

Most simply, CBOs are organisations that originate within a community to meet its specific needs. As compared to NGOs, they tend to remain focussed very locally and to operate with little formalised structure, using the time and resources of community members to undertake their activities. NGOs, on the other hand, are usually more structured organisations with their own staff and locale, a wider mandate covering a greater geographic area and a range of activities which does not necessarily directly benefit the staff or members of the NGO. NGOs also need to be registered with the relevant government authority in their country, which requires that they have certain organisational and financial controls, and abide by state regulations governing the administration of NGOs.[1] Community-based organisations rarely face any such official requirements.

NGOs can be classified in many ways. David Korten has classified NGOs based on the types of activities they undertake;[2] Frits Wils has devised criteria for classifying NGOs by their size;[3] still others have classified NGOs by their origins, sectoral focus or sources of funding. In this book, the most relevant distinction is between NGOs of different geographic origins: specifically, between NGOs from the North and NGOs from the South.

Throughout the last century, NGOs originating in the North have grown from a small number of post-war relief organisations to a major industry of large, multinational organisations with relief and development mandates both at home and abroad.[4] Many of these NGOs are operational, meaning that they run their own development projects in both their home countries and abroad. I will call these groups, originating in the North, but with international mandates throughout the South, international NGOs, or INGOS. NGOs originating in the North can also be strictly non-operational in the South, in which case they tend to concentrate on advocacy and lobbying activities in their home countries and on providing funding and expertise to NGOs in the South. I will call these NGOs, northern NGOs, or NNGOs. This distinction between operational INGOs and non-operational NNGOs will become increasingly important later in this book, when we consider how the presence and activity of many INGOs in Africa has prevented their NGO counterparts in the South from attaining power.

Until the 1980s, it was these types of foreign NGOs which were 'the most prominent non-governmental organizations operating in Africa, Asia, the Caribbean and Latin America' (Smillie 1995: 60). More recently, however, NGOs originating in Southern communities have become a prominent force in international development. In some developing countries, like India and Bangladesh, they now rival their INGO counterparts in terms of their size and impact. This book focuses on these NGOs originating in the South, or what I call local or indigenous NGOs.

[1] This definition is not without its problems. If a human rights NGO is deemed by its government to be 'interfering' in politics, and, as a result, denied official government registration, is it any less an NGO than one which has been registered? Nonetheless, I did use official registration as one of the minimum requirements for the inclusion of local NGOs in the sample I studied, as this hurdle represents the commitment of an NGO to honest financial management and to pursuing long-term goals. In the field-work countries, even those NGOs which had the most antagonistic of relationships with government had still been officially registered as NGOs or voluntary associations.
[2] See Korten's now classic generational groupings of NGOs, based on programming strategies (Korten 1987).
[3] See Wils' taxonomy of 'Big NGOs' (Wils 1995).
[4] Some of today's largest international NGOs began in this way: Save the Children UK was created in 1919 to provide relief to children in parts of Europe devastated after World War I; Oxfam in Great Britain and Care in the United States were started in 1942 and 1945, respectively, to provide food and other relief to post-World War II Europe.

Fowler (1988: 3) is very strict in his usage of the term indigenous NGO, using it to denote only those organisations 'which are derived from forms of social co-operation which are indigenous or traditional to the communities concerned'. I will be much less restrictive in my classification of indigenous NGOs, using the term for all NGOs that are founded by nationals of the state in question for the benefit of that state's development and which employ a majority of indigenous staff. For while a rural African NGO undertaking maternal and child health outreach services might model itself on a successful urban INGO, this does not reduce its potential to do valuable work, incorporate local labour and be responsive to local community concerns. This echoes Paul Wangoola's (1991) definition of an indigenous NGO as one borne out of local problems and using local skills and resources to solve them.

In considering questions of NGO power, the distinction between indigenous NGOs and international NGOs is an important one. Many INGOs are incredibly powerful organisations which set the tenor of international debates and whose influence is said to be so great that they 'are able to push around even the largest governments' (Mathews 1997: 53). International NGOs have been the catalysts for successful recent global campaigns on issues from international debt relief to access to essential medicines. As opposed to local NGOs, international NGOs tend to receive regular funding from their home offices in the North, have a higher level of human resources at their disposal and be less susceptible to the whims of the governments of the countries in which they work (Tandon 1991, Manji 1997). And while INGOs may lack power in their relationships with their own donors, the operating environment in which they work is considerably different from that of the majority of local NGOs (Lister 2000). These profound differences between NGOs from the North and the South make it impossible for one study to consider the power of both types of NGOs equally. Accordingly, this book will focus on the experience of indigenous NGOs.

While indigenous NGOs and the forms of organisation on which they are based have existed throughout the developing world since before colonialism, it was only in the 1970s that they experienced a global rise in prominence. At this time, the industrialisation strategies pursued by developing country governments as a means of economic growth showed few signs of success, and the expected 'trickle down' effects of this growth had made little impact in alleviating poverty. International approaches to development shifted in focus from economic to social development and placed increased importance on the participation of the poor in development initiatives. These trends opened the door for a global increase in the number and range of local NGOs active in the developing world.

Local NGO sectors in the South continued to expand in the 1980s, amidst the resurgence of free-market ideology among Western governments and the international financial institutions. Free-market thinking advocated a reduction in the role of the state and, as they had done in other sectors like energy and agriculture, donors sought a competitive, private-sector alternative to the state within development. NGOs provided just such an option and donors were quick to channel increasing amounts of development funding and attention to them (Anang 1994, Riddell and Robinson 1995, Therkildsen and Semboja 1995, Hulme and Edwards 1997).

The belief in the supremacy of democracy, central in the Cold War era, furthered donor support for NGOs in development. In pursuing their own individual goals, NGOs were seen to inject a pluralism into the political systems in which they worked and to contribute to the strengthening of civil society (Hearn 2000, Goldsmith 2001). Where Western donors were on poor terms with the national governments of developing countries, the presence of NGOs in the South had an additional advantage, as it allowed donors to contribute to development while bypassing hostile states (Charlton *et al.* 1994). NGOs were invaluable to donors in allowing them to further their altruistic and political aims throughout this era, and so benefited from increased financial support.

By the 1990s, international frustration over the corruption and weak capacity of many developing country governments provided a further impetus for donors to channel their aid monies through NGOs. As agents of development, NGOs, with their relative small size, flexibility and access to local expertise, came to be perceived as possessing a comparative advantage over inefficient and increasingly bureaucratic governments. This alleged comparative advantage of NGOs over governments in development went far beyond the financial; it was seen to include their ability to better reach the poor at the grass-roots level, to form close and lasting relationships with beneficiaries, to ensure meaningful participation by beneficiaries, and to empower and strengthen local people and their institutions (Fowler 1988, Farrington *et al.* 1993, Sandberg 1994, Fowler 1995a, Riddell and Robinson 1995). While these comparative advantages of NGOs in development can, but do not necessarily exist, they are often taken for granted in the field and their promise has convinced many donors to channel their monies through NGOs over governments.[5] Coincidentally or consequently, the number of local NGOs has also increased steadily and their activity has expanded into new regions, sectors and partnerships.

Today, Southern NGOs are key players in international development, major contributors to development processes within individual countries

[5] The evaluation of both Northern and Southern NGO projects has yet to become an entrenched part of development. To a great extent, it still depends on the practices of individual project donors, the amount of funding involved in a project and the NGO running the project (Padron 1987, Fowler 1995b, Riddell and Robinson 1995). Riddell (1987) estimates that less than 15 per cent of all ODA has ever been evaluated, which makes it difficult to either prove or disprove assertions about the comparative advantage of NGOs. Within the field, however, it is generally accepted that NGOs can possess several advantages over governments in the provision of development services.

and are continuing to grow. Flows of official development assistance (ODA) from the North to the South may have declined over recent years, over 11 per cent between 1994 and 2001, but the proportion being channelled through NGOs is increasing steadily (Fowler 1991, Smillie 1995, OECD 1998, OECD 2002). Worldwide, it is NGOs and not governments or the United Nations agencies, which are the most prominent advocates of international human rights, and what one writer calls the 'very soul' of their promotion and protection (Nchama 1991: 114). The impact of NGOs is similarly strong in individual country contexts: in Bangladesh, one single NGO's health and nutrition programme touches over 30 million people, or roughly half of the population of the United Kingdom (BRAC 2000). In other countries, Southern NGOs have become an institutionalised part of society (Fowler 1997). The Grameen Bank in Bangladesh, SEWA in India and Madres de Plaza de Mayo in Argentina possess brand names that are as recognisable in their countries as those of Microsoft or Manchester United.

The United Nations, once the holder of a monopoly on formal development activities, has recognised this growing role of NGOs in development. The UN's Economic and Social Council now grants consultative status on its work to 2,234 NGOs from around the world, up from 41 in the 1940s (Chege 1999, ECOSOC 2003). The administrator of the UN Development Programme (UNDP) recently praised NGOs for their 'their knowledge of issues, capacity to mobilize communities at all levels and ability to invent solutions to complex problems', as the UNDP embarked on a large-scale initiative to facilitate NGO partnerships with governments and the private sector (UNDP undated: 1). Even the World Bank, often primarily focussed on large-scale development and infrastructure projects, recognises NGOs as vital to its work. In 1998, 50 per cent of the projects it approved incorporated NGO participation, a marked increase from 1973, when only 6 per cent of Bank projects involved NGOs (Malena 2000).

The growth in number, scope and profile of African NGOs over the last thirty years mirrors these general trends among Southern NGOs. Of all the regions of the developing world, it is Africa that has experienced the most marked proliferation of NGOs in recent years – rapidly expanding NGO sectors have been a phenomenon of Ghana after its economic collapse, Zimbabwe after independence, and South Africa after apartheid (Smillie 1995). In large part, this has been as a result of the weakness of African governments.

As dictatorships and military governments heavily in debt and saddled with unwieldy bureaucracies lacking implementation capacity, many African states have lost the confidence of international donors, who have chosen to fund development through NGOs instead. The additional burden of structural adjustment programmes on African governments has similarly created openings and opportunities for local NGOs to become involved in development (Fowler *et al.* 1992). Reflecting this trend, Africa is home to the largest proportion of World Bank projects involving

NGOs (Gibbs *et al.* 1999). And as human suffering on the continent has worsened with famines, natural disasters, armed conflicts and HIV/AIDS, donors have targeted more funds at social development, providing a further impetus to NGO growth. Many international and northern NGOs, religious groups and development associations have fuelled the development of local NGOs, funnelling aid from the North into local projects and programmes that were later spun off into autonomous local NGOs.

The impact of local NGOs in Africa reflects both their considerable expertise and the levels of donor support from which they have benefited. Somalian NGOs have been an important part of post-civil war rehabilitation and reconciliation programmes in that country; NGOs in Kenya now provide more than half of the countries' health services; and South African NGOs have played a pivotal role in the campaign to improve the access of the African poor to life-saving essential drugs (Therkildsen and Semboja 1995, Abdillahi 1998). One study of African states and NGOs characterises the importance of African NGOs in this way: 'Domestically NGOs are now taking their places alongside political parties, elite bureaucratic factions, executive styles of governing, class struggles, ethnic and other interest group rivalries, military offices, trade unions, and peasants as a new focus for understanding important domestic actors in Africa' (Sandberg 1994: 3).

The importance of local NGOs in Africa seems likely to grow given the increasing prominence afforded to NGOs in donor funding plans. While net ODA receipts in Africa have fallen by more than 30 per cent since 1994, NGOs are increasingly the recipients of the donor funding that does arrive on the continent (OECD 1998, OECD 2002). In 1999, both the American and Dutch governments decided to channel an increasing proportion of their development aid in Africa away from governments and towards NGOs (Chege 1999). As these trends illustrate, the perceived corruption, ineffectiveness, and overall weakness of African governments has led Western governments, donor agencies and international financial institutions to focus significant attention on NGOs as instruments of development, and has contributed to the rise of NGOs on the continent. With donor funds moving further away from government coffers in many countries and NGOs virtually replacing government in certain development sectors, it is no surprise that the balance of power in African development is changing. But has it yet changed to allow for the development of powerful local African NGOs?

The political economy of power in the African NGO sector

Development associations and NGOs date back to several decades before colonisation in many parts of Africa. The emergence of local associations continued during the colonial era, stimulated by pre-colonial secret societies, early movements for independence and the flourishing of hometown community development associations which accompanied increasing urbanisation in the early twentieth century. In this era, most NGOs found their niche in providing the social services that colonial states ignored in favour of revenue extraction (Hyden 1995, Fowler 1995a, Ishumi 1995). These NGOs were predominantly centred on social and welfare services, particularly within health and education, and were often church or missionary society based (Chazan 1994, Jenkins 1994, Van Rooy 2000). Posing little threat to colonial governments and seeking little power for themselves, these NGOs met with little opposition and continued on in their service-oriented missions, largely unhindered by government. This allowed many local NGOs and civil society organisations to play significant roles in national independence movements.

From the colonial era, however, the balance of power in African states has lain with government; civil society organisations have rarely been independent loci of power in their own right. The power of the African state is largely due to the competitive nature of the colonial contest for Africa, which required colonising nations to have a strong physical presence in their colonies to exclude rival powers (Young 1988, Young 1994). The cost of maintaining this presence and the absence of existing revenues or infrastructures for revenue extraction made the imposition of centralised and authoritarian state structures imperative. At independence, it was these autocratic, patrimonial and extractive states that were bequeathed to post-colonial governments and maintained the existing balance of power between the state and society (Callaghy 1986, Wunsch 1990, Chabal 1992).

The post-independence rise of African socialism in much of the continent further cemented the power of the state over society and reduced the space available to civil society groups. Different socialist leaders stressed different socialist values, depending on their particular aims and strategies, but most proclaimed the importance of hard work, unity within and among African states, equality of all peoples, and co-operation and communal responsibility for the common good (Dia 1964, Nkrumah 1964a, Nkrumah 1964b, Nyerere 1964, Senghor 1964). The single-party state adopted by most of these governments was proclaimed as the embodiment of socialist principles and as the return of these newly independent countries to traditional African forms of governing (Onuoha 1965).

The centralist state was also, however, a practical response of new governments to their widely dispersed populations and to the threat that ethnic, regional, religious or linguistic division posed to their power (Herbst 2000). It made possible the restriction of pluralist activity in a way that preaching the traditional principles of unity and co-operation alone would not. This monopolisation of political power reduced the ability of civil society organisations like NGOs to obtain access to the state and state actors and to impact directly state decision-making processes (Chazan 1988, Wunsch and Olowu 1990, Howell and Pearce 2001). The diverse societal interests which had been represented by political parties and civil society groups were co-opted into the dominant political party – which set up official wings for women, youth, students and workers (Tripp 2001). This allowed governments to increase their control over the space available to civil society and deter the growth and development of independent civil society organisations.

During this era, the centralised post-colonial African state also attempted to reduce dependency on the government by encouraging communities to rely on their own resources and hard work. This process of state propelled disengagement replaced existing civil society movements with government sponsored programmes for popular mobilisation, further restricting civil society access to the state and reducing the ability of civil society organisations to command resources from the state (Azarya 1988, Olorunsola and Muhwezi 1988). While rural participation in these rural mobilisation plans – such as *harambee* in Kenya and *ujamaa* in Tanzania – was initially high, so too were people's expectations of participating in both resource creation and resource allocation (Mbithi and Rasmusson 1977, Hyden 1980). As these movements came to be increasingly bureaucratically controlled and politically motivated, rural support for them waned. By this time, however, civil society organisations were few.

The legacy of the overdeveloped state inherited by post-colonial regimes and reinforced by their subscription to African socialism has had a lasting impact on development in Africa. One result has been the encroachment of a strong and often bloated centralised government into civil society, and the resultant weakening and marginalisation of civil society. Civil society, particularly as applied to Africa, is a concept fraught with debate: its relevance, its suitability, its usefulness, its existence or absence and its very definition are regularly debated.[6] Van Rooy (1998) for example, highlighted the difficulty of defining the term 'civil society', illustrating the various meanings, from a value, to a historical moment, a space for activity and an antidote to the state, that are ascribed to the term and the many biases inherent in choosing any one definition. Many others have criticised the unquestioning use of a term with Western roots and biases to represent the realities of the developing world (Chabal and Daloz 1999, Howell and Pearce 2001). While not diminishing the importance of their arguments, for the purposes of this investigation of the power relations inherent in African NGO sectors, however, I will use the term 'civil society' as it is most commonly used in our field: as a collective noun which represents the collection and arena of extra-state actors involved in creating positive change in their communities (Van Rooy 1998).

[6] See Chazan 1994, Harbeson *et al.* 1994, Fatton 1995, Hutchful 1995, Gyimah-Boadi 1996, Hann and Dunn 1996, Fisher 1997, Stewart 1997, Howell 2000, and Howell and Pearce 2001 for an elaboration of these debates on African civil society.

What Jean-François Bayart (1986: 112) called the 'hegemonic imperative which drives the state and the self-proclaimed dominant social groups to seek to control and to shape civil society', has made Africa distinct among regions of the developing world today for the relative weakness of its civil society (Dunn 1986). This weakness is evident in the absence of the material, organisational and ideological means required for civil society activity (Rothchild and Lawson 1994). Civil society groups in Africa often lack access to capital resources or to supporters able to accumulate the capital which is fundamental to the material dimension of civil society (Bratton 1994a, Kasfir 1998). They similarly often lack the participation, co-ordination and leadership necessary to fulfil the organisational and ideological dimensions. The difficulties of planning and co-ordinating across competing ethnic, linguistic and religious communities, for example, have plagued civil society groups across the continent (Gyimah-Boadi 1996). A lack of access to high quality human resources has further plagued many civil society organisations in Africa. In the post-colonial era many high quality university graduates chose employment in burgeoning governments and nationalised industries – in some countries, the numerous non-monetary perks available to government employees mean that these trends persist (Bayart 1986, Ayoade 1988, Copestake 1993, Gueye *et al.* 1993).

The weakness of indigenous NGOs in Africa could thus be considered as nothing more than a reflection of the weakness of civil society in Africa. Yet over the last two decades, civil society organisations including NGOs have played crucial roles in liberalisation and democratisation in several countries, benefited from increasing levels of donor interest and become more relevant to international decision-making processes in development. To Haynes, 'civil society aims to balance the state's tendency to seek ever greater amounts of power, by achieving a measure of power in its own right. Civil society, in short, functions as the citizen's curb on the power of the state' (1997: 16). If the recent trends which have seen NGOs rise in prominence across the continent signal that civil society organisations, moved by public frustration, discontent and what Célestin Monga (1996) calls 'anger', are beginning to achieve this counterbalance to the power of the state, then we might well expect a reorganisation of power relations in African development – one that would result in more powerful African NGOs.

But African NGOs have not gained the power we would expect them to have, the power that their counterparts in other parts of the developing world now wield. When we think of powerful NGOs at work in sub-Saharan Africa today, it is multinational and international organisations that we think of, whether international NGOs originating in the North, like CARE, Save the Children, the International Union for the Conservation of Nature (IUCN) and the Intermediate Technology Development Group (ITDG), or multinational NGOs or NGO networks originating in the South, like Six-S, ENDA Tiers-Monde, the Council for the Development of Social Science Research in Africa (CODESRIA), and the African Medical Research Foundation (AMREF). So why have local African NGOs been unable to gain power? And how has their lack of power impacted local development on the continent?

The case studies

The answers I propose to these questions are based on fieldwork undertaken in Zimbabwe, Tanzania, and Senegal during 1999 and 2000.[7] Within each of these countries I met with and interviewed the directors, or other similarly high-ranking officials, of a wide range of local NGOs. The goal of these interviews was to gain a detailed understanding of the evolution of local African NGOs, their project and programme experiences and their relationships to their stakeholders. Across the three case study countries, I interviewed over sixty local NGOs. Interviews were also conducted with other relevant local development actors in each case study country, including officials and representatives from different layers of government, international NGOs, key donor agencies, church movements, academics, beneficiary groups and media organisations. As a basis for comparison, I conducted an in-depth examination of a local Bangladeshi NGO in July 2000, interviewing several of its key staff, donors and counterparts in development. In total, I interviewed over 130 members of the NGO communities in Zimbabwe, Tanzania, Senegal and Bangladesh, and generated several hundred hours of taped interviews.[8]

---

[7] These countries were chosen for their relatively stable recent political histories and NGO sectors which encompassed a range of NGOs diverse in sectoral focus, regional distribution, size and age. They are also broadly representative of three different regions within sub-Saharan Africa. While the representativeness of these countries of their regions (namely Southern Africa, Eastern Africa and West Africa) could be called into question, as could the general practice of using regional labels to imply ties between countries beyond simple geography or climate, in choosing three countries for this study it seemed appropriate to consider as diverse a set of countries as possible.

[8] Direct quotes from many of these interviews appear throughout this book. Because of the confidentiality assured to interviewees, their words appear anonymously and are marked only by the date on which their interview took place. Because of my confidentiality arrangements, I have been unable to attribute these quotes, even where the revelation of their source would add to the power of the statements presented. I am aware that this can make it seem as though the NGOs interviewed are part of some sort of NGO witness protection programme. But I am confident that the candid words of these NGO representatives, about their finances, relationships to donor agencies and difficulties with national government, will more than compensate for the obscuring of their precise identities. I have reproduced quotations exactly as they were given to me, and have attempted to portray the context and spirit in which they were given as accurately as possible. The names and affiliations of interviewees who agreed to be quoted on the record appear alongside their words. Quotes from interviews conducted in French, as were the majority in Senegal, have been translated literally into English. In some cases, to reflect the power and accuracy of interviewee statements in both English and French has meant that quotations are grammatically incorrect or lack proper sentence structure.

It is worth taking a few moments here to address the issue of generalisation, specifically as it relates to the applicability of research done in three African countries to the sub-Saharan context at large. Each country in sub-Saharan Africa has a unique cultural context and social, political and economic history, and there is a great deal of variation among sub-Saharan NGO sectors, as reflected in Table 1.1.

Table 1.1. Selected indicators for the case study countries

	Zimbabwe	Tanzania	Senegal
Colonial power	Britain	Germany/Britain	France
Date of independence	1980	1964	1960
Population (millions) 2001[a]	12.8	35.6	9.6
GDP per capita (PPP US$) 2001[a]	2,280	520	1,500
Official development assistance per capita (US$) 2001[a]	12.5	34.7	43.5
Life expectancy at birth (years) 2001[a]	35.4	44.0	52.3
Percentage of population living below international income poverty line ($1 US a day)[a]1	36.0	19.9	26.3
Percentage of adults living with HIV/AIDS (age 15–49) 2001[a]	33.73	7.83	0.50
Average age of the local NGOs sampled	12	9	14

(a) UNDP 2003
[1] Based on the most recent data available for each country from 1990-2001

Senegal, for instance, the eldest of the case study countries, gained its independence a full twenty years before Zimbabwe, the youngest in the sample. The average age of NGOs in the three case study countries also varies, with the oldest in Senegal and the youngest in more recently liberalised Tanzania. Such variations are important in the context of this research, which relates the power of the NGO sector to highly specific characteristics such as civil society strength, the character of government and national human resource availability. Yet, while sweeping generalisations across the continent would be difficult to support, this book contends that many NGOs across Africa are excluded from power by very similar obstacles and actors.

Moreover, I will argue that the lessons learned from NGOs within specific country contexts should be disseminated to NGOs in other parts of the continent and to civil society organisations at large. They may, because of general similarities in the political economy of African development sectors, prove useful to a range of civil society groups formulating their own strategies for gaining power. Michael Lipton (1989: 352) makes this point succinctly: 'the persistence of generalizations about SSA – by Africans as well as foreigners; among the wise as well as the foolish; on price policy, nutrition and democracy as well as on agricultural research priorities – strongly suggests that there is some set of 'African' experiences, problems or opportunities that is worth generalizing about.' Some of the components of this 'set' of common African realities may include: economically, the high significance of agriculture within national accounts and the post-independence rise and subsequent decline in economic growth; politically, the common experience of colonial rule and more recently of authoritarian government; and socially, increasing populations and poverty rates (Wellard and Copestake, 1993).

The history of power relations between African states and civil societies suggests two possible explanations for the absence of power among local African NGOs. The first is that African governments, in trying to protect their power, their 'paramountcy', had struggled against the ascendancy of local NGOs and prevented them from gaining power (Bayart 1986). In his consideration of state-NGO relationships in Kenya, Stephen Ndegwa characterises this phenomenon as less a contest for power than a full-out 'assault on organisations in civil society by a regime seeking to consolidate power and neutralise potential independent agents of agitation' (1996: 25). If the efforts of weak African governments to consolidate their power had led them to control and restrict NGO activities perceived as threatening, to engage in patrimonial behaviour and patron–client relationships which had displaced NGOs from the political arena, or even to be unable to provide an enabling environment for NGO activity in their countries, then this might have constrained the ability of African NGOs to develop power. A second possibility is that while NGOs have increasingly curried favour with international donors and governments, they have remained plagued by the weaknesses and inefficiencies that hinder civil society organisations as well as many public and private enterprises across the continent. They lack strong supporting institutions, have lost potential leaders to government, the private sector and well-paid careers abroad, suffer from the low enfranchisement and mobilisation of the masses as well as from the lack of a distinct culture of, and role for, civil society organisations on the continent.

Yet interviews with local NGOs in Zimbabwe, Tanzania and Senegal revealed that neither of these hypotheses adequately explained why local African NGOs have been excluded from power, nor the degree to which this lack of power has undermined development on the continent. While many local NGOs in these countries did share common organisational and operational shortcomings with much of African civil society, power was seen wanting even among those NGOs which had overcome these weaknesses. This indicated that the widespread lack of power among local NGOs in Africa could not simply be dismissed as symptomatic of the weakness of its civil society at large.

Furthermore, the experiences of the local African NGOs I met suggested a second unexpected conclusion: that government antagonism on its own could not explain the absence of power among African NGOs. Governments and NGOs in the field-work countries did struggle against one another to pull the balance of power in their favour. But it was the fight for space, financial independence, international links and access to political issues within development, often indirect and involving actors other than government, that had prevented local NGOs in Africa from achieving power.

2

NGO Power

In considering the power of local NGOs in Africa, we must first determine what we mean when we talk of NGO power. Is power security? Influence? Respect? Or something else entirely? Surprisingly, given that international aid is a multi-billion dollar industry, and NGOs are one of its key actors, there is no generally agreed definition of NGO power. In a field which has long been predicated on concepts of charity, benevolence and voluntarism, discussions of power, with their Machiavellian connotations, have seemed somehow out of place. When it comes to NGOs, we prefer to immerse ourselves in the warm and comfortable discourse of participation and partnership than to engage with questions of power and politics. Yet with the number of actors, politics and dollars involved, there are plenty of power games at play in the development sector. And NGOs, whether international or local, are a part of them.

What is power?

Questions of power have occupied great thinkers and political scientists throughout history. What is power? How is power developed? How is power wielded? How can power be measured? Even today, power continues to be among the most important, widely used and regularly debated concepts in politics, economics, sociology, business and management. But what aspects of power are particularly relevant to the experience of NGOs and civil society actors? In developing a definition of NGO power which will be useful in our analysis of local NGOs in sub-Saharan Africa, we can benefit from a brief examination of several of the theoretical debates that surround the concept and its applications.

The Prince, Niccolo Machiavelli's sixteenth-century treatise on how a sovereign can gain and hold onto power, has dominated Western political thought and framed our understanding of political power as encompassed in the state. For Machiavelli, power was the sovereign's superiority, authority and ability to rule, and was absolute. While his name has come to be synonymous with power achieved through ruthlessness and cruelty, for Machiavelli protection of this power was fundamental, and as such, he sanctioned unpleasantness towards one's subjects where it reinforced the position of the Prince, and force where it was necessary to protect against foreigners (Machiavelli, 1997). A similarly strong and active, albeit less militaristic, defence, can play an important role in NGO power, allowing an NGO to capture or protect space and resources by reducing or eliminating its competitors. An effective publicity and marketing campaign, focussing on an NGOs' accomplishments and unique knowledge or expertise is but one example of such a strategic defence.

While it was the power of a ruler that also fascinated Thomas Hobbes a century later, this power was not just achieved, but rather conferred, by the united consent of subjects, each of whom possessed power as an individual. For Hobbes, 'The power of a man (to take it Universally,) is his present means, to obtain some future apparent Good' (Hobbes [1651] 1985: 150). In other words, power lies in one's present capacities, the abilities one has and can put to use. Hobbes' work is important to the present debate as many of the individual component powers that he cited in 1651 are qualities that we might still today consider to confer, or at a minimum, characterise power: strength, prudence, eloquence, riches, reputation, friends. Several of these elements will reappear later in this chapter when we consider what a powerful local African NGO would look like. Hobbes' work offers one more insight into power which may be useful in our reflection on NGO power, however: that 'the nature of Power, is in this point, like to Fame, increasing as it proceeds; or like the motion of heavy bodies, which the further they go, make still the more hast' (Hobbes [1651] 1985: 150). Indeed, as we will see, power reinforces itself in the NGO world. NGOs use their power to increase their financial resources and to increase the freedom with which they use these financial resources, and this in turn further amplifies their power within the international development community.

Other major thinkers have expounded different theories of power that are also relevant to our current consideration of power in the NGO sector. John Locke, who wrote about political power and government's right to wield it, saw the right to exercise power as linked to its being exercised for the public good (Locke [1690] 1967). Locke's view of power, if extended to NGOs, could suggest that the only local NGOs that will develop power are those which succeed in serving the needs of their communities. Foucault also saw power as extending beyond simple relationships of opposition or domination; to him it was both positive and negative, and in different circumstances, individuals could be both powerful and powerless (Hindess 1996, Foucault 2000). He argued that true power was generative, creating new forms of behaviour, discourse and knowledge. I will return to this idea when we consider innovation, the creation of knowledge and the ability to capture space as crucial elements of NGO power. BRAC –

one of the powerful local NGOs in Asia which we will examine shortly – has partly developed its power by pioneering new methods and strategies for meeting the needs of its beneficiaries and encouraging new ways of thinking among donor organisations.

Steven Lukes' more recent consideration of power is also useful to our present discussion of what NGO power is. While power has traditionally been conceived of as one's ability to exert his/her will over that of another when the two are in conflict (whether overt or covert), Lukes stresses that a significant aspect of power is not merely resolving conflict, but rather preventing it from arising (Dahl 1957, Bachrach and Baratz 1962, Lukes 1974). In the NGO world, for example, this might mean that where the majority of local NGOs face regular challenges from their donors over spending decisions and planning directions, the donors to a powerful NGO are so eager to work with it that they accept the conditions which the NGO itself sets down for accepting funds. In this way, donors cede their rights to scrutinise the operations of the powerful NGO and potential conflicts between the two groups are reduced. More recently, Hayward (1998: 2; 2000) has sought to 'de-face' power, moving from the notion of power as 'an instrument powerful agents use to alter the free action of the powerless', to a new conception of power as 'a network of social boundaries that constrain and enable action for all actors'.

What do all of these concepts of power mean for NGOs? First, they all reflect that the powerful are able to achieve their ends irrespective of the preferences of others (Scruton 1996). Second, common to all of these is the notion that power does not exist in a vacuum – it exists only as one exists in a world with others – over whom one is able to exert influence, for whom one is able to do good, with whom one is able to avoid conflict. NGO power, therefore, must reflect the freedom and ability of an NGO to achieve its ends despite or because of the efforts of those around them. I will define NGO power as *the ability of local NGOs to set their own priorities, define their own agendas and exert their influence on the international development community, even in the face of opposition from government, donors, international NGOs and other development* actors. This definition incorporates both the many understandings of power as based on opposing or conflictual aims, as well as alternative conceptions of power as based on networks of norms and boundaries.

NGO power can be created, transferred and lost. Power is not conserved and the amount of power in the world is not constant. A simple way to understand this might be to consider power as the opposite end of the spectrum from energy – which cannot be created or destroyed – and the conservation of which is one of the fundamental laws by which we understand our universe. While the total amount of energy in our universe is constant, the amount of power is not. Power is not a zero-sum game, where the power gained by one actor has been lost by another, or where there is a finite amount of power for which actors compete. This is a crucial point.

Where NGOs gain power by decreasing, eliminating or reshaping the social boundaries or constraints that affect them, thus being better able to set their own priorities and exert their influence, then these actions will not necessarily reduce the power of another actor. Other actors may simultaneously benefit from their changed environment and likewise gain power. As Gaventa and Cornwall (2001: 72) write: 'power may have a synergistic element, such that action by some enables more action by others. Challenging the boundaries of the possible may in some cases mean that those with relatively less power, working collaboratively with others, have more.'

Of course, gaining power does not always occur without conflict or struggle. For example, as Migdal (1994: 4) writes in his study of power struggles between states and societies: 'some interactions between state segments and social segments can create more power for both. Some, of course, favour one side over the other. Some vitiate the powers of each side.' Migdal's model of state–society relations sees the possibility of different combinations of weak and strong states coexisting with weak and strong societies (Migdal 1988). Within the realm of NGOs, similar variations in the synergies and rivalries for power are possible. Indeed, were NGOs to only gain power at the expense of other relevant groups, like the state, for instance, it would be difficult to argue in favour of NGO power. In the case studies of local NGOs in Zimbabwe, Tanzania and Senegal which follow in the next several chapters we will attempt to discover the groups with which NGOs experience the greatest synergy in attaining power, and the groups which regularly engage in a contest for power with African NGOs.

Agency is at the heart of NGO power: the ability of a local NGO to exert its influence over others to further its ends, rather than its ability to accrue the resources necessary to force others comply with its will. Of course the control of resources can be key, and the balance of power in an NGO's relationships is often seen to lie with the party which controls the bulk of the financial resources (Lister 2000). Indeed, a powerful local NGO will be one able to free itself from the financial control of others. But as the case studies of local NGOs in Zimbabwe, Tanzania and Senegal will illustrate, NGO power does not seem to be achieved by a Hobbesian accumulation and aggregation of individual attributes, resources or component powers. This seeming contradiction is one of the most interesting aspects of NGO power in Africa: many NGOs that have achieved the individual characteristics that most observers would consider key components of power nonetheless remain quite powerless.

Given the international nature of development work, as development activities in the South are funded by a myriad of governments and donor agencies from the North, staffed by individuals from around the globe, and based on conventions and priorities decided at international conferences, I have defined NGO power on an international scale. While indigenous NGOs may be influential in their local communities or national arenas, until they are able to influence the many international processes which affect them, their donors and their governments, they will not be truly able to set their own priorities and define their own agendas. As such, it is power on an international scale – an influence over international development discussions, debates and decision-making – that I will consider as NGO power.

NGO power allows local NGOs to assert their own agendas and influence, even when they are in conflict with the priorities or norms of other groups. The main actors in international development include multinational institutions, governments, donor agencies, international and local NGOs, a diverse range of civil society organisations like labour unions, church groups and student movements, and beneficiaries and their communities. Relationships between these groups are generally hierarchical and characterised by asymmetric levels of power. A brief examination of the relationships in which local African NGOs lack power at this point will help to better understand both what NGO power is, and what power would mean to a local African NGO.

When it comes to relationships between NGOs and states in Africa, it is most often the state which holds the balance of power in its favour. This is certainly the case in interactions between the majority of African states and local African NGOs. While certain authors have begun to argue that the influence and impact of NGOs can decrease the power and legitimacy of the state, their examples generally come from countries and regions outside of Africa (White 1999, Mercer 2002). The control that governments exert over the NGO registration process and their ability to monitor and deregister local NGOs in their countries is the most obvious manifestation of this power in Africa. While several international NGOs at work on the continent, like Greenpeace and Amnesty International for example, can exert considerable power over national governments, their local counterparts rarely have a similar influence (Strange 1996). For these groups, the achievement of power is not about controlling the state or supplanting its role in development, nor is it to be gained solely at the cost of the state. Rather, power is an aim which would allow African NGOs to criticise or engage with their governments without jeopardy, to be valued, recognised and rewarded partners of government in national development activity, and to have real policy influence over the governments in their countries – all with the ultimate aim of advocating for, and with, the poor and marginalised in their countries.

Donors similarly wield great power in the international development community, and they traditionally dominate in their direct relationships with both Southern governments and NGOs (Elliott 1987). As Terje Tvedt (1998: 224) writes of the power distribution facing NGOs, 'the donors in general call the tune, because of financial resources, conceptual dominance and the unequal distribution of sanctionary instruments. NGO aid, like other donor channels, always produces unequal distribution of sanctionary instruments.' It is donor agencies that generally dictate contract terms and often even project design; they decide what capacity-building their partners need, how they will report, how they will be monitored and evaluated, and how their performance will be measured (Fowler 1998, Lister 2000).

Other NGO observers reinforce this idea of a power relationship which slants away from local NGOs, writing that Northern donors 'have an enormous amount of power. They are able to shape the lives of the organisations they support, not simply because they fund them, but also because of the processes and disciplines they require the organisations to become involved in. The term "partner" only obscures what remains a very real power relation. The egalitarian label does not change reality' (Ford-Smith 1989: 186). This unequal power relationship described by Ford-Smith was aptly demonstrated during 2003, as foreign aid and development assistance became part of the national security agenda in the United States. American NGOs receiving USAID funding have been told to see themselves as an 'an arm of the US Government' (InterAction 2003a). Those NGOs that fail adequately to promote their links to the US Government and its foreign policy could face the loss of their funding. Even for well known and well resourced international NGOs, donors at times not only pull the strings, but wield the axe. It is easy to see that this phenomenon is only compounded in Africa, where the absence of a local donor community or giving public make local NGOs largely dependent on donor organisations for their financial resources.

In terms of the three instruments for wielding or enforcing power identified by John Kenneth Galbraith (1983), namely punishment, compensation or conditioning, donors are able to use all three in their dealings with African NGOs. Both the threat of withdrawing or reducing funds, or the promise of providing new or additional funds can dictate the areas in which NGOs are active and the types of projects they undertake. Similarly, the culture of international aid is such that donor interests can be passed on to their partners – including NGOs, but also national recipient governments – by custom, persuasion or targeted education (such as through training or capacity-building curricula and programming). Steven Lukes stresses that a significant aspect of power is not provoking conflict, but rather preventing it from arising (Lukes 1974). In the NGO context, donors do not just exert their power over local NGOs by getting them to do something they would not otherwise do, but by influencing them to the extent that the NGO itself willingly rethinks its priorities to fit the mould provided by its donors. The case studies from Zimbabwe, Tanzania and Senegal which follow in the next three chapters will provide examples of African NGOs which, because of this unequal power relationship with donors, have variously focussed their work around gender issues, environmental conservation and economic development in order to reflect the changing priorities of their donors. Donors to powerful NGOs, however, are so eager to work with these groups that they are willing to accept the conditions set down by the NGOs for their funding. In this case, donors accept the norms dictated by their NGO partners, ceding their rights to scrutinise NGO operations, and reducing potential conflicts between them.

The relationships between local African NGOs and their international counterparts can also be generally characterised by asymmetric levels of resources and power. There are hundreds of international NGOs at work in Africa today and the largest of them command annual revenues of several hundred million US dollars – many times over what the average African NGO could hope to see in its lifetime (Lindenberg and Bryant 2001). International NGOs are also able to rely on influential directors and board members who amplify the reputation, voice and resources of the NGO. While an ideal of partnership is widely touted as the norm between international and local NGOs, this sentiment can often be little more than rhetoric used opportunistically by INGOs to maximise their resources, and is not representative of a genuine interest in mutual learning and co-operation (Lewis 1998). As described in later chapters, the notion of partnership further obscures a power relationship in which international NGOs create their own local divisions rather than work with established local NGOs, offer financial incentives to encourage beneficiary participation in their projects over those of local NGOs, and compete with their local counterparts for donor contracts and funds – phenomena which all serve to marginalise local NGOs in African development. Were African NGOs to gain power in these relationships, Alan Fowler's vision of 'a sellers' market for aid' in which it is the work of local NGOs 'which holds the key to the legitimacy of northern aid agencies' would be achieved (Fowler 1998: 150). For those who see power as inextricably linked to resources and capabilities, whether Thomas Hobbes in the seventeenth century, Karl Marx in the nineteenth century, or political economists today, legitimacy is one of the local NGO resources which can help to counterbalance the donor and international NGO resource of funds on the scales of power.

Multinational institutions like the United Nations and the international financial institutions (IFIs) generally wield the greatest power in the international development community. These groups are the most widely recognised, best funded and largest-scale development actors in the world. Which of us, when explaining to new acquaintances that we work in 'international development', hasn't been met with the reply, 'Oh, you mean with the United Nations?' As Susan Strange writes, 'The annual meetings of the World Bank and the International Monetary Fund draw literally thousands of journalists every year. Their readers no longer have to be told what these bodies are; 'IMF' is already in the translingual, global vocabulary, along with STOP, Fax or Coca-Cola' (1996: 161). In so far as they can control both resource flows to local NGOs and to their governments, these organisations exert tremendous power over African NGOs.

With its ability to provide for local NGO involvement in the projects it supports, the World Bank, for example, is able to influence both the finances that will be allocated to individual NGOs and the activities they will be involved in, as well as set the tone for government–NGO relationships in its project countries (Malena 2000). The power of these groups over local NGOs is not limited to their control of financial resources, however. Their publications, such as the UNDP's Human Development Reports and the World Bank's World Development Reports, create global development trends, influencing the sectors of development that first-world governments and northern NGOs will decide to fund and either creating or reducing the space available to local NGOs by the themes they choose for their reports. Moreover, their ability to define the terms of development debates and, in many cases, the debates themselves, gives the international organisations the power to influence the very place and relevance of local NGOs in development (White 1999).

Of course the relationships described above are not constant across Africa, and will depend on the unique development space in each country. They are also not fixed in time. Consequently, the relationships between local NGOs and the other actors in their development space may be different from one location to another (e.g. urban to rural) and from one year to the next. Yet across all of these contexts, local African NGOs lack power. We will return to consider in depth how the absence of power has affected NGOs on the continent and undermined development in Africa in Chapter 6. The examination of the link between power and sustainability in Chapter 7 will be a key part of this discussion, and will be especially significant for both local NGOs themselves and for those INGO and donor groups which prioritise the goal of sustainability in their support for local NGOs.

While local NGOs in Africa lack power, many examples of internationally powerful indigenous NGOs exist in Latin America and Asia. The Self-Employed Women's Association (SEWA) and Working Women's Forum (WWF) in India, the Bangladesh Rural Advancement Committee (BRAC) and Proshika in Bangladesh, Madres de Plaza de Mayo in Argentina, the Instituto Brasileiro de Análises Sociais e Econômicas (IBASE) and Federaçao de Orgãoes para Assistência Social e Educacional (FASE) in Brazil and the Centro de Estudios y Promocion del Desarrollo (DESCO) in Peru, though involved in a diverse range of activities and sectors, are all notable for the power they wield in both local and international development. While this is not an exhaustive list of powerful Southern NGOs, their examples can help us to understand what it means for a local NGO to be powerful and how local African NGOs could develop power.

What does power look like? An introduction to powerful local NGOs

The NGOs that come to mind when we try to picture powerful Northern NGOs are groups like Oxfam in Great Britain and the United Way in America; groups which have become 'institutionalised in the sense that they are a recognised and valued part of society' (Fowler 1997: 21). Powerful local NGOs are a similarly visible, respected and entrenched part of their societies. It is difficult to participate in a conversation on development in Bangladesh, India, Argentina, Brazil or Peru that does not make mention of local NGOs. It is even more difficult to participate in a conversation on NGOs in these countries that does not make mention of BRAC or Proshika, SEWA or the Working Women's Forum (WWF), Madres de Plaza de Mayo, FASE or IBASE, or DESCO. These powerful local NGOs have very different histories, work in different environments and have their own unique goals; yet they all share several distinguishing characteristics which signal their power and which we can use to identify powerful local NGOs across the globe.

Size

In Bangladesh, which houses one of the world's largest NGO sectors, BRAC and Proshika stand out as among the largest of these organisations (Sobhan 1997). BRAC's rural development programme works with over three million people, and over one million children attend its schools (BRAC 2000). To serve its beneficiaries, BRAC employs 60,000 people, not including its volunteers. Proshika, the country's second largest NGO, counts over 1.7 million members in its village groups and employs over 4,000 staff members (Khan *et al.* 1993, DFID Bangladesh 2000, Smillie and Hailey 2001). These two groups alone work with a client base roughly equal to the population of London. India's most powerful local NGOs are also each a giant in their own right. SEWA and the Working Women's Forum each have a membership of around 250,000 but touch many more people through their programmes. More than one million people have borrowed credit from SEWA and more than 1.6 million people have been touched by the Working Women's Forum grass-roots health programme (Edwards and Hulme 1995, Working Women's Forum 2002). While big NGOs in Latin America tend to have smaller staffs and client bases than their counterparts in Asia, the most powerful among them are still notable for their size (Wils 1995). Over 3,000 women, for instance, belong to the Madres de Plaza de Mayo in Argentina (Skaar 1994). And both DESCO, the largest research NGO in Peru, and FASE in Brazil have over 100 staff members (Fowler 1997, Meyer 1999, FASE 2002).

The reach of these powerful local NGOs is equally remarkable. BRAC's four core programmes, in rural and urban development, education and health, cover all 64 districts of Bangladesh and reach more than 50,000 villages. It has now also started to run programmes in neighbouring Afghanistan. Proshika is active in 57 of Bangladesh's districts and estimates that 10 million people have benefited from its programming (Proshika 1999, Proshika 2001). From their roots in Ahmedabad and Madras respectively, SEWA and the Working Women's Forum also have a tremendous reach across India. The Working Women's Forum has members throughout Southern India and SEWA is now a truly national

NGO with offices from Ahmedabad in the west to Bhagalpur in the east, and from Delhi in the north to Trivandrum in the south. Powerful local NGOs in Latin America have a similarly large reach. FASE has offices all the way along Brazil's expansive coastline as well as in its interior Amazon basin and DESCO in has offices or projects in 17 of Peru's 24 administrative regions (DESCO 2002, FASE 2002). With the advent of the internet and the growth of transnational networking and coalition building, the reach of many of these local NGOs is almost limitless and they are on their way to becoming truly global organisations.

As these NGOs have grown in size, they have also grown in scope: moving between sectors of development and incorporating new areas of interest into their portfolio of services. They each offer their clients or beneficiaries a wide and often diverse range of services. IBASE and DESCO, while predominantly research and advocacy organisations, focus on a range of social and political issues including gender, human rights, democratisation, food security, social responsibility, and the environment (Ribeiro 1998, IBASE 1999, DESCO 2002). Even SEWA and WWF, while organised around employment and labour issues, incorporate other aspects of their members' livelihood and security into their work, undertaking projects on credit, food and water, housing, insurance, legal aid, child care and health care (Rose 1992, Ramesh 1995, Bhatt 1998). With their financial, political, environmental and social foci there are few services that BRAC and Proshika in Bangladesh do not provide to their members. BRAC advertises that it provides a 'holistic approach to poverty reduction', one of its donors calls it a 'multinational superstore' amongst 'corner stores' (BRAC 2000: 13; Interview with Representative, International Donor Agency, Dhaka, 19 July 2000).

As the size of these powerful NGOs has reinforced itself, these groups have been able to diversify with little risk to the strength of their organisations. This is certainly a part of innovation, which, though often thought to be greater among smaller NGOs, is, according to Sobhan (1997), more a characteristic of large NGOs, whose resources and structures make them more able to assume risk and to cope with failures. In turn, the variety of innovative programming that these big NGOs offer has drawn more people to them. Research conducted by BRAC highlights its size, variety and depth of programming as key to its ability to attract more clients, particularly in communities in which several NGOs are providing overlapping development services (Chaudhury 1999). As NGOs like BRAC have grown, and their ability to diversify, innovate and attract greater numbers of beneficiaries increased, so too has their attractiveness to donor agencies.

Donors recognise that big NGOs will be able to absorb large amounts of funding relatively easily, by scaling up their operations and replicating existing programmes. This makes them very attractive to donors, who lack the human resources to make a large number of moderate grants to small NGOs, each of which will require regular support, monitoring and evaluation (Sobhan 1997, Holloway 1998). Donor agencies also recognise that, because of economies of scale, only NGOs of a certain size will be able to undertake large scale or high technology projects. So donors fund these large, powerful NGOs, they absorb larger amounts of funding and grow even bigger, and the cycle continues with their size being reinforced and their power self-perpetuated (Pfeffer 1981).

Many in the international community are now beginning to question the flexibility, responsiveness and links to the grass-roots of local NGOs as they grow in size, and to wonder how many of the competitive advantages traditionally associated with NGO movements are circumscribed as their organisations and bureaucracies grow. But BRAC, which has always thought in terms of solving the problem of poverty on a national scale in Bangladesh responds to advocates of the 'small is beautiful' NGO philosophy in this way:

> Over the past 16 years BRAC has grown large, compared to the width and depth traditionally associated with NGDOs. On the other hand, it has not sacrificed its innovative, low-cost and politically independent policies. BRAC argues that issues concerning underdevelopment are so complex and multifarious that small programmes can hardly make a difference. BRAC's aim is to be *significant* and not necessarily beautiful. [...] Small is not always significant (BRAC 1992: 58, original emphasis).

The 60,000 staff members and four million beneficiaries with whom BRAC now works are certainly significant in both a national and an international development context.

Wealth

A second distinguishing characteristic of powerful local NGOs is their wealth. By any NGO standard, these groups are very wealthy organisations, whose budget sheets read unlike most other local NGOs' the world over. BRAC's 1999 budget, for instance, was 131 million US dollars, more than the expenditure of many donor agencies. The wealth of powerful local NGOs manifests itself in several ways. Firstly, these groups are able to attract and absorb a staggering amount of donor funding. In 2000, BRAC and Proshika alone absorbed over half of all donor funding given to NGOs in Bangladesh and perhaps even more significantly, stood head and shoulders above the other big NGOs in the country (DFID Bangladesh 2000). According to a recent DFID study, BRAC and Proshika reaped 86 per cent of the funding given to the largest 11 local NGOs in Bangladesh, each a giant in its own right with at least 30,000 clients. Given the trend of donors channelling the bulk of their funding through a small number of very large NGOs in Bangladesh, and given BRAC and Proshika's ability to capture the greatest percentage of it, the funding these two NGOs have at their disposal is astounding (Sanyal 1991, Sobhan 1997, DFID Bangladesh 2000).

But the wealth of these two powerful local NGOs is not only a result of the sheer volume of donor funding they have received; it is equally a result of their ever-increasing levels of power and control over their donors. BRAC and Proshika have succeeded in getting the donors for their largest programmes to work together in funding consortia, over which each donor, as an individual, has very little power. In BRAC's consortia, each donor is presented with an identical programme proposal and budget, usually for five years, which includes all project costs and all overhead, or core, costs for the proposal. Each donor then contributes to this proposal in common with all the other donors, and none has any say, once the proposal is accepted, on how their funds will be spent. Sobhan (1997: 16) describes this type of consortium as 'maximum flexibility' funding, where 'core funds [...] are provided to an NGO to be used at their discretion often within the context of a [longer-term] plan, and are not ear-marked for a specific project.'

For most local NGOs, and certainly the African NGOs which will be examined in later chapters, it is nearly impossible to get donors to pay for overhead expenditures, to have the freedom to move around previously allocated donor funds as project needs change, and to be assured of five years of future funding. For BRAC and Proshika to have accomplished this is already a major coup among NGOs. To achieve this not only with individual donors, but with whole consortia, in which donors have little say over individual components of a long-term programme and must accept it as a whole, where donors all receive the same standardised reports, and where donors sacrifice the individual prestige often available to them as the funders of a particular project or campaign, is a feat which is rarely matched by other NGOs.[1]

BRAC also receives funding from outside its consortia. Some donors who work in the consortia decide to contribute additional funds to BRAC, and others, unwilling or unable to work in a consortium, decide to fund smaller BRAC projects and programmes. Not only is BRAC not dependent on any one donor or type of funding, it is not even dependent on its own donor consortia for funding! Avoiding dependence has been a key concern for BRAC, which does not accept funds in excess of 20 per cent of its annual budget from any one donor (Luz 1991). While 20 per cent of 131 million US dollars is still a considerable amount of funding, BRAC could easily obtain far more from many of its donors.

But while declining a portion of the funds that a donor wishes to give you might spell the end of a funding relationship for another local NGO, it does not for BRAC. This is one of the most potent indicators of its power. As Sarah White (1999: 321) writes of BRAC, 'its size means that it is effectively independent of any single donor, and the scale of some

[1] All donor consortia do not, by definition, enhance the power of local NGOs. Smillie (1995) and Perera (1997), for example, examine the rather unsuccessful donor consortium experience of Sri Lankan NGO Sarvodaya Shramadana.

donors' commitments to BRAC mean that a break-down in that relationship would be as much a disaster for the donor as it would be for BRAC itself'. Some donors seem to have taken this to heart, and today BRAC has donors who have been funding its various programmes for over twenty years, with no foreseeable end to that funding relationship. Meanwhile, under the rhetoric of supporting NGO 'sustainability', many of these same donors limit their funding contracts with other Bangladeshi NGOs to the course of a single project or programme (Sanyal 1991). A long-term commitment to BRAC may be one reason why its donors have felt willing not only to contribute to its core costs, but also to support its capital purchases, which have ranged from a printing press in 1975 to a twenty-storey office tower in more recent years.

As a characteristic of powerful local NGOs, wealth is perhaps most significant when it indicates an organisation's financial security and independence from donor agencies. Despite the large amounts of donor financing that BRAC absorbs, these account for only 25 per cent of its budget expenditures; BRAC provides the other 75 per cent of its budget by itself, through revenues from its programmes and commercial activities. Other powerful local NGOs in South Asia and Latin America have similarly built up their wealth by generating revenues internally. NGOs that offer credit and financial services, like Proshika, SEWA and the Working Women's Forum, recoup a large proportion of their administrative and operating expenses through interest and service payments on the loans they offer. The Working Women's Forum is able to completely cover the cost of operating its credit programme through income from its loans and says that it now maintains a 134 per cent level of financial self-sufficiency (Ramesh 1995, The Microcredit Summit Campaign 2002). Proshika's revolving loan fund has played a similarly important role in its financial security. Proshika plans to reach achieve 100 per cent institutional self-sufficiency by the end of their current 1999–2004 programme, and to fund half of this five-year programme, budgeted at over 400 million US dollars, with earnings from its credit and savings activities (Proshika 2001).

In addition to generating income by extending credit, the powerful NGOs we have been looking at have added to their wealth and independence from donors by strategically using their experience and areas of expertise to create other sustainable forms of revenue. IBASE funds 44 per cent of its budget from commercial activities, which include operating a Rio-based internet node whose network has users in more than 35 countries (Fowler 1997, Ribeiro 1998). DESCO has created a professional services wing which capitalises on its reputation for high-quality research and analysis and offers monitoring and evaluation, research, and capacity-building and training services to local and international organisations. It undertakes more than 70 such consultancies each year, making it a significant form of revenue-generation for the NGO (DESCO 2002). Even Madres de Plaza de Mayo has ventured into commercial waters, starting a bookshop and printing project focussed around human rights at their head office.

All of these powerful NGOs have played some role in ensuring their wealth, whether generating income from microfinance activities, commercial activities, consulting services or programme support activities designed to complement their social services or to link their beneficiaries to the market. Their wealth has allowed them to diversify their social programming and economic opportunities and has continued to reinforce itself. Wealth is therefore another one of the most obvious outward signs of an NGO's power.

Reputation
Powerful local NGOs like BRAC, SEWA and Madres de Plaza de Mayo have reputations that precede them both at home and in development circles the world over. Those reputations are a key sign of their power. Nationally, BRAC is a brand name known in virtually every household in Bangladesh. It is a trademark that appears on a vast range of goods from dairy products to home furnishings to internet servers to schools, hotels and a bank. It may yet be possible to find villages in Bangladesh which have never heard of Coca-Cola; to find villages which have never heard of BRAC would be a far more challenging task. As BRAC's 'Aarong' craft shops export products into Europe and North America, it may not be long before its brand name is as well known outside Bangladesh.

How have the powerful local NGOs gained their reputations? First and foremost, by being good at what they do, and having superior knowledge and experience in the fields in which they work. Evaluations of the work of groups like Proshika and SEWA speak of the high quality of their projects as well as of their impact on project beneficiaries. A 1995 study of the chronic economic difficulties of SEWA members concluded that 'women who had been members of SEWA for longer periods, who had savings accounts in the SEWA Bank, and who contributed a greater share to total family income had a lower incidence of [economic] stress' (Bhatt 1998: 158). Proshika's health programmes have assisted with the installation of close to 90,000 tubewells and latrines and its loan programmes have generated more than 350,000 employment opportunities (Hashemi 1995). A comparison between Proshika's 1995 and 1998–9 impact assessment studies shows that the average income of its group members has doubled, and that the literacy rates for its male and female members have risen from 39 and 22 per cent to 64 and 47 per cent respectively (Proshika 2002). Proshika's donors recognise the quality of Proshika's work, and one of its main donors highlighted the strength of Proshika's advocacy and social mobilisation activities in his discussions with me (Interview with Representative, International Donor Agency, Dhaka, 25 July 2000).

Part of the reputation of powerful local NGOs comes from their ability to do what an NGO is expected to do, and to do it well. But another part of that reputation has developed because the impact of these powerful

NGOs extends beyond their immediate effect on their clients to include their influence on their national social, economic and political arenas. Observers of development in Argentina have variously called the Madres de Plaza de Mayo 'the symbol of resistance to military dictatorship', 'an important development in the national political scene, not only in terms of women's problems but in relation to the whole political panorama' and 'the back bone of the human rights movement in Argentina' (Navarro 1989: 241, Feijoo and Gogna 1990: 85, Skaar 1994: 144). SEWA's lobbying activities have forced the Indian government to recognise the labour rights of self-employed workers and to give priority to the products of women's groups when purchasing goods for government departments (Rose 1992, Acharya and Thomas 1999). Moreover, in 1988 the political influence of the Working Women's Forum convinced the then-Prime Minister of India to visit WWF twice in one year to meet with its members (Haynes 1997). BRAC's policy impact in certain areas is undeniable as well and BRAC's pioneering of non-formal primary education in Bangladesh is but one example of how BRAC programmes have catalysed national changes in government and civil society approaches to development (Howes and Sattar 1992, Ahmad 1999).

One of the most visible marks of the power of these local NGOs is that their reputation stands out not only among other local NGOs in their countries, but among all NGOs, local and foreign, working in those countries. BRAC, for example, has already begun to replace international NGOs in many arenas of development in Bangladesh, and is fulfilling their previous roles as intermediary organisations administering donor grants and providing technical support to local NGOs (Sobhan 1997). Several donors who see local NGOs eventually fulfilling this intermediary role on a permanent basis support BRAC's efforts in this respect. As one donor said, 'we see no reason to support international NGOs when Bangladeshi ones can do most of, if not all of what the international ones can do' (Interview with Representative, International Donor Agency, Dhaka, 24 July 2000). This support is not just in principle, but in terms of financing as well. It is only in Bangladesh and the Philippines for example, that the EU has permitted individual local NGOs to access direct funding from them; throughout the rest of the world, local NGOs must always undertake a co-financing arrangement with a European NGO approved by the EU. And, significantly, the possibility has been raised of BRAC becoming the new local representative for Oxfam, one of the world's largest and best known international NGOs, replacing its existing Bangladesh office. While the future of INGOs, as local NGOs grow and develop their capacities, has often been called into question in a general sense, Bangladesh is one of the first countries in which the debate is of immediate consequence. In 1995 BRAC set up an 'NGO Co-operation Unit', and became a direct donor itself, using its own funds and technical expertise to support small NGOs throughout the country (BRAC 2000). As BRAC begins to delve into the domain of donor organisations as well, perhaps it is not just the future of INGOs, but that of donor agencies which is also at stake.

In terms of their reputations, powerful local NGOs are as well known on the international stage as they are in their local ones. Madres de Plaza de Mayo have truly 'attracted the world's attention' (Skaar 1994: 142); they are regularly courted by organisations across Latin America and Europe for speaking tours, have spawned auxiliary groups in Australia, Canada and the Netherlands, have a square named after them in Amsterdam and have been awarded prizes in Italy, Germany, Spain, the United States, Argentina, Brazil and Cuba, in addition to receiving the 1992 Sakharov Prize for Freedom of Thought from the European Parliament and the 1999 UNESCO Prize for Peace Education. (Bouvard 1994). SEWA, which one observer writes, 'has emerged as one of the leading organizations of poor working women in the Third World', is similarly well-known on the international stage, not least because it has spawned its own offshoots in South Africa, Yemen and Turkey (Spodek 1994: 193).

These powerful local NGOs are also unusual in the degree to which they have courted partnerships with the international community – partnerships in which they play the lead roles. Most local NGOs are brought in on the projects of international organisations, like the UN agencies, as junior partners, or contractors, with a specific predetermined role to play. With their levels of power, however, these groups can design their own large-scale projects, which they then offer international bodies the opportunity to become involved in. And where the majority of local NGOs are the subjects of the work of external researchers, usually commissioned by their donors, each of these powerful local NGOs plans and undertakes high quality research that is widely disseminated and relied upon. Proshika, IBASE and FASE each also publish their own journals, known as *Discourse*, *Cidadania* and *Proposta*, and DESCO, which publishes two regular journals, has published over 250 titles since its first publication in 1972 (DESCO 2002). In addition to sharing their research and expertise through their publications, NGOs like BRAC and SEWA add to their international reputations by bringing development leaders from across the world to their flourishing training centres in Bangladesh and India. (Spodek 1994, BRAC 2000). The amount of attention afforded to these local NGOs in journals and at conferences, the number of replications of their projects currently underway throughout the developing world, the number of international development professionals attending their training courses, and the number of donors clambering to work with them, are all telling signs of their reputations and illustrate how their power has reversed the typical international 'partnership' relationship in which northern groups dominate.

A willingness and eagerness to promote one's self has been invaluable to these groups in building their reputations. As one observer of powerful organisations has noted 'the appearance of power can actually provide power' (Pfeffer 1992: 44–5). It is the curse of many local NGOs to toil in obscurity for year upon year, and too often local NGOs believe that to share their success with others would brand them arrogant and proud. As we will see in later chapters, self-promotion is something that local NGOs in Africa shy away from, believing that the impact of their work should speak for itself. Powerful local NGOs like the ones discussed here, on the other hand, have packaged their successes and shared them with the world. In a description of its work which was published among the profiles of NGOs from around the world, BRAC (1992: 53) wrote that it had 'grown into a multi-disciplinary development agency, leading both within the country and abroad'. That may be true, and indeed, one of the main points I am trying to make, but it is rare to find a local NGO willing to make such a claim. It may well be that it is only powerful NGOs that are able to tell the world about their successes because they are the only NGOs confident and powerful enough to withstand the resultant onslaught of attention from the international development community and be certain that even their critics will be unable to discredit their claims.

The charisma and contacts of an NGO's leader can also make a major contribution to its self-packaging and reputation. F.H. Abed, BRAC's founder is well respected the world over. One donor, when asked what impressed him most about BRAC, responded in this way, 'Abed is the most impressive asset of BRAC.' (Interview with Representative, International Donor Agency, Dhaka, 26 July 2000). Organisational promotion is certainly made easier by having someone of Abed's prominence and vision at the helm of the NGO. The fact that Abed is as well-known as BRAC also makes it considerably easier for him to assert himself in dealings with the whole of the development community and to cultivate individual friendships which reinforce the reputation of BRAC throughout the world. The contacts and experience of IBASE founder Betinho de Souza, Proshika founder Qazi Faruque Ahmed, WWF founder and prominent ex-politician Jaya Arunachalam and SEWA founder Ela Bhatt have been similarly important to enlarging the reputations of their organisations (Haynes 1997, Bailey 1999, Smillie and Hailey 2001). Rose (1992: 264) writes of Ela Bhatt that, 'one can measure the enormous progress made by the women's development movement by tracing her work'; in 1986 she was appointed as Chairperson of a National Commission on Self-Employed Women and in 1987 was appointed a Member of Parliament in India's upper house. As the ability to build a strong international reputation is often contingent on an NGO's power, the reputation of an NGO and its individual officers is yet another characteristic which we can use to identify powerful local NGOs.

Ability to write and rewrite the rules
The NGOs I have been describing are notable for their rare talent for challenging the *status quo*; they have developed their power not simply by offering an especially high quality range of existing development

services,[2] but by encouraging relevant actors to approach development from new and alternative perspectives. They have collectively rewritten the rules on what an NGO is meant to look like and how it is meant to behave. While most local NGOs do valiant work providing some welfare service to the poor and marginalised, both SEWA and the Working Women's Forum in India have been clear since their inception that their goal was not just 'to help, but to empower poor women and to enable them to challenge the existing exploitative and oppressive power structures in society' (Ramesh 1995: 95). These NGOs are not afraid to confront unions, governments and international organisations in their efforts to organise and mobilise poor women workers. Ela Bhatt of SEWA has voiced her organisation's goals as follow: 'We not only want a piece of the pie, we also want to choose the flavour, and know how to make it ourselves' (Smillie 1995: 81). SEWA has lobbied the Indian government all the way to the Supreme Court in order to recognise the rights of hawkers and vendors and has similarly influenced the International Labour Organisation (ILO) and the International Confederation of Free Trade Unions (ICFTU) to extend their attention and their protections to self-employed and home-based workers (Clark 1991, Rose 1992, Datta 2000).

Madres de Plaza de Mayo has similarly challenged the status quo in Argentina. The first group to condemn state-sanctioned disappearances in that country and to pressure authorities to release information on the disappeared, the Madres staged gutsy public marches at a time when 'demonstrations of any kind were forbidden' (Navarro 1989: 250). In making it an ethical obligation of the people to oppose Argentina's military dictatorship, they 'transformed the [disappeared] into an issue that no political party could ignore or could afford to negotiate' (Navarro 1989: 255), and played a significant role in the downfall of the regime (Feijoo and Gogna 1990, Chinchilla 1992). In doing so, the Madres have forever redefined political activity in the country, especially in terms of the role of women in the public sphere, and have changed all the rules for organised dissent (Feijoo and Gogna 1990, Navarro 1989, Chinchilla 1992, Craske 1999). Even today they continue to challenge the idea of what an NGO is meant to do, recently starting up their own private university in Buenos Aires.

Powerful NGOs are also distinct for their ability to rewrite the rules that govern how an NGO should relate to government. While many local NGOs either choose to be uncritical bedfellows or constant opponents of their governments, NGOs like SEWA, IBASE and Proshika have developed

[2] Many local NGOs have actually fought against this. Margarita Bosch (1997: 234) writes of NGOs in Brazil that, 'the development of a stronger identity among Brazilian NGOs has been based on a distinction from, or even opposition to, social welfare. [...] The tension between the provision of material services on the one hand, and the struggle for civil rights and influence over government policies on the other, has been particularly intense, with "assistencialism" ("welfare") being the "evil spirit" to be continuously exorcised by NGOs in their work.'

much more nuanced relationships with government. SEWA's efforts to pressure the Indian government for legal and policy changes that benefit its membership have not prevented it from collaborating with various levels of government on its projects and from working within government, in Parliament and on a national commission (Rose 1992, Spodek 1994). Similarly in Brazil, IBASE works with government agencies on various social initiatives and is a regular paid contractor for government programmes; yet it is not afraid to lobby government for changes or to speak out against government social policies, even when it means losing government consulting contracts (Bailey 1999). Each month IBASE also compiles 'a critical evaluation' of the government's most recent policies and performance, which it distributes to 3,000 different organisations, including government departments (IBASE 1992: 217).

Proshika's relationship with the government of Bangladesh has evolved greatly since its early days of mistrust and animosity. While harshly criticised for taking an aggressive anti-government stance with one government regime and then an overly-close relationship with its successor in 1996, Proshika has maintained that 'development cannot be separated from obvious and clear issues of governance' (Smillie and Hailey 2001: 23). While many observers questioned Proshika's politicisation in that era, they now consider its advocacy programme to be one of its major strengths (Interview with Representative, International Donor Agency, Dhaka, 26 July 2000). In the words of one of Proshika's major donors, as they 'have criticised very vociferously some of the things that [government] have done, this has proved what Proshika has said all along: that they are political, but not party political' (Interview with Representative, International Donor Agency, Dhaka, 24 July 2000).

Even the generally antagonistic relationship between Madres de Plaza de Mayo and successive governments in Argentina diverges from the norm: where it is usually NGOs who work in opposition to government, in this case the reverse is true. As one set of observers write, the Madres 'derive their power not so much from opposing the state as by the fact that the state has systematically opposed them' (Calderón *et al*, 1992). At the hands of government they have endured political ridicule, being dubbed 'the madwomen of the Plaza de Mayo', and ongoing oppression in the form of imprisonment, police harassment, the raiding of their offices and even the kidnapping of their members (Navarro 1989, Feijoo and Gogna 1990, Bouvard 1994). Yet the Madres are as comfortable today speaking out against their democratically elected government as they were speaking out against the military junta (Taylor 1998). By necessity they have rewritten the rules on how NGOs ought to relate to government, and how governments ought to relate to NGOs.

Powerful local NGOs also create their own rules when it comes to enduring criticism or withstanding scandal. Despite their reputations, each of the powerful local NGOs we have been looking at has at one time or another faced criticism from government, the media or other NGOs over their size, their lack of transparency or their economic or political involvement. Yet unlike most, these NGOs have seldom lost a donor, a partner or a publication over any of the allegations. BRAC and Proshika's well publicised and ongoing struggles with Islamic groups and certain factions of government, for instance, rarely caused worry among their donors, despite the severity of the conflicts. While the NGO sector as a whole has been targeted by Islamic fundamentalists, during 1994, for example, when the 'Society against Atheists and NGOs' objected to the aims of several NGOs, it is these two NGOs which have faced the majority of this opposition. Proshika plant nurseries and trees used by BRAC in its sericulture programmes were destroyed, at least 50 BRAC schools were burnt down and BRAC was compared to the East India Company by one daily newspaper and accused of fronting foreign forces trying to take over the country (Holloway 1998, Tvedt 1998, Interview with A.M.R. Chowdhury, Deputy Executive Director, BRAC, Dhaka, 23 July 2000). Similarly, in 1997, the backlash to a BRAC poster campaign led to demonstrations against BRAC, religious condemnation of its work and the assault of its personnel (Rafi and Chowdhury 2000). Yet support of all kinds continued to pour into these NGOs. The controversies over BRAC's use of donor funds to support its various commercial enterprises have caused a similar uproar in the press, yet have failed to deter the NGO's many supporters.

But in today's development climate, many good local NGOs continue to retain their supporters, their friends, even in the face of local opposition. Quality NGOs are supported by other civil society organisations in their region, Northern NGOs, donors and in some cases by their governments as well. In fact, the degree to which local NGOs have become the automatic and favourite friends of donor organisations has caused some concern for the future of the Bangladeshi state (Hashemi 1995, Sobhan 1997, White 1999). To have friends who will stand by you in the midst of opposition is one mark of power. But a truer test is to have friends who will stand by you when you implicate yourself in inefficiencies, poor management and financial scandals. Powerful local NGOs have just those kinds of friends.

One of the biggest complaints of local NGOs throughout the world is the uncompromising focus of their donors on the rhetoric of aid: accountability, sustainability, logical framework analysis and the like. NGOs that are late with a quarterly report, appoint too congenial a board member or embrace too hierarchical a form of decision-making often face censure from their donors. One of the biggest surprises in examining the powerful local NGOs we have been discussing is not that they are powerful, but rather that they are powerful while still suffering from many of the weaknesses commonly pointed out in other local NGOs – weaknesses that donors recognise, but ignore. One key donor agent illustrated this incongruity with respect to BRAC: 'They actually deliver the goods. They have such a vast network that they are actually able to reach out to various parts of the country where it's not political for other people to bother with it.' Yet they were also quick to point out many of BRAC's shortcomings: 'It's a very long, slow, painfully tortuous process for BRAC to get a proposal together. They're not able to'; 'BRAC is so big one hand doesn't know what the other is doing. One director doesn't know what the others are doing'; 'BRAC is probably one of the worst NGOs, along with [another large local NGO] in terms of choosing new members for boards'; 'Their staff policy is in the dark ages. It's very weak' (Interview with Representative, International Donor Agency, Dhaka, 19 July 2000). Another donor described a similar frustration with BRAC:

> They never send anything on time. That's not quite true [but] they either choose not to, or they don't quite have the capacity to deal with donors in the way you would expect an organisation of that size to. And I suspect it's more they choose not. Because if you look at a lot of the stuff [... like] their annual report, the publications which they put out themselves, they're extremely well written, very glossy, and have a very good level of analysis compared to some of the stuff they send to donors. And I quite understand why they do that, because we're stupid enough to carry on funding them. So why should they spend any more effort giving us any more than they need to get away with it (Interview with Representative, International Donor Agency, Dhaka, 24 July 2000).

Yet it is BRAC, and not the many local NGOs in Bangladesh with faultless administrative and accountability systems, which is able to maintain its donors year after year and benefit from ever improving terms of aid. So how do powerful local NGOs like BRAC manage to get away with what are, for most NGOs, capital crimes? Firstly, by being very good at what they do. These NGOs deliver on their promises and their size means that in funding one NGO, donors are touching multiple sectors, regions and types of beneficiaries. Every donor needs to be seen to be supporting this type of highly 'successful' local NGO. One donor echoed this sentiment in explaining BRAC's allure for them:

> They are successful. And donors need to be able to trot out successful projects to keep getting the money. And I don't think any donor would deny that. They wouldn't be able to say it to BRAC perhaps, but that really is the bottom line. Everybody needs a success story. And BRAC certainly is one of the most successful stories (Interview with Repre-sentative, International Donor Agency, Dhaka, 19 July 2000).

Secondly, there are few substitutes for these NGOs, whether BRAC in Bangladesh or DESCO in Peru. International NGOs in Bangladesh, for example, offer little competition to local NGOs in terms of the breadth and depth of their programming, and are slowly being replaced by their local counterparts. Government, on the other hand, has yet to develop a widespread and comprehensive development agenda. According to one donor agent, their government is 'not convinced that the Bangladeshi government has a sincere commitment to poverty reduction', and in the words of another, 'the government is not doing anything. I mean provision of services, almost any kind of service, is so sub-standard. [...] So thank God for the NGOs' (Interview with Representative, International Donor Agency, Dhaka, 24 July 2000, Interview with Representative, International Donor Agency, Dhaka, 26 July 2000). So donors face a difficult choice: continue to support powerful NGOs and accept their organisational shortcomings and shrewd tactics, or end these funding relationships and face the wrath of a head office which expects super-star NGO names to be listed on its annual report. Donors need powerful local NGOs as much as the NGOs need donors, if not more. Donor agencies need to invest their funding in the world's poorest countries, and in the face of government impotence, they need to be funding the actors who are making a difference in that country's development. For them, these powerful local NGOs are the obvious choice. This ability to rewrite the rules of the game, to the point that donors need their beneficiary NGOs as much as the beneficiaries need the donor, is therefore another distinguishing characteristic of powerful local NGOs.

These brief case studies of local NGOs with power, as demonstrated by their size, wealth, reputation and ability to rewrite the rules on acceptable NGO behaviour, has helped us to understand better what NGO power looks like and what it enables local NGOs to do. The examples of these powerful local NGOs from Argentina, Bangladesh, Brazil, India and Peru have also generated some interesting and unexpected details about NGO power. First, power is not just about being good at what you do and obeying the rules. There are dozens of very effective and efficient local NGOs in Africa which still lack power. If anything, powerful local NGOs have achieved many of their successes by refusing to play by the book. Second, there is an important distinction between the good and the powerful. Lots of good NGOs are not powerful. And powerful NGOs are not always good. They have faults and weaknesses like any other NGO, and perhaps even more than some. None of the powerful NGOs studied here are infallible or always perfect, and each has at some time disappointed its stakeholders. Yet they have each managed to achieve and retain power. We turn now to consider the evolution of these local NGOs: the aspects of their histories which place them apart from other local NGOs in their countries and have been key to their development of power.

How is power developed? The evolution of powerful local NGOs

No two of the powerful local NGOs we have been considering share the same history. Some, like SEWA, FASE and Proshika, emerged out of other existing organisations, both local and international. The Self-Employed

Women's Association, for example, began its life as an initiative of the women's wing of the Textile Labour Association (TLA), an Indian union of textile workers. It spent nine years aligned with the TLA, before a range of conflicts culminated in the parent organisation severing all its ties to SEWA (Rose 1992, Smillie 1995, Datta 2000). In Brazil, where the Catholic church played a leading role in human rights and democratisation movements during the period of authoritarian rule, it was the Catholic Relief Services organisation which gave birth to FASE, one of the country's 'first purely Brazilian NGOs working in community development' (Smillie 1995: 65, Meyer 1999, Hanashiro 2000, Houtzager 2000). Proshika, on the other hand, originated out of an international organisation, the Canadian University Service Overseas (CUSO). Proshika was initially a CUSO project, 'without ambitions of autonomy, and without expecting to become a role model for others' (Smillie 1995: 66, Smillie and Hailey 2001). Today it is one of Bangladesh's largest NGOs. Other powerful local NGOs like the Working Women's Forum or DESCO, however, were started expressly to address particular needs and service gaps in their countries and are today recognisable as older, more experienced versions of the same organisations as which they began.

Powerful local NGOs also vary in the degree to which their focus, strategies and programming have changed over their lifetime. Soon after it was created, BRAC found that its relief and rehabilitation operations failed to truly address the deeper, underlying issue that plagued Bangladesh: poverty (BRAC 1992, BRAC 2000). So BRAC modified its focus from emergency relief to community development, and in doing so, mirrored the transition from first generation to second generation NGO work as first described by David Korten. For Korten (1987: 147), there is 'an underlying direction of movement' for NGOs, from a first generation focus on relief and welfare, to a second generation focus on small-scale local initiatives, to a third generation engagement with larger debates on inequality at the political and policy level. BRAC's evolution to the present seems to generally coincide with this progression, and from a community development focus, the BRAC programme has moved towards a strategy of empowerment of the rural masses, including economic, social and political empowerment activities (Howes and Sattar 1992, Luz, 1991). Madres de Plaza de Mayo, on the other hand, has from its inception been a resistance organisation firmly situated in human rights and democratisation activities which Korten would consider as belonging to the third generation of NGO work.

Despite their different origins, however, all of these local NGOs share certain common elements in their histories. Firstly, they all emerged in contexts in which there were few 'competitor' organisations on the scene. Originating in Brazil in 1961, Peru in 1967 and Argentina in 1977 respectively, FASE, DESCO and the Madres were among only a handful of local NGOs at work in their countries in those eras of civil society repression and autocratic rule.

Created just after independence in Bangladesh in 1972, BRAC found itself in a country in desperate need of relief and rehabilitation. Thirty million people were homeless, refugees streamed over the new borders from India and Pakistan, and starvation and illness were rife (Islam 1981). Infrastructure, both social and economic, was in ruin, and the newly independent government inherited a 'near stagnant economy with little capacity for internal resource generation' (Sobhan 1982: 3). The country was in need of levels of relief and rehabilitation that the government alone could not provide. Yet few local development organisations had yet been created and few international NGOs had remained in the country through its period of civil war. Many of the foreign organisations which did remain were treated with suspicion because of their Western roots and direct ties to Christian churches (Shailo 1994, Jamil 2000). As such, considerable uncontested development space was available to BRAC and, like its South American counterparts mentioned above, it gained a head start over other NGOs. With few local role models to follow and no accepted division of labour among existing development organisations, these groups also had the chance to set their own priorities for their work and to take that work in whatever direction it wanted. No matter what activities BRAC, DESCO or FASE decided to incorporate into their work, they could be confident that they would not find themselves competing with another organisation already working in that area.

A second element common to these NGOs' history is their almost immediate interest in linking both themselves and their clients to mainstream economic systems. For SEWA, Proshika and WWF, started in 1972, 1976 and 1980, and long before microcredit became in vogue in international development circles, this meant offering credit. Their banks and credit programmes have not only had a tremendous impact on the welfare of the clients of these NGOs but have also improved the financial security and self-sufficiency of their organisations. Today the credit and banking activities of these three organisations are arguably the pro- grammes for which they are most renowned. They, and their powerful counterparts, have been equally interested in linking themselves to the market. BRAC and IBASE run internet service providers, DESCO and IBASE conduct consulting contracts for a variety of local and inter- national agencies, and BRAC, Proshika, SEWA and WWF all market their clients' products, ranging from milk to silk to handicrafts, both locally and internationally. BRAC's Executive Director explained how this strategy has been critical to his organisation:

> Right from the beginning we thought that we shouldn't be totally dependent on the donors. [...] So in 1974, I remember writing a proposal for a printing press to be funded by some donors. A number of donors said all right, since you're in education and you'll need a printing press we'll give you a printing press. So that's how we started our first income-generating project. And then of course all the

businesses that we have done were all related to helping the poor to link to the market. (Interview with F.H. Abed, Executive Director, BRAC, Dhaka, 25 July 2000)

Throughout their histories, powerful local NGOs have also prioritised links to other key development figures in their home countries and abroad. Some of BRAC's earliest projects, for example, linked it to civil society organisations, such as the Bangladesh Institute of Development Studies and the International Centre for Diarrhoeal Disease Research, as well as to the government of Bangladesh itself. Links to other civil society organisations in Bangladesh have been furthered by BRAC's wide network of ex-employees and partners. BRAC is committed to training and hiring large numbers of young development professionals in Bangladesh, and as these employees have moved to other NGOs, donor agencies and the private sector, BRAC has gained bonds with these other organisations (Clark 1991, Interview with F.H. Abed, Executive Director, BRAC, Dhaka, 25 July 2000).

Similarly, this group of local NGOs has carefully cultivated ties to international organisations. From the INGOs, unions, United Nations agencies and IFIs, with whom all of these groups have worked and groups like DESCO have undertaken contracts for, to the academic bodies around the world with whom these NGOs have collaborated on research, to the governments in Spain, the Netherlands and the European Parliament which have been strong supporters of Madres de Plaza de Mayo, to the global corporations like IBM and American Express with which BRAC and IBASE have collaborated, to the international offshoots which SEWA, BRAC and the Madres have spawned, these NGOs have expansive networks of international contacts (Bouvard 1994, Bailey 1999, BRAC 2000). While most local NGOs in the developing world work in relative isolation at some period in their history, these groups stand out for having consistently capitalised on opportunities to link themselves, their clients and their programmes to others. Their standing as among the few local NGOs in their countries through much of their histories has certainly contributed to this trend, as foreign organisations looking for local partners would have naturally turned to them.

One last historical aspect which has set powerful local NGOs apart from the many other NGOs in their countries is their engagement with politics. Political activity is at the very heart of their work of groups, like SEWA, WWF and FASE, which attempt to redress social, economic and legal inequalities and have been active in organising their members and beneficiaries into unions (Houtzager 2000). Even the language in which SEWA describes its mandate is highly political; Ela Bhatt, SEWA's founder sees the NGO as pursuing 'the twin strategies of struggle and development' (Bhatt 1998: 147). The activities of Madres de Plaza de Mayo have been similarly political from the outset. In an environment in which all political activity was banned, political parties outlawed, judges dismissed and opposition politicians imprisoned, their marches in defiance of the law and in opposition to the government moved the dis-appearances of their children from the realm of the private to that of the public (Navarro 1989, Elshtain 1995). They also contributed 'to a redefinition of what constitutes political activity or 'doing politics' in Latin America' (Chinchilla 1992: 41).

In pursuing their social, economic and research aims, the leaders of organisations like IBASE and Proshika have also engaged their organisa-tions with the political process in their countries. Despite the economic and political costs to their NGOs, both have openly criticised their governments over their development policies; Proshika's founder and director, for example, called for the resignation of the Bangladeshi government in both 1990 and 1996 (Bailey 1999, Smillie and Hailey 2001). Even NGOs like BRAC, which originally organised around local socio-economic issues, have taken on a decidedly political slant, with BRAC reorganising its village groups into large-scale committees focussed on higher-level political issues including 'wage bargaining, political representation, protest action and pressure for local government services' (Luz 1991: 123). In a 1992 article, BRAC explained its interest in politics as one of 'identifying the power structure as a constraint on rural development' in a section they entitled 'Empowerment of the Poor...is a political act' (BRAC 1992: 57). While BRAC officials shy away from overt political opposition to the government and have, for example, banned BRAC employees from contesting elections, they maintain that BRAC is a political organisation: 'Party political no, political yes. I mean, whenever you are trying to change a society in any way it is political' (Interview with F.H. Abed, Executive Director, BRAC, Dhaka, 25 July 2000).

So the present day power of local NGOs in the developing world seems most linked to four aspects of their histories. Firstly, the availability of development space has enabled these NGOs to set their own agendas and decide what kind of work they wanted to concentrate on. Having little competition BRAC, for example, was able to gain a competitive advantage in that work and quickly distinguish itself with donor agencies and the government. Secondly, the decision of NGOs like IBASE to engage with economic markets has helped them to gain a measure of financial independence early in their history. This increased their freedom and confidence and minimised the influence of donor agendas on their choice of development activities. Thirdly, links to the international development community, such as those fostered by the Madres de Plaza de Mayo, have helped these NGOs to develop international reputations within the field of development, making them sought-after local partners and helping to protect them from government repression. As their publicity and reputation have increased, demand for the services of these NGOs has multiplied, boosting their power considerably. Lastly, as with all the local NGOs we have been considering, SEWA's engagement with development as a political issue has helped to set it apart from many of its counterparts in India and to gain considerable power.

Are these circumstances the recipe for power; are they replicable in other local NGOs? Obviously, individual elements are not. BRAC's power is in many ways a result of the particular conjuncture of circumstances and events in which it found itself. In a country recovering from a devastating war of independence and plagued by natural disaster and famine, BRAC was able to access large amounts of external aid and was helmed by an intelligent and well-liked leader with the right kinds of contacts both at home and abroad. Today, few local NGOs will find themselves alone on their national development scene, with little competition from other local NGOs, INGOs or government as BRAC did in 1971. The particular circumstances that gave rise to the Madres in Argentina, for example, are similarly unlikely to be reproduced exactly in other developing countries. Moreover, the few local NGOs that I have highlighted here are not the only powerful local NGOs in the world and theirs is not the only path to power. Nor is it the case that size or wealth is a desirable or necessary goal for all local NGOs. But as NGO power conveys certain crucial benefits to Southern NGOs and to development processes in the South, it is an end which is worth understanding and pursuing. The details of this group of local NGOs' progression have important lessons to teach us about power and NGOs and can be used to construct a general picture of what a powerful local NGO in Africa would look like.

A picture of a powerful African NGO

Based on the history of local NGOs like SEWA, BRAC, IBASE and DESCO, I can identify four factors which could be expected to lead to power among local African NGOs.

1. A powerful African NGO would possess its own space within development
Space, niche, competitive advantage – a powerful African NGO would be one that was fulfilling unmet demand for development services. It might have found this space by starting its operations immediately after independence or political liberalisation, before other similar civil society organisations were at work. It might have developed a niche for itself, providing development services that no other organisation provided, providing services in a different region or language, or using a novel approach to development in its work. Or it might have pursued a competitive advantage for itself, specialising in a particular area of development, and gaining a level of skills, training, experience and contacts in that field that no other development agency could match. Regardless of the particular strategy or circumstance, a powerful African NGO would be one that found or created room for itself on the development scene.

The ability of a local African NGO to develop space might coincide with its government's weakness in addressing development concerns at large or in responding to a particular sector or geographical area. Perhaps national government has only meagre resources at its disposal or more pressing political concerns, while local levels of government lack strength and a sense of purpose. The absence of competition from government would considerably increase the room in which a local African NGO could manoeuvre. Similarly, for a local African NGO to develop power it would also have to outcompete international NGOs. Since INGOs tend to be better funded than local NGOs, an African NGO would rarely outcompete an international NGO in terms of resources. It would therefore have to provide development services that INGOs could not or would not provide. As will be illustrated shortly, highly politicised development services often fall into this category.

Perhaps the most effective way for African NGOs to capture their own space within development – and one which has been crucial to NGOs like BRAC and SEWA – is through social innovation.[3] NGOs which are able to make an impact by generating and articulating new ideas, methods and knowledge, linking old ideas and processes in new ways, reframing issues and bringing people to view will automatically create their own niche. They will attract the support of government agencies and other like-minded groups, and find their knowledge and experiences in demand by NGOs, academic institutions and donor groups around the world – thereby reversing the traditional flow of ideas and resources from the North to the South. But most importantly, innovative NGOs will gain the respect and solidarity of their beneficiaries, as they are better able to serve their needs and represent their interests.

The lack of competition and availability of development space that faced many of the world's most powerful local NGOs in their early years allowed them to create a niche for themselves and expand it, capitalising on donor funds and diversifying their areas of activity. As they grew, they were able to create new space for themselves, while guarding their traditional domains, and as this cycle has continued, their power has been further reinforced. While local African NGOs might never be the first development organisations at work in their countries, as were many of their counterparts in South Asia or Latin America, their ability to succeed as social innovators is limited only by their imagination, their understanding of the needs of their beneficiaries and their willingness to experiment.

2. A powerful African NGO would be financially independent
To have the power to determine and follow its own priorities, a local NGO must have a degree of financial independence from its donors. Some elements of such independence include: relying on no single donor for funding, but working with multiple donors of different sorts (e.g. official aid agencies, private foundations and northern NGOs) and from different

---

[3] I am grateful to David Brown for his suggestions on this section.

home countries; accepting only basket or untargeted funding; and negotiating funding contracts which include overhead or core funding, and are of medium- to long-term duration. Such strategies help an NGO to avoid the pitfalls of upwards accountability or 'standardisation' – the adoption by an NGO of the practices and priorities of its funders – to which even international NGOs with large donating publics can be susceptible (Wallace *et al.* 1997).

To achieve financial independence, a local NGO must also be able to survive without donor funds, either by tapping into alternative sources of funding or by generating its own funds. In local development, where governments rarely fund the work of NGOs and donating publics are rare, few alternative sources of NGO funding exist. To survive without donor funds is often, therefore, to be able to generate your own funds. A powerful local African NGO would be expected to generate revenue internally, through its involvement in economic projects or commercial enterprises. Local NGOs involved in micro-credit programmes can generate considerable funds through the interest they charge on the loans they make. With a 15 per cent service charge on the loans it disburses, and loan disbursements of over 965 million US dollars, BRAC, for instance, has raised a significant amount of money (BRAC 2000). Powerful local NGOs not involved in the credit sector would be predicted to be generating revenue for their organisation through commercial activities. These might be enterprises linked directly to their programmes, such as marketing handicraft or agricultural products, or side businesses in consulting or training, which capitalise on the knowledge and experience of the staff of the NGO. IBASE in Brazil raises almost half of its funding from such commercial endeavours (Fowler 1997).

With the relative amount of financial security that independent sources of income can provide, a local NGO can avoid being buffeted by frequently changing donor priorities or by offers of funding which might divert it from its main areas of focus. Reducing financial dependence on donors can also help local NGOs to gain legitimacy in the eyes of their beneficiaries and the state, as the influence of Western donors on their agenda is lessened and conflict with a government that perceives donor funding for NGOs as lost government revenue is reduced (Atack 1999). And as declining aid flows begin to affect developing countries around the world, independent sources of funding will help NGOs to continue their work and maintain their influence and impact should they one day find themselves in a 'beyond aid' scenario (Aldaba *et al.* 2000).

3. A powerful African NGO would have strong links to the international development community
There are hundreds of thousands of local development NGOs in the world today. To become one of the few that are powerful a local NGO has to make itself indispensable, not only locally, but internationally. In other words, it must occupy development space both at home and abroad.

Creating ties to development actors throughout the world is one of the ways to achieve this international space.

There are several different kinds of international links that one would expect to find in a powerful local NGO in Africa. First, perhaps, would be links to other NGOs, NGO umbrella bodies, civil society organisations and government agencies at home, as well as links to a wider range of African organisations working in the same field of development. These kinds of local and regional links can be crucial to an NGO, facilitating the sharing of work, resources and experiences in good times, and providing financial and political support in times of difficulty.

Secondly, powerful local NGOs would be expected to have cultivated links to development organisations further afield. Links to academic institutions can be important in helping an NGO to develop its research capacity, get the results of its research published, and further train and educate its employees. Alliances with non-operational NNGOs, international organisations and multinational corporations can be similarly important, as they provide project funds and equipment, professional and technical expertise, and international support for local development campaigns. Relationships with the international media can also be crucial in helping local NGOs to develop a name and reputation in the countries where donors and donating publics live and where most development policy is determined. These ties to the international press often also help to ensure the safety of an NGO's staff and beneficiaries in times of conflict with the government.

Finally, as transnational networks and social movements have become increasingly active and influential in international development and global politics, we would expect powerful local NGOs to participate in these movements around issues of interest. Just as the increasing rate of globalisation has made it necessary for a business in one country to plug into the changing global business context to succeed, the development community has also become more international, and local NGOs can benefit from being more connected to their counterparts in other countries. Transnational networks, backed by large numbers of people from around the globe, play a significant role in shaping the international development discourse, influencing the decisions of states and multilateral agencies, strengthening civil society groups and, through their advocacy or protests, placing cross-border development issues such as human rights, debt relief or dam creation on the international agenda (Keck and Sikkink 1998, Anheier *et al.* 2001, Edwards and Gaventa 2001, Lindenberg and Bryant 2001, Khagram *et al.* 2002). Southern NGOs gain valuable contacts, information, solidarity, support, international exposure and access to international systems from participation in such networks. They can also benefit from building an identity beyond that of a service provider. Being identified with a popular movement of core relevance to an NGO's mandate and its beneficiaries' interests can add to the legitimacy of an indigenous NGO in the eyes of its clients and allow it to play a truly transforming role in society.

4. A powerful African NGO would be willing to engage with the political aspects of development

Moyo (1992a: 10) claims that 'if NGOs are to be effective, they should be politically involved'. This is a controversial claim and, applying it to the present context, suggests that an indigenous African NGO would have to engage with politics in order to become powerful. The powerful local NGOs featured earlier in this chapter are distinct for having a political mandate in their work and an influence on development policy. Their examples illustrate that a powerful NGO is one that does not shy away from challenging elite interests and linking political arrangements to social and economic development in line with its projects and programmes. But it is also one which does so without becoming the government's unofficial political opposition and speaking out against it at every opportunity.

An important reason why powerful NGOs tend to be those which engage with political debates in development is that they are able to create and access development space for themselves in working on these issues. International NGOs are active and operational in education, health, agriculture, credit and almost all fields of development activity across Africa. But for many reasons, including their dependence on the goodwill of foreign governments to remain and work in their countries, INGOs are rarely willing to include rural empowerment, mass mobilisation, lobbying and advocacy activities in their portfolio of development activities.[4] This allows local NGOs one field of development activity in which they face no competition from INGOs or from the government against which they tend to be mobilising. Based on the examples of several powerful local NGOs in the developing world, then, a powerful local African NGO is one which, while not necessarily focussing on development solely as a political issue, is willing to include political activity, where necessary, as part of its approach to development.

This model is built on four key factors which, based on the experience of powerful local NGOs around the world, would be expected to lead to power among NGOs in Africa. Obviously these are not the only variables by which power will be gained and the confluence of circumstances in any one context at any one time may be such that even NGOs that have achieved these elements of power nonetheless remain powerless. As such, I would consider these four factors to be necessary, though not always sufficient, to gain power.

How do these four cornerstones of power relate to each other?[5] And is there a hierarchy of importance or sequence in which they need to be achieved in order to build power? As I have suggested, the achievement of individual elements of power can be of significant benefit to an NGO in achieving others. For example, strong links to the international develop-

---

[4] Auret (1993), for example, identifies increased government control as one of the repercussions of advocacy work for international NGOs in Zimbabwe.

[5] I am grateful to Sam Hickey for his suggestions on this section.

ment community can lead to the forming of relationships with northern donating communities, businesses and private philanthropists thus increasing an NGO's independence from traditional aid donors. Engaging with the political aspects of development can help an NGO to carve out its own distinct space in development. Equally, by being a social innovator, a local NGO may not only create space for itself, but also attract a diverse range of partners from around the globe.

All four of these elements are intimately connected, and I would be reluctant to rank them in terms of their importance. However, I would consider the attainment and protection of space to be the foundation for the other three building blocks of power. While an NGO could grow to gain power even if it began its life as isolated, unwilling to engage with the political elements of underdevelopment, and tied to donor funds, it would be difficult for an NGO to be able to set its own priorities, define its own agenda and exert its influence, despite opposition, without having its own space. And though the model itself is flexible, for the majority of NGOs, I would anticipate that the four dimensions of power that I have identified would be achieved in the order in which they were presented. For many of these groups, it will only be with the achievement of space and financial independence that they are able to invest in international bridge-building – which can be an especially costly endeavour in Africa. In certain contexts, it will also be the case that adopting a more politicised work agenda and assuming what is often a considerable risk, will only be possible for African NGOs with financial independence from donor agendas and strong support from the international development community.

Some final thoughts on powerful NGOs

Powerful local NGOs do indeed exist and the factors which have influenced their rise to power are identifiable, if not exactly replicable. The experience of a small sample of powerful NGOs from across the developing world suggests that several factors, including space, financial independence from donors, solid links to the international development community, and a willingness to engage with the political aspects of development work are relevant to NGO power. Their examples also illustrate that while these NGOs are powerful, they are not immune to the difficulties that plague most local NGOs whether in terms of confrontational governments or struggles to achieve donor standards in administration and management. Power and efficiency are not equivalent, and the fact that the donors of these powerful NGOs recognise and accept their inefficiencies is symbolic of the power they wield in their relationships with donors.

Traditional explanations for the weakness of local African NGOs tend to make this mistake, confusing power and efficiency. Richard Sandbrook considers the 'debilitating weaknesses' of African NGOs to be their small size, relative isolation and poor funding, their role as representatives of the weakest and most vulnerable strata of society, and government attempts to control the NGO sector (Sandbrook 1993: 4). Yet the ways in which powerful local NGOs in Asia and Latin America have progressed to their current position of power, and the picture of a powerful local NGO that their experiences have helped to develop, suggest that Sandbrook's explanation of local NGO weakness in Africa does not adequately explain the phenomenon of power among local NGOs in Africa. In the next three chapters, these explanations of power will be studied alongside the experiences of local NGOs in Zimbabwe, Tanzania and Senegal.

3
The Power
of Local NGOs   in Zimbabwe

The power of a country's local NGO sector is often most related to the historical place of social movements and civil society organisations in its national landscape. In Zimbabwe, however, it is as much related to very recent political developments in the country. In February 2000, President Robert Mugabe's ruling ZANU-PF party suffered its first defeat since it assumed power in 1980, shortly after Zimbabwean independence. Voters in a national referendum defeated proposed changes to Zimbabwe's constitution, which would have increased the power of the state over all elements of civil society. From this moment on, the fate of NGOs and their fellow civil society organisations was irreversibly altered. Within days, the government was supporting and often encouraging widespread and violent invasions of white-owned commercial farms by ZANU-PF followers and members of the War Veterans' Association.

The country was in crisis by June of that year, when the Mugabe government maintained a narrow majority in national parliamentary elections. Political killings, torture and intimidation characterised the election campaign, as supporters of ZANU-PF, the government's Central Intelligence Organisation (CIO) and even police officers attempted to intimidate members of the government's main opposition party (Krieger 2000, Amnesty International 2001). In the following months, private sector businesses, the independent press, the judiciary and the NGO community were also to suffer at the hands of war veterans and government forces, all of whom were granted immunity by the President for any role they played in politically motivated crimes.[1]

Since 2000, political turmoil has reigned in Zimbabwe. After incidents like the raiding of NGO offices, the abduction of the head of an

---

[1] Raftopoulos (2000) and Blair (2002) provide detailed and insightful descriptions of government antagonism towards groups as diverse as telecommunications companies and department stores, private hospitals, journalists, Supreme Court justices and international NGOs.

international aid agency and the ill treatment of a Canadian diplomat, many donor countries have reduced or frozen both their official aid to Zimbabwe and their funding to its NGOs (Blair 2002). Zimbabwe's once thriving tourist industry has all but collapsed. With the additional decline of the agriculture industry, the elimination of official aid and export financing and the imposition of international sanctions, Zimbabwe has fallen further into economic turmoil. Flows of investment capital have dried up, foreign currency reserves are depleted, inflation exceeds 60 per cent, and unemployment rates have climbed above 70 per cent (*The Zimbabwe Independent*, 23 January 2002).

Enjoying a relatively high per capita gross national product (GNP) and human development index compared to most countries in sub-Saharan Africa, and labelled a country with 'plenty of economy potential' by one of its donors, Zimbabwe would not be the first African country to come to mind when considering underdevelopment (DFID 1999: 1). Yet like its neighbour South Africa, and the oil-rich Nigeria, Zimbabwe's wealth is unevenly distributed across its population. Its per capita income is high in sub-Saharan African terms, but the gap between the rich and the poor has continued to widen since independence (UNDP Zimbabwe 1999). More than one third of the population lives below the dollar a day poverty line, more than a third of the adult population is HIV positive, and women continue to be disproportionately affected by the deteriorating social conditions in the country (UNDP 2002, ZWRCN 1998).

According to one political expert at the University of Zimbabwe, 'There is general discontent in all sectors of society. The country has never been in a deep crisis as it is now. The vast majority of people are very unhappy with the government because it cannot even afford to provide them with basic needs' (*The Financial Gazette*, 19 November 1998). The state's financial resources have been strained by the loss of official aid monies and depleted by its support for the government of the Democratic Republic of Congo in its civil war. The ruling party, meanwhile, continues to blame foreign governments, Western donors, domestic critics and subversive white 'Rhodesians' for undermining the economy. In this context, civil society organisations play key roles in meeting the country's development needs.

Historical setting

Social movements and the precursors to today's local NGOs date back to well before Zimbabwe's independence. Burial societies, savings groups, women's clubs and professional organisations have operated consistently in the country since the early twentieth century, and many indigenous welfare and self-help groups, churches and labour movements, were crucial actors in Zimbabwe's liberation struggle (Moyo 1992b, Mushauri 1997). The number of NGOs in the country mushroomed after independence and over the last decade the estimated number of local and international NGOs at work in Zimbabwe has expanded to 850 (Moyo 2000a). While early NGOs were predominantly concerned with relief and welfare, in the last ten years they have developed more prominent roles, especially in the areas of human rights, HIV/AIDS and the environment – three issues around which government has been unable or unwilling to act.

Despite their number and the strength of their presence, however, local NGOs still tend to lack policy influence and opportunities to participate in higher-level decision-making in Zimbabwe. Like their counterparts across sub-Saharan Africa, they have been excluded from power. This chapter will explore the reasons behind this lack of power and determine where power does lie within the Zimbabwean development sector.

The local NGO sector in Zimbabwe

Zimbabwe's long struggle for independence, only fairly recently achieved, the increasingly adversarial relationship between its government and its civil society organisations, and its relatively high levels of human development, wealth and inequality, combine to create an unusual development space in the country today. This makes Zimbabwe an important and especially interesting case study in considering the power of local NGOs in Africa. During 1999, I interviewed representatives from a variety of relevant development actors in the country, including a sample of over twenty local NGOs, with an average age of twelve. This section will explain the results of this field work, focussing on the sectoral distribution, human resource base, financial situation and network of relationships that local NGOs build with other development actors. It aims to develop a clearer picture of local Zimbabwean NGOs, the roles that they play in national development and the power that they wield.

In what sectors are Zimbabwean NGOs most active?
One of the most striking characteristics of the local NGO sector in Zimbabwe is the degree to which the majority of its NGOs specialise. While many local NGOs in other countries regularly alter their focus and their types of programmes, as the competing interests of their donors and beneficiaries change, Zimbabwean NGOs provide a rather unique contrast to this phenomenon (Brown 1988). Even NGOs that are struggling for survival seem to hold tightly to a very focussed mandate. This strategy has obvious funding implications. By specialising and restricting their activity to one sector of development, NGOs in Zimbabwe also restrict the number of donors on which they can rely for funding – since most donors tend to have very focussed and limited areas of interest.

Not surprisingly, given that most Zimbabwean NGOs specialise narrowly, there is relatively little overlap of NGO activity in the country.

While almost half of the local NGOs active in the capital Harare either specialise in providing business and credit services or work in the field of natural resources and the environment, most groups within the latter sector have developed a niche of their own. The focus of NGOs active in this field includes providing environmental education for schools and industry groups, researching and lobbying on land reform, undertaking sustainable forestry, and wildlife-use projects. As a result of this special-isation, competition within the sector is limited and several NGOs have been successful in developing a national influence and reputation for innovation. This group of NGOs has evolved considerably since 1994, when Vivian wrote that: 'most [Zimbabwean] NGOs are followers rather than leaders on environmental issues' (1994: 186). Within the business and credit sector, however, most local NGOs have yet to develop their own particular speciality or niche, and regularly compete with each other for both donors and clients. This crowded space could explain why few individual NGOs within the credit sector have a particularly strong voice in Zimbabwean development.

Interestingly, a large number of Zimbabwean NGOs seem to be special-ising in relatively new and untraditional areas of development activity – such as small-enterprise support and democracy-building – and moving away from the welfare sectors of development traditionally associated with NGOs.[2] Instead, it is government bodies and international organisa-tions that are undertaking the majority of projects in 'first-generation' development fields like education, health and agriculture. Even those local NGOs which do engage with these welfare fields tend to do so at the nexus between welfare and advocacy or empowerment; education activities are often in voter education or business literacy, and health projects are regularly at the cutting edge of HIV/AIDS awareness, advocacy and research.

One explanation for this trend could be that donors have changed their funding priorities, moving their focus away from welfare and towards empowerment and advocacy activities. However, a quick look at the funding priorities of donor agencies currently in Zimbabwe indicates that this has not been the case. While they have added fields like governance and human rights to their funding portfolios, it is still only education and health, (especially important in light of Zimbabwe's debilitating level of HIV prevalence), that are funded by the majority of donor organisations in the country.

This suggests that it might be the availability of space that has encouraged Zimbabwean NGOs into alternative sectors. Emerging deve-lopment fields, such as advocacy and human rights, have few existing NGOs, but face increasing levels of demand from both local community

---

[2] This illustrates a marked change from 1993, when the majority of the Zimbabwean NGOs involved in a UNRISD/ACDI survey saw themselves as filling gaps in the government's provision of social services (Vivian 1994).

groups and international movements. Meanwhile, in more traditional welfare-based areas of development work, local NGOs face competition for resources from schools, hospitals, church and evangelical groups, government agencies, and international NGOs, whose activities predate Zimbabwean independence. Choosing to be active in less traditional development work is, therefore, one way for local NGOs to secure adequate space, funds and clients for their projects.

While Zimbabwean NGOs tend to specialise in terms of their sector of activity, they spread that activity over a diffuse geographical area. In addition to undertaking development work in multiple regions of the country, many local NGOs also create their own regional or provincial offices with which they can share decision-making and programming responsibilities. The low cost and relative ease of travel and communications within Zimbabwe is one factor which contributes to this phenomenon. Good roads traverse the country and its telecommunications infrastructure is one of the best on the continent. A second reason is that indigenous NGOs need to be seen as serving and representing the two largest ethnic and linguistic groups in Zimbabwe. Ethnic tensions, often inflamed for political purposes, are still of great relevance in the country, and any organisation interested in representing constituents of both the Shona majority and the Ndebele minority cannot remain in one centralised Harare office. Several of the organisations I met had achieved nationwide representation, with offices in all Zimbabwe's provinces. Those with fewer resources have striven at least to provide representation in both Harare and Bulawayo, the largest city in Ndebele territory.

Zimbabwe is unique among the three African countries studied in this book for its sectorally specialised but geographically widespread local NGOs. It is perhaps their very degree of specialisation which allows these NGOs to expand their operations around the country. They know that wherever they go, they will not meet with additional competition, for there are relatively few other civil society organisations which will be working in their specific sub-field. By contrast, in Tanzania and Senegal, the subjects of Chapters Four and Five, there is much greater overlap between the activities of different development organisations. Unable to find a niche for themselves based solely on the kind of development projects they undertake, local NGOs in these countries tend to work in only one region, sub-region, or town, in order to find space of their own.

How strong are the human resources of Zimbabwean NGOs?
Moyo and Katerere (1992: 2) claim that 'the single greatest constraint to NGO effectiveness is their inability to attract and retain the right calibre of staff.' Yet the majority of local NGOs in Zimbabwe are highly professional organisations, particularly with respect to the nature and quality of their human resources. All of the local NGOs I encountered had a full-time and fully salaried director. While this may not seem

remarkable, Zimbabwe was the only country in which this was the case. Few directors had previously worked in the NGO field, but each had a university degree and the specialised skills necessary to carry out their job and to guide the work of their organisation. The directors of research organisations came from university positions; the directors of credit organisations from the private-sector banking industry; and the directors of legal and human rights NGOs were former lawyers and magistrates.

The continuation of a founder or founding member of an NGO as its director several years after its creation is common in the NGO world. Yet in Zimbabwe, few NGO directors had actually founded the NGO they were now leading. The absence of this trend may be a further indication of the professionalism of Zimbabwe's NGOs. Quite in contrast to the common portrayal of local NGOs as dominated by highly personalistic connections, these groups are run by qualified individuals who have been hired expressly for their skills and experience.

In addition to employing a skilled and experienced director, the majority of local NGOs have also succeeded in attracting high-calibre staff. This can often be a genuine difficulty for local NGOs since the salaries they are able to offer are significantly lower than those offered by international development agencies or the private sector and come with fewer perks than government positions. In Zimbabwe, however, the salaries offered by local NGOs are unusually generous – only slightly lower than those offered by international NGOs and roughly comparable to those offered by government agencies and public sector businesses. The work environment fostered by these NGOs has similarly helped them to attract and retain high-quality employees. The benefits of the NGO work environment, as described by the staff of various local NGOs, include security of employment, opportunities for professional development and the absence of bureaucracy. NGO directors also recognise the importance of the open and supportive work environment they foster, as reflected in this interview excerpt:

> [Our NGO] is an exciting place to work. Being a fairly new organisa-
> tion, we're much more flexible than either government can be, or than
> perhaps some very well established organisations are. And therefore
> we can adapt and take on new ideas much more readily and stuff like
> that. And I think people really like that, they really feel that they can
> contribute and that their voices are heard and lead to real change
> (Interview with Executive Director, Local NGO #6, Harare, 18 August
> 1999).

These advantages of working in the NGO sector, combined with the ability of local NGOs to provide their employees with adequate salaries, have made it possible for Zimbabwean NGOs to count on a strong, professional and relatively secure staff complement. In Tanzania and Senegal, on the other hand, many local NGOs rely on volunteers for their survival. NGO work is regularly planned by a part-time or unpaid director and undertaken by volunteers during their spare time. It is quite normal to walk into the office of such an NGO and find no one there but a receptionist. In Zimbabwe, however, local NGOs have all the accoutrements of professional life: full-time staff; a permanent location; a telephone number; and basic publications about the organisation. This disparity between the high quality of NGO human resources in Zimbabwe and that generally ascribed to local African NGOs means that while the phenomenon of 'briefcase NGOs' is a recognised problem throughout sub-Saharan Africa, it is rarely applied to Zimbabwe.

How are Zimbabwean NGOs financed?
The high quality of the human resources found in Zimbabwean NGOs is largely due to their financial strength. While local NGOs are stereotyped as living hand to mouth, few of the organisations I encountered in Zimbabwe were consistently short of funds. This is not to say that none of them faced difficulties in obtaining funding from time to time, for particular projects or aspects of their programming; nor that they had all been able to secure core funding for their organisational expenditures. But it is a potentially important trend, when considering the power of local African NGOs, that the majority of those in Zimbabwe appear to have achieved some degree of financial security. In Harare, for instance, over a quarter of the local NGO directors I interviewed said that they had more funding, or the promise of more funding, than they could presently use. NGOs in other African countries seldom face this dilemma and it is indicative of the special relationship between local NGOs in Zimbabwe and their donors, which will be analysed shortly.

The ability to seize or create opportunities for internal income generation is one characteristic of powerful NGOs. Yet few local African NGOs are able to generate funds for themselves. Membership fees, heavily constrained by the limited means of NGO members, are often their only source of internally generated income. In Zimbabwe, however, local NGOs across sectors, regions and levels of experience have already developed strategies and capitalised on opportunities for sustainable internal income generation. These opportunities are varied and include undertaking research and consultancy work for donors and international organisations; conducting training sessions for government and the private sector; and renting out parts of NGO premises for workshops and conferences. One local women's NGO in Harare has been able to construct a large conference centre, complete with meeting rooms, guest bedrooms and a commercial size kitchen and banquet room, all of which provide it with a steady income. The financial independence from donors promoted by these kinds of income-generating activities increases the ability of local NGOs to determine and follow their own priorities. Creating such opportunities is a primary goal of many Zimbabwean NGOs.

With whom do local Zimbabwean NGOs form relationships?

No NGO can survive in isolation from other actors in development, whether other NGOs, government structures or donor organisations. As NGO power can only be measured with respect to other development actors, the relationships that local African NGOs form with these groups will undoubtedly impact on their ability to wield power. Who are the individuals and organisations that most affect the work of local Zimbabwean NGOs, and what sorts of links exist between them?

Other local NGOs

Relationships between local NGOs in Zimbabwe are strong and provide considerable mutual support. The majority of indigenous NGO directors I met mentioned other local NGOs first when asked about the groups that best support their work. This support is rarely material. Most frequently, steady relationships between Zimbabwean NGOs are considered important as they facilitate the sharing of labour on common projects and allow NGOs to present a unified voice when lobbying.

Regular networking and strong relationships are most pronounced among NGOs involved in gender issues. Every one of these groups that I interviewed highlighted the importance of their relationships to other local NGOs, especially other women's NGOs, to their work. The same was true of NGOs involved in human rights work, whose well built links added strength of numbers to their advocacy activities. One last set of local Zimbabwean NGOs that recognise the importance of inter-NGO contacts is the group of NGOs working on issues around natural resources and land. Indeed, this group has institutionalised their informal relationships into a communally funded body which is very active around land redistribution – one of the most important and controversial issues in Zimbabwe today.

The successful relationships built between local NGOs in Zimbabwe are attributable to the efforts of these NGOs alone. The National Association of Non-Governmental Organisations (NANGO), Zimbabwe's NGO umbrella group, has had little impact on coordination and collaboration within the sector (Rich Dorman 2001). While NANGO claims over 300 paid member organisations, both local and international, and undertakes training and communication activities for the sector as a whole, only one of the NGOs I encountered even mentioned it to me.

NANGO is the subject of much criticism within the Zimbabwean development sector. While it claims to 'promote and facilitate collaboration and co-operation between NGOs and Government', NANGO is usually seen as having closer ties to government than to the NGOs themselves (NANGO undated). In 1995, NANGO failed to inform its members of the Zimbabwean government's Private Voluntary Organisations (PVO) Act until after it had been passed by Parliament. The act gave the government widespread powers to deregister NGOs and suspend their executive committee members. NANGO's only reaction to the PVO Act is said to have been a suggestion that the government change its title to the 'NGO Act' (Rich Dorman 2000). And as of 1999, NANGO still received the majority of its funding from the government.

NANGO has also been criticised for its decision to become involved in providing front-line development services, moving beyond its mandate of supporting and coordinating NGOs. As an operational NGO working in multiple areas of activity including HIV/AIDS, land reform, constitutional reform and children's rights, NANGO now competes directly with other local NGOs for resources, clients and space. This directly conflicts with what Stremlau sees as the role and responsibility of NGO co-ordinating bodies: 'their *raison d'etre* is to work for the interests of their members, not themselves to operate at project level' (1987: 221). NANGO recognises these shortcomings and its Director has summarised NANGO's performance from 1991 to 1995 as characterised by poor vision, communication and decision-making by its leadership, and by an unprofessional management, insensitive to the needs of member NGOs and staff (NANGO 1999). A more drastic contrast between NANGO and CONGAD, the NGO-co-ordinating body in Senegal, would be difficult to find. In Senegal, not only is CONGAD an independent, non-operational body, with a strong and respected voice in all affairs relating to NGOs in the country; it is also a key partner for NGOs.

Strong relationships between local NGOs and international NGOs active in Zimbabwe are rare. During my fieldwork, I was only able to identify two local NGOs that had received support, whether material or non-material, from an INGO – in both cases from the same one. It is a surprising trend that so few local NGOs seem to have had any support from the international NGOs they work alongside. Moreover, operational INGOs rarely mentioned local NGOs when discussing the organisations they worked with most closely. While this is partly caused by the reluctance of international NGOs to share their funding with local counterparts, in certain fields this is also due to the divergent philosophies of development adopted by the two types of organisation. For example, in the prominent and highly politicised sphere of natural resource conservation, INGOs have tended towards protectionism, ignoring the sustainable use approach favoured by the majority of Zimbabwean NGOs and their beneficiaries (Duffy 2000). Despite the rhetoric of partnership that resounds in the international development community today, local and international NGOs continue to act as rivals for funding, clients and space within the Zimbabwean development sector.

Civil Society Organisations
Local Zimbabwean NGOs do not focus solely on building strong relationships with their fellow NGOs; for many of them, relationships with other civil society organisations are just as crucial to their success. One set of regular collaborators is researchers and research centres at the University of Zimbabwe. They provide technical assistance to NGOs, advising them

in the fields of education, health, land issues and agriculture, and helping them to undertake their own research projects. Labour and church movements are also important partners, especially in the often sensitive and difficult fields of lobbying and advocacy. Labour has been a visible and well respected voice in Zimbabwe for many years. Its partnership with local NGOs working in the areas of human rights, constitutional reform and land redistribution has made it possible for civil society organisations to gain a stronger voice in relevant debates with the government (Raftopoulos and Phimister, 1997). Similarly, certain church organisations in Zimbabwe (perhaps most notably the Catholic Commission for Justice and Peace) have been outspoken proponents of human rights, speaking out against offences throughout Zimbabwe's history (Moyo 1996). Their support for the human rights efforts of local NGOs has similarly strengthened the voice of human rights campaigns in Zimbabwe, and has added to the collective security of local NGOs working in that field.

Another set of key relationships for several Zimbabwean NGOs are those that they have cultivated with industry and private sector enterprises. While the number of NGOs involved in private sector partnerships is still quite small, this is nonetheless an important trend, unique to Zimbabwe among the three case study countries. Private enterprises, ranging from tea manufacturers to tourism operators, have partnered local NGOs working with communities to develop economic opportunities based on the sustainable use of natural resources. Perhaps the strongest private sector–NGO partnership I observed was that between an environmental NGO and heavy industry companies in Zimbabwe. In addition to its regular environmental awareness activities with schools and rural communities, this NGO had developed a programme for environmental management in industry, to improve links between industries and communities and to supplement its income. It is now helping a range of industries to adopt eco-labelling programmes, develop strategies for preventing and reacting to environmental damage, and to comply with new and changed environmental legislation in the country. In the current climate of globalisation, these kinds of relationships, which help local NGOs to increase their financial self-sufficiency and to develop a reputation with powerful national and international companies, will only continue to grow in importance.

Donor agencies

In Zimbabwe, the largest proportion of funding for local NGOs comes from official sources: embassies and government development agencies. Every local NGO I encountered received funds from at least one of these groups. Throughout the last decade, NGOs have benefited increasingly from donors' growing inability or refusal to work with the Zimbabwean government on development projects. President Mugabe's increasingly frequent attacks on donors as subversive have certainly expedited this trend.[3] The most visible donors in Zimbabwe are NORAD, NOVIB and DANIDA, while both CIDA and USAID are active within particular sectors. Private funding agencies are also a relatively large presence, with American organisations like the Ford and Carnegie Foundations, the German Konrad Adenauer and Frederick Ebert Foundations, and the Dutch HIVOS all funding local NGOs in several sectors.

While INGOs are increasingly perceived as donors to local NGOs in the South, especially early in their life, they very rarely fund local NGOs in Zimbabwe (Lewis 1998, Smillie and Hailey 2001). Not one of the local NGO directors I interviewed in the country named an INGO as an important financial partner. For the majority of them, receiving funding from an INGO is inconceivable, as demonstrated by the words of this local NGO director: 'We've collaborated on one or two things with [an INGO], but they would never provide money to us. [...] NGOs are too competitive, they're not going to raise money for, and they're not going to give money to, another NGO' (Interview with General Secretary, Local NGO #3, Harare, 10 August 1999). So in addition to the poor levels of contact between INGOs and local NGOs in Zimbabwe, the majority of INGOs are operational organisations undertaking their own projects, rather than support organisations, helping to fund and develop the skills of their local counterparts.

Of all of the official donor agencies and private development organisations which did fund local NGOs, three stood out as consistent favourites: the American Ford Foundation, and the Dutch NOVIB and HIVOS. Zimbabwean NGOs favoured these three because of their caring personnel and their flexible approaches to funding. These agencies work closely with their partners and offer them advice, but avoid stifling NGO creativity and intruding on the ownership of projects. Their willingness to include funds for institutional development and their partners' overhead costs within their grants was also highlighted. Despite the relatively strong financial situation of the majority of local NGOs in Zimbabwe, nearly all of them still have difficulty finding donors willing to fund their core expenses and so regularly find themselves surreptitiously moving project funds into overhead accounts. The words of this NGO director described her difficulty in finding core funds and were echoed by many others:

> We have another donor who is supporting the revolving loan fund alone. And you tend to ask yourself, how can somebody say I can only support the revolving loan fund? Who in, for heaven's sake do you think is going to run that revolving loan fund? Is it God himself? You

---

[3] As but one example, the government-run Sunday Mail ran a front page article with the headline 'US, UK conspire to oust Mugabe?' in April 1999 (*The Sunday Mail*, 11 April 1999). It contended that donors were part of a plot to bring down President Mugabe after several donors, along with the World Bank and several American NGOs and academics, attended a one-day conference entitled 'Zimbabwe at the Crossroads'.

fail to understand the reasoning behind [donor policy] sometimes you know. And [donors] will just stand their ground and say, oh, we are only funding the revolving loan fund, that's all. If you don't have money for administration, too bad, better look for money for administration. But you go to the other donor and you say you want money for administration. And they will say no, but we can't just give you money for administration [...] And this is incredible. It's such a vicious circle (Interview with Director, Local NGO #17, Harare, 9 September 1999).

Local NGOs also struggle to sustain long-term links with their donors. Personal relationships are key to ensuring the success of partnerships. Yet many donor agencies have a rapid turnover of the programme officers responsible for working most closely with local NGOs, while in others, the programme officer is an entry-level position to which they assign only their most junior personnel (Fowler 1998). The difficulty of cultivating strong relationships with a donor agency, when its front-line representatives are changing constantly, is explained by this NGO director:

This is the problem with the funders. When they change programme officers or heads, then you go back to square one, unfortunately. [...] The thing is that you have to get the right person on the line, and then it works, but they don't seem to have a culture of this in any of these funding organisations. So then [with each] new one, you have to start building that relationship [again] to move forward (Interview with Co-ordinator, Local NGO #4, Harare, 10 August 1999).

The absence of strong donor co-ordination and harmonisation of donor funding practices poses another problem. Donor agencies interviewed agreed that, but for specific crises, they spent far too little time sharing information and building collective strategies. The achievement of BRAC and Proshika in getting the donors in their consortia to accept standardised reporting and common pool funding may not seem especially remarkable in the abstract; but is an accomplishment that local Zimbabwean NGOs have been unable to replicate.

While many local NGOs throughout Africa find it difficult to secure core funding for their activities, build strong long-term relationships with their donors and co-ordinate the various demands of their donors, one aspect of the donor–NGO relationship in Zimbabwe does stand out as remarkable. It is generally accepted that donors are reluctant to become involved in funding the work of highly charged or politically controversial NGOs (Edwards and Hulme 1996, Stewart 1997). Indeed, many such local NGOs in Zimbabwe experienced difficulty in finding donors in their early years, and one lost all of its prior donors in its transition from an INGO project to a registered local NGO. What seems to be particular to Zimbabwe, however, is that most of these NGOs now find themselves with adequate funding to carry out their activities. This is especially significant given the antagonism between national government and the local NGO sector. The Zimbabwean government has levelled allegations (ranging from financial mismanagement to treason) against local NGOs, which would have been sufficient grounds for donors to terminate their funding arrangements with these organisations. Yet few local NGOs have ever lost donors because of their politicised development activities and conflict with government. The uncharacteristic decision of donors to fund such NGOs in Zimbabwe, despite courting controversy and threats is in large part due to the relationship between local NGOs and the Zimbabwean government.

Government bodies

> For any NGO to succeed the most important aspect is the political environment: that the government of the day allow their existence (Interview with Executive Director, Local NGO #14, Harare, 1 September 1999).

By the logic of this statement, (by the director of one of the best known local NGOs in Zimbabwe) the local NGO sector in Zimbabwe stands very little chance of success. Local NGOs in many countries suffer from restrictive legislation governing their activity and an onerous and inhibitive registration process; but local NGOs in Zimbabwe often have far more serious worries when it comes to their relationships with government. While the relationship between government and NGOs in the early post-independence era was amicable, government officials and civil society personnel having fought side by side in the war for independence, it soon deteriorated with five years of state-sponsored violence in the Ndebele minority region of Matabeleland.

The 1996 Private Voluntary Organisations Act, which governs NGO activity in Zimbabwe, reflects the government's increasing distrust of NGOs. It leaves complete discretion for registering and deregistering NGOs with a director within the Ministry of Public Service, Labour and Social Welfare, allowing that individual to deregister an NGO if they deem 'it is necessary or desirable to do so in the public interest' (Government of Zimbabwe 1996: 89). In Zimbabwe, however, the pretext of the public interest is often used to legitimate the government's self-interest.

The government now regularly issues stinging condemnations of NGOs and civil society organisations, particularly over their support of political pluralism. The state-owned media has been a major facilitator of the government's campaign against civil society activity, publishing front-page exposés on allegations of NGO corruption.[4] One of Zimbabwe's

---

[4] For instance, the government-run Sunday Mail ran with the headline 'Misuse of Funds Alleged at ZimRights' (*The Sunday Mail*, 18 July 1999). ZimRights was, at the time, one of the country's best-known human rights NGOs. The government newspapers did not cover the NGO's subsequent audit and evaluation, and the independent auditor's press release entitled 'No Misuse and Abuse of Funds' days later (*The Daily News*, 29 July 1999).

independent newspapers has accused the government of 'using the state media to attack [its] foes' and of forming a group 'to organise demonstrations against journalists and media deemed to be unpatriotic' (*The Independent*, 1 April 1999). This suggests that the government's real fear is not the potential mismanagement or corruptibility of local NGOs, but their potential to expose its shortcomings and to provide political opposition. Until the launching of the Movement for Democratic Change (MDC) in 1999, official opposition parties in the country were either weak or absent and NGOs and civil society organisations were increasingly called on to engage with political issues (Sithole 1997). The government has perceived this new role for NGOs as a challenge to its domain, and the Africa Rights organisation blames the Zimbabwean government's desire to monopolise political space for its repressive attitude towards civil society (Africa Rights 1999). A political approach to development is an expected characteristic of powerful African NGOs, partly because of the space it allows local NGOs to capture *vis-à-vis* other civil society development groups. But in Zimbabwe, the government seems to be challenging NGOs for this space.

Not surprisingly, the NGOs that have had the greatest difficulties with the government are those perceived as a political threat and those which can be exploited to further government's political power. The first group includes local NGOs that are relatively successful and run by white Zimbabweans. The white minority, which controls a disproportionate amount of wealth, is regularly branded unpatriotic and used as a scapegoat by the government to explain the widespread poverty and economic stagnation in the country (Raftopoulos 1996). Successful NGOs run by white directors are therefore in a precarious position – even when they are the only white members of the organisation. This is of particular importance in the environmental sector, where the majority of NGOs are led by white Zimbabweans (Duffy 2000). One such director described the situation facing his NGO as follows:

> I'd have to say that we, and particularly I, walk a political tightrope all the time. [...] Our strength [racial diversity] is also a soft spot. And I am a very easy target if someone really decides they want to hit out at [us]. I know they could just lash out at me, just like that. [...] Anyway, I sort of have a feeling that, inevitably, one day that will happen (Interview with Director, Local NGO #9, Harare, 25 August 1999).

Local NGOs working directly to promote human rights and democracy have faced similar difficulties with the government. The directors and staff of these organisations have become used to working in a culture of fear. They often find exposés of their personal lives in the pages of the state newspapers and the government's Central Intelligence Organisation, once used to destabilise its official opposition, is now a regular presence in the country's NGO sector (Sithole 1997, Rich Dorman 2000, Amnesty International 2001). The director of a very strong, well-known NGO working on democracy-building described the culture of fear fostered by the government in this way:

> We are constantly followed. My phone, all my phones are tapped. I believe they have tapped this office, somehow. I have had my locks changed almost on a regular basis, which doesn't help, because we are dealing with a very powerful system. They used to follow me to my home. [...] We've had our donors being pushed into corners while supporting this group and ended up being ravaged in the papers. All sorts of irregularities have occurred, especially where the state secret agents are concerned. And they have tried to infiltrate [our NGO]' (Interview with National Coordinator, Local NGO #20, Harare, 17 September 1999).

Government–NGO relations in Zimbabwe are made all the more interesting when relationships between local levels of government are included in the equation. Even in the face of this overt fight with national government for political space, Zimbabwean NGOs often develop strong positive relationships with government at the local or ministerial level. The contrast between this relationship and that of local NGOs with central government reflects Van Rooy's (1997) contention that NGOs have historically had stronger relations and influence with weaker members of government bureaucracies. It also reflects the greater development space available to Zimbabwean NGOs at a local level.

At the local level, government bodies such as village development committees and rural district councils are key partners for NGOs, and the two types of organisation work hand in hand. Most of the NGO directors I interviewed cited the loan of local government buildings, such as schools or village halls, and the tacit support of local authorities as critical to their success. Several local NGOs also used government extension workers to undertake work on their rural projects. While many local African NGOs receive technical advice and support from government extension workers, in Zimbabwe, these government employees actually take on NGO project duties, usually training and monitoring, and incorporate them into their regular schedules. This benefits both parties. The government workers are given a small stipend, vehicles, supplies and, (often critically), motivational support. The NGOs gain a field worker with good knowledge, experience and connections in the area and are able to reach very rural areas at a lower cost than would otherwise be possible.

This type of government–NGO cooperation continues at the level of individual ministries. Joint programmes with government ministries provide local NGOs with the opportunity to gain experience and raise their profile while also making crucial contacts with donors and multinational organisations like the World Bank. In the fields of HIV/AIDS services and business and credit, collaboration between the government and NGOs reached new levels of trust and esteem as the government contracted various local NGOs to provide HIV awareness training to its employees and to administer its loan funds. Several NGOs working in the fields of gender and the environment are also often called on to work closely with individual ministries, offering an NGO perspective on government committees and commissions. But often, even those organ-isations enjoying good relationships with government see little tangible benefit from these ties. The director of a local gender issues NGO put it like this:

> Government, as I said, it was very hostile in the beginning with [us]. Now, I suppose, with international pressures, they are also into women's issues, so we enjoy moral support. And when there's some-thing going on, governments are requested to bring their NGOs together with their government [officials, on] the government delegation. So they're bound to put us in there. So we enjoy moral support, I suppose, by default. [...] But besides moral support, we don't get anything else (Interview with Director, Local NGO #5, Harare, 17 August 1999).

The relationship between local NGOs and the government, therefore, seems to depend on the type of activities that the NGO is involved with and the space available to the particular layer of government or govern-ment body in question. For the majority of local NGOs, relations with the government seemed to lie at one of the two extremes of antagonism and close collaboration.

International development community

Relationships with international organisations outside Zimbabwe are also significant to local NGOs. NGOs in Zimbabwe consider their strong connections with other local NGOs in southern Africa and their good networks of information sharing and support very important to their work. These connections are most numerous among gender and environ-mental NGOs and can extend to local NGOs throughout the continent.

International links are also advantageous for Zimbabwean NGOs working in human rights and democratisation (Thomas 1996). The Western media, in particular, has played a significant role in raising global awareness of their work and achievements, thereby protecting the NGOs from government retaliation. This has been crucial to the survival of many local NGOs in the recent era of government opposition, threats and violence. One NGO director I interviewed described the importance of the international media to his organisation as follows:

> One of our advantages is that we have had a good press coverage. We've had not only local, but also international coverage. So [govern-ment] can't target someone like me and hope to get away with it with-out the press and the whole international community coming down [on them] (Interview with National Coordinator, Local NGO #20, Harare, 17 September 1999).

International links thus seem to be flourishing within the Zimbabwean local NGO sector.

Power

Local NGOs in Zimbabwe stand out for their sectorally focussed, yet broad geographic approach to development, their high-quality staff complements and their years of experience within their chosen field. They provide quite a contrast to Sandbrook's picture of the weak African NGO, which suffers because of its small size, relative isolation and poor funding. But is the inner strength of local NGOs in Zimbabwe and their ability to provide for the development needs of their beneficiaries, proof of their power? The experience of other powerful local NGOs suggested that to become powerful, local NGOs in Africa would have to gain space; a degree of financial independence from donors; solid links to the international development community; and a willingness to engage with the political aspects of development work.

Space
With their many strengths, local NGOs in Zimbabwe should easily be able to create or locate a secure niche. But this is a problem for many. Most have steady donor funding and many are exploring promising opportunities for income generation, but local NGOs still regularly find themselves competing with operational international NGOs for funds. Sam Moyo (2000a) writes of the direct competition between local and international NGOs in sectors as varied as relief, poverty alleviation and the environment. Donors rarely make a distinction in their funding portfolios between supporting local NGOs and supporting international NGOs, and most INGOs possess a considerable advantage over their local counterparts in terms of presenting proposals to suit donor trends and building inside connections with donor agencies.

Competition from INGOs and foreign organisations has most affected the space available to local NGOs working in the same welfare sectors as foreign NGOs. This has rarely been a problem for local NGOs working in fields such as human rights, the environment and women's issues. In these fields, in which local ties and experience are necessary to develop credibility and legitimacy in the eyes of beneficiaries, local NGOs have the edge over their northern counterparts, many of which choose not to work in these sectors. They still have to contend with competition from government, however, which can be fierce in Zimbabwe's current political climate.

As the government has sought to repress local NGOs working in the areas of lobbying and advocacy, donor confidence in the government has waned and donors have increased their support to NGOs. This has resulted in conflict, both over money and over political space and power, between the government and certain sectors of local NGOs. In a country which was, for many years, a *de facto* one-party state, the reasons for government antagonism towards the human rights and democracy building sector may be obvious. The reasons for government resentment of the environmental sector are perhaps less so. Other factors may contribute to this, but one key reason is that local NGOs in Zimbabwe working on environmental and natural resource management today all address questions of land distribution and land reform (Mutepfa *et al.* 1998, Marongwe 1999).

This has been an issue of critical importance in Zimbabwe since the struggle for independence. As evidenced by the occupation of commercial farms from early 2000 and subsequent civil unrest in the country, land is undoubtedly still one of the most sensitive issues facing the government (Herbst 1992, Vudzijena 1998, Bowyer-Bower and Stoneman 2000). NGO projects dealing with land are highly politicised and the government of Zimbabwe has been quick to seize on land reform as its signature issue, monopolising the political space in which questions surrounding land can be raised and silencing those attempting to criticise its land reform policies. In these ways, then, while many local NGOs do exhibit financial and organisational strengths, they still lack adequate space in which to manoeuvre and grow – space which is crucial to developing power and which INGOs and the government of Zimbabwe seem unlikely to yield in the foreseeable future.

Financial independence from donors
Financial independence from donors is another characteristic of powerful local NGOs. Many Zimbabwean NGOs are currently developing and pursuing strategies for generating income which should increase their ability to determine their own priorities and to follow them through. The majority of these NGOs are, unsurprisingly, located in the field of credit provision and business services, where revenue from interest payments and user fees is relatively easy to collect and arrives with some regularity.

But local NGOs working in advocacy and empowerment activities have very few opportunities for internal income generation, because of the nature of their work. Without a defined set of beneficiaries, to which they directly provide a well defined service or product, these NGOs are unable to charge user fees or to sell their services. Their specialist skills are similarly unconducive to professional opportunities with other development or private sector organisations, most of which require trainers and consultants within their own particular subject areas. As a result, this kind of NGO finds itself dependent on donor funds for survival. Donors to Zimbabwe have generally been eager to provide support to such NGOs, and none of them are in urgent need of funds, but their future financial sustainability is nonetheless uncertain (de Graaf 1987, Fowler 2000b). Many donors have seen NGOs as essentially playing the role of the official opposition in Zimbabwe and have felt it important to continue to fund them as such. But with the rise of the MDC opposition party, which now holds over one-third of the seats in parliament, donors may well reduce or redirect their spending on democracy-building. In this way, local NGOs which seem financially secure today, could tomorrow be in serious danger.

The goal of increasing their internal income generation was common to almost all the local NGOs I interviewed in Zimbabwe. NGOs which already have revenue-generating activities (such as consulting or selling publications) aim to increase the regularity and predictability of these incomes, so that projects and programmes can be planned around them. Organisations which have rarely been able to generate their own funding are also looking to develop such opportunities in the short term, most of them focussing on modifying their offices to be able to capture rental income. The guaranteed and untied pools of funding that internal revenue generation can supply to a local NGO can make it possible for it to invest in the kinds of longer-term or experimental programmes that donors may be reluctant to fund. In other words, determining and following its own priorities. This element of power is still in its infancy among local NGOs, with few of them able to count on substantial and sustainable amounts of revenue. Financial dependence on donors is therefore another reason why strong Zimbabwean NGOs have failed to develop power. However, the professed commitment of these organisations to pursue new and more creative opportunities for revenue generation may soon help them to achieve increased levels of power.

Links to the international development community
Continuing to build links, nationally, regionally and internationally, and pursuing an increased profile at all of these levels will also be necessary for Zimbabwean NGOs. Ties between local NGOs are strong and are an important resource in a variety of circumstances. Environmental and gender NGOs share information and experience in strong networks throughout southern Africa, and the Western media has been of considerable support to advocacy NGOs in the country (Duffy 2000). But these ties are still weak in comparison to links and influence over the international development community that powerful NGOs in South Asia and Latin America have developed. For the majority of NGOs in Zimbabwe, linkages tend to be national or regional. Organisations in only a few sectors have been able to achieve higher level international links, and these often only spring to life around particular issues or events.

If local NGOs in Zimbabwe were able to achieve their stated goal of building more strategic relationships with out-of-country organisations and increasing their international reputation, they could not only increase their power, but also their space and their opportunities for greater financial independence. International exposure and recognition will help local NGOs to secure greater space and funding in Zimbabwe, as their reputation for experience and results begins to rival that of their operational INGO counterparts. An international reputation, and being considered a leader in their field, could also increase demand for an NGO's research and consultancy services by other NGOs, multilateral institutions, donors and government bodies.

But in order to build a strong global reputation, local NGOs in Zimbabwe must be willing to undertake publicity for their organisation and its work. The majority of the local NGOs I met in the country resented the need to publicise their achievements, and preferred to let the impact of their work speak for itself. Until they can cultivate this sort of publicity and increase their connections to the international development community, local NGOs in Zimbabwe will continue to lack power.

Engagement with the political aspects of development work
The power of NGOs like Proshika, SEWA and IBASE is due, in part, to their willingness to engage with political debates in development. In Zimbabwe, a number of local NGOs across the fields of gender, health, the environment, human rights and democracy-building have incorporated political activity into their work. This has been crucial in helping them to capture space *vis-à-vis* international NGOs in the country. The activity of this group of NGOs around issues of constitutional reform and land redistribution illustrated the extent to which they, as a group, have succeeded in being timely and relevant, creating their own niche and gaining space in Zimbabwe. The director of one of the NGOs I interviewed considers that it is only with the advent of politically focussed NGOs that civil society as a whole in Zimbabwe has started to develop power.

With the events of the spring of 2000 unfolding in the country, not least the defeat of the government-proposed constitution in the national constitutional referendum, it seemed that civil society in Zimbabwe had achieved a critical mass from which its collective voice had become difficult to ignore. But like their civil society counterparts in the media, the judiciary and the private sector, NGOs face considerable opposition from a government trying to curb their power. The hostility of the government towards local NGOs and overt conflict between the two groups over political space still makes it difficult and dangerous for individual local NGOs to be seen as engaging with the political causes of underdevelopment. So while the local NGO sector may continue to gain momentum in the coming years, the nature of the current government regime makes it unlikely that individual local NGOs working in politicised fields will be able to act unchallenged and unmolested until a more open government is elected.

Conclusion

While many local NGOs in Zimbabwe have developed strong organisational structures, significant levels of influence, and have achieved numerous successes in their fields, they have yet to develop power. NGOs in the human rights sector are able to develop strong links to international organisations and their own space *vis-à-vis* INGOs, but they face numerous difficulties in achieving financial independence from their donors and in securing political space. Certain NGOs in the credit sector are relatively successful at generating revenue internally. But these groups have yet to find their own space and link credit issues to political inequalities: a step that helped the Grameen Bank – one of the world's most powerful credit-based NGOs – to develop power. Overall, none of the local NGOs I encountered in Zimbabwe have been able to find and protect their own space, achieve a significant level of financial independence from donor organisations, build solid links to the international development community and incorporate political activity into their work. Ultimately, none of them have been able to replicate their Asian and South American counterparts' successes in developing power. It seems that while donor agencies, INGOs, mass social movements and even local NGOs can each gain power in different developing country contexts, the balance of power in Zimbabwe's development sector is still firmly in the government's hands.

4

The Power
of Local NGOs   in Tanzania

The power of local NGOs in Tanzania and their place in national development, relative to community groups, government agencies and international actors, is inextricably linked to the history of social organisation
in the country. Tanzania has traditionally had a strong associational life
and burial societies, dance and music troupes, voluntary associations and
ethnic societies flourished even during colonialism (Tripp 1992, Meena
1997). Working with labour unions and workers' groups, many of these
organisations were key forces in the country's independence movements.
As such, Tanzania had a vibrant civil society when independence was
achieved in 1961 (Havnevik 1993, Ngware 1997). In the years following
independence, however, the strength of local organisations was restricted
by government and over the next twenty years their influence and numbers
declined.

Historical setting

Kiondo writes that 'from 1964 until the early 1980s Tanzania was the site
of one of Africa's furthest-going forms of statism, that is, of systematic
efforts by the state to penetrate/dissolve civil society and remould it in
the image of the state itself. In this process voluntary associations were
either suppressed or incorporated within the state' (1995: 110). In 1965
the ruling Tanganyika African Nationalist Union (TANU) declared Tanzania a one-party state, effectively eliminating the space for autonomous
civil society organisations. From 1967, when the government adopted the
Arusha Declaration, and its tenets of socialism, self-reliance and freedom
through hard work, or *ujamaa*, any surviving associations, like the
country's co-operative societies, were dissolved and replaced by parallel
state structures (Nyerere 1968).

Over the next twenty years, *ujamaa* in Tanzania meant different things
to different communities, depending on the region and era. But it always

implied some form of collectivisation – most notably villagisation – designed to encourage communal production and to facilitate the provision of state services. The success of Tanzania's *ujamaa* strategy, both in terms of encouraging self-sufficiency and improving the quality of life for Tanzanians, was limited. In the years that followed the Arusha declaration, the government became increasingly authoritarian. As state structures proliferated, it became more rather than less hierarchical; and while social services improved in the late 1960s, by the late 1970s Tanzania was in an oil-price triggered crisis. Agricultural production stalled; debt levels soared; social welfare deteriorated; and public support for socialism waned (Havnevik 1993).

In the mid-1980s, under pressure from donors and the IMF, the government began to reduce the role of the state sector and liberalise the economy. Starting with Canada in 1987, Tanzania's largest donors all made democratisation a condition of their aid (Vener 2000). By 1992, Tanzania had officially become a multi-party state and social and political associations were once again free to organise. As the number of political parties, independent media organisations and other social organisations has mushroomed from the early 1990s onwards, so too has the number of NGOs (TANGO 1994, Lange *et al.* 2000). The most recent estimates suggest that there are about 8,000 NGOs in Tanzania today (Kelsall 2001). With over 40 per cent of the population under the national poverty line, rising rates of unemployment and inflation, and slow economic growth, Tanzania's development needs are great and these NGOs play an important role in meeting them (TGNP 1997, UNDP 2002).

The Local NGO Sector in Tanzania

Tanzania's strong history of social co-operation and collectivisation has created a present-day society in which the principle of organisation for the common good is embraced. It is, however, a principle that has most often been fulfilled through the auspices of the ruling TANU party and at the level of individual communities. How have NGOs been incorporated into this development space and to what extent have they been able to develop power in national-level development? This chapter presents a snapshot of the local NGO sector in Tanzania, based on interviews in 2000 with a wide range of development actors and a diverse sample of local NGOs with an average age of nine.

In what sectors are Tanzanian NGOs most active?
Tanzanian NGOs have a very focussed mandate and a highly specialised approach to development work. As a result, the local NGO sector is characterised by very little duplication. Each individual NGO within a sector of development seems to have found or developed its own niche. This is illustrated by local NGO activity in the fields of gender and of

natural resources and the environment, which are the two most crowded sectors of the Tanzanian NGO scene. NGOs working within the general domain of gender issues each address a different problem from a different angle, variously focussing on the role of the media, educational institutions, economic structures, legal and justice systems, or land and tenure systems in promoting gender equality. The large group of environmental NGOs is similarly diversified across aspects of environmental stewardship, education and advocacy. These organisations rarely find their projects in direct competition with each other. Strong ties between organisations working in the same field (which are especially visible among local NGOs focussed on gender) are key in preventing overlap and duplication of efforts.

The sectors in which Tanzanian NGOs specialise are the same as those in which the majority of local NGO activity in Zimbabwe is found. Both tend away from the more traditional welfare spheres of development. In Dar es Salaam, for example, only a handful of local NGOs work in traditional welfare fields, and two of the best known are heavily involved in advocacy and lobbying in addition to their respective services for AIDS sufferers and street children. It would be misleading, however, to suggest that welfare and service-based organisations in Tanzania are scarce. The majority of local groups which call themselves NGOs are involved in caring for the sick, disabled and elderly, with varying degrees of professionalism and success. However, these social welfare organisations lack any engagement with the wider issues of underdevelopment, are tied to international movements or have no official organisational standing, and as such, were not considered local NGOs for the purposes of this study. Some of these groups will be discussed in a later section on the activity of community-based organisations. For now it will suffice to say that as in Zimbabwe, social welfare activities are not the focus of the majority of local NGOs in Tanzania.

The largest sector of local NGO activity is gender. Since before independence it has held an important place within mainstream political discourse. Women play a larger role in the local NGO sector in Tanzania than in the two other African case study countries and nearly half of local NGOs are run by female directors. Government recognition of the role of women in achieving national independence and in building post-independence Tanzania is one factor which has played a catalytic role in the development of women's NGOs (Geiger 1997). Others include high levels of education among women in urban Tanzania, the physical proximity of the 1985 World Conference on Women in Nairobi, and the key role played by a Tanzanian woman in the 1995 World Conference on Women.[1] Other sectors with significant representation include legal and

---

[1] Gertrude Mongella, the Secretary-General of the United Nations World Conference on Women, held in Beijing, China in 1995, is a Tanzanian and is well-known in Tanzanian NGO circles.

human rights, and natural resources and the environment. Credit and business services, which is one of the best represented sectors of NGO activity in Zimbabwe is, however, very small in Tanzania. This is unsurprising given the slow emergence of private business and entrepreneurial sectors in the country.

While the discussion above indicates that there is a fair degree of resemblance between local NGOs in Tanzania and those in Zimbabwe, in terms of their sectors of activity and degree of specialisation, there is an immediate and important contrast to be drawn between the two countries in terms of their NGOs' geographical areas of activity. While the majority of local NGOs in Zimbabwe have regional offices and decentralised activities throughout the country, the majority of local NGOs in Tanzania have a much more narrowly focussed geographic target zone. For many local NGOs this is limited to one urban centre, usually Dar es Salaam, and a handful of smaller districts or villages. These smaller villages are often localised in the wealthy areas around Kilimanjaro and Arusha. In these areas, high, regular income from tourism has made organisation for communal economic benefit much easier – an African reflection of the Northern trend of voluntarism as a luxury of the wealthy. Since most urban NGOs lack permanent field offices or field workers in rural areas, however, their activities there are usually short-term and irregular interventions such as holding training courses and workshops. Similarly, those local NGOs which originate in rural areas or inland urban centres tend to remain localised in these same regions. This inability of local NGOs to reach beyond their immediate location to the rural-based majority of Tanzanians has been a major criticism of the local NGO sector (Mercer 1999, Lange *et al.* 2000).

Many observers decry the elite-centred nature of Tanzanian NGOs as the cause of this trend. But the high cost and difficulty of travel in many regions of the country and the absence of infrastructure such as roads, telephones and electricity also contribute to the dearth of decentralised NGO structures in the regions, and to the general urban focus of local NGOs. Not only are the costs of geographic expansion in Tanzania higher than those faced by NGOs in Zimbabwe, but the resources which Tanzanian NGOs have at their disposal to meet these costs are considerably lower. While it is common for local NGOs in Zimbabwe to possess their own vehicles, the same is not true of local NGOs in Tanzania. As such, the NGOs which are present in remote rural areas tend to be INGOs which have the means to make travel to, and communication with, those regions possible. Sectoral and geographical specialisation, therefore, is one way in which local NGOs in Tanzania can secure a niche for themselves in spite of the widespread presence of operational INGOs.

How strong are the human resources of Tanzanian NGOs?
In Tanzania, as in Zimbabwe, the trend of sectoral specialisation among local NGOs can be attributed to the specialist skills and previous

experience of NGO staff. In Tanzania, however, this high quality of human resources is not always accompanied by the 'professional' image that local NGOs in Zimbabwe have cultivated. An important distinction exists in Tanzania between local NGOs which exist only in name and those which are registered and active. Talk about the NGO sector is common across social, economic and political spheres and most Tanzanians living in the capital, Dar es Salaam, know someone working in the NGO sector. However, the actual number of local NGOs with a permanent office, staff and level of activity is quite small. The exercise of identifying and locating local development NGOs in Tanzania can be extremely difficult, partly because very few local NGOs are full-time organisations.[2] Many of them exist in name and proposal only. The notion of 'briefcase NGOs', due in part to proliferation of local NGOs in Tanzania, permeates all discussions of its local NGO sector.

The unusual organisation of even the most well known NGOs in Tanzania has contributed to the perception by INGOs, donors and government of the local NGO sector as characterised by unstable briefcase NGOs. This unusual method of organising can best be described as a part-time approach to development work. It is visible at the level of the director and staff of local NGOs, as well as at the level of its projects and programmes. A great many local NGO directors only work with their NGO on a part-time basis; they continue to occupy full-time positions, most often in government or academia, and work on NGO business in their free time. Few Tanzanian NGOs have a full-time staff complement, with the majority having only full-time support staff, such as a secretary or receptionist. In these cases, most of the actual project work of the organisation is undertaken by 'members' – individuals employed else-where, who identify with the goals of the NGO and volunteer their time to its activities. More than half of the NGOs I encountered in Tanzania relied on volunteer members to carry out their mandates.[3]

These members and directors are often highly skilled, experienced professionals who are committed to the work of their NGO and involved in all aspects of that work, from conceiving and planning projects, to fundraising and implementing projects. However it is impossible to ignore the fact that the dependency of these organisations on part-time inputs affects the work that they can accomplish. The time frame in

---

[2] While TANGO's membership of 450 could be taken as an approximation of the number of active NGOs in Tanzania, the government and other observers claim that there are more than 8,000 NGOs in the country (*Daily News*, 8 April 1998, Kelsall 2001). This number likely reflects both the mushrooming of NGOs in Tanzania since liberalisation as well as the tendency of a great variety of social organisations to call themselves NGOs. It should also suggest to the reader the difficulties faced in locating legitimate and active NGOs for this study.

[3] In this light, the relatively common practice among academics and development professionals of using paid or employed staff as a defining characteristic of NGOs (especially as distinct from CBOs or grass-roots organisations (GROs)) seems ill-suited to reflecting the reality of the Tanzanian NGO sector – and, I suspect, the nature of many useful African NGOs across the continent.

which such NGOs can complete projects, their ability to adapt quickly to changes and their ability to undertake large-scale programmes are all circumscribed by the fact that most of their human resources are employed elsewhere. More 'professional' NGOs would certainly be expected to perform faster and with more consistency than an NGO whose employees are volunteers, facing conflicting demands on their time from their jobs and their families. This contrasting view of the abilities of different types of NGOs is not just theoretical; it confronts the majority of donor organisations in Tanzania when they decide whether to invest their funds in local NGOs, subject to these constraints, or in international NGOs which maintain large full-time staff complements. This unfavourable comparison has had serious repercussions for local NGOs in terms of the space they are able to hold and, consequently, the power they are able to wield.

The widespread phenomenon of NGO work as a part-time endeavour is unique to Tanzania among the case study countries and is extremely important in understanding the workings of the sector and its national reputation. The first obvious question that arises when considering this trend is why individuals, interested in the issues and types of work carried out by the NGO sector, continue to work in other forms of employment. One answer is that the benefits of work in other sectors, especially government, include not only higher or more secure incomes, but also perks such as health care benefits, subsidised housing and easier access to licences and permits. Despite efforts at civil service reform, the government bureaucracy in Tanzania remains very powerful and government jobs offer a host of benefits and powers to employees and their extended families (Danielson and Eriksson Skoog 2001). In addition, the stability of employment in government is rightly perceived as greater than that in the very new and often chaotic NGO sector. As one university professor, long active in the NGO sector suggested to me, it would be preposterous to choose contract employment in the NGO sector in a culture of lifetime employment with government (Interview with Professor, University of Dar es Salaam, Dar es Salaam, 10 November 1999). So the decision to 'straddle' two sectors – remaining employed in academia, government or business, while devoting considerable time and effort to a cause of great personal worth – is an important survival strategy for individuals in the local NGO sector in Tanzania.

This survival strategy is not new. The founders of several prominent local NGOs took indefinite leaves of absence from their posts in government when they created their NGOs, so that they would have a job to fall back on if the NGO failed. More than a decade on, many of these NGO directors are still technically on leave from the civil service. According to one donor, the quest for survival in the local NGO sector has meant that 'everyone has their fingers in other pies' (Interview with Programme Analyst, Canadian International Development Agency, Dar es Salaam, 25 October 1999).

Why then, do the majority of these NGO directors not remain in the security of a government job and volunteer a few hours a week to an existing NGO? Simply put, in the years since economic liberalisation in Tanzania, government has also become a less secure place to be employed. Over recent years, threats of widespread civil service retrenchments have been regularly issued. By creating their own NGO, many highly skilled government workers are hedging their bets against both sectors. This trend of local NGOs being developed as the pet projects of civil servants in insecure governments posts – who have the political know-how, contacts, and literacy skills to be a success with donors – has given rise to much of the furore over briefcase NGOs (Cooksey 1997, Kelsall 2001). The proliferation of this type of NGO, combined with the part-time nature of even the most successful local NGOs in Tanzania, has fuelled the scepticism of donors and government over the longevity of local NGOs and their potential to carry out anything but the most short-term development projects. This has had many immediate consequences for Tanzanian NGOs, including a negative impact on their ability to secure stable funding.

How are Tanzanian NGOs financed?
If the part-time nature of many local NGOs has endangered the seriousness with which they are perceived by donors and government and their ability to access donor funds, it has at least helped to reduce the level of funding that they require to survive. With few overhead costs, especially in terms of salaries or large office space, local membership-based NGOs in Tanzania do not have to constantly search for the funds that many of their more 'professional' counterparts around the world require. Only a small number of the local NGOs I met faced a real shortage of funds, which is surprising given that many of them lacked vehicles and some even computers.

This philosophy of making-do dominates the sector and it seems that few NGOs complain about their lack of funds, not because they do not lack money, but because they see their role as one of doing the best they can with what little they have. It is possible that this trend is part of the legacy of socialist rule in Tanzania and its self-help philosophy; but it could equally be a reflection of the realistic expectations of the directors of these local NGOs, who are well aware that new vehicles and electronic equipment are unlikely to be a part of the next grant they are offered. Whatever the reason, it is because of a strong spirit of voluntarism that local Tanzanian NGOs survive. Members donate their old computers, sacrifice their personal vehicles for organisation activities and do odd-jobs for the NGO, such as photocopying and telephoning, at their regular place of employment. The spirit of voluntarism and community-mindedness not only created the majority of Tanzanian NGOs and kept them running, it also kept them financially viable.

But while the amount of funding that most local NGOs in Tanzania require is smaller than might be expected, their ability to generate these funds internally is also weak. Many local NGOs in Zimbabwe generate considerable income from rent on their properties, but any opportunity to generate money based on capital purchases is beyond the reach of the majority of Tanzanian NGOs. They lack adequate financial resources to pay staff, let alone buy conference centres. Similarly, the full-time careers of NGO members conflict with opportunities for NGOs to conduct research or short-term consultancies for international organisations and private sector companies. Moreover, with a very poor clientele, these local NGOs are either unable to charge user fees for their services at all or are only able to charge such a small amount that these fees contribute very little to the overall financial needs of the organisation. Thus, while Tanzanian NGOs could survive without donor funds, many directors still see their organisations as 'totally donor-dependent' (Interview with Co-ordinator, Local NGO #30, Dar es Salaam, 2 December 1999).

With whom do local Tanzanian NGOs form relationships?
I have already alluded to the importance of linkages among local NGOs in Tanzania, as they play a role in minimising NGO project duplication and overlap. The next section examines these and the other relationships on which local NGOs rely in order to conduct their projects and programmes.

Other Local NGOs
In all the case study countries, local NGOs have built strong relationships with each other. In Tanzania, inter-NGO linkages are strongest among NGOs working on gender issues. These NGOs consistently cite connections to other women's NGOs, including those in the wider regions of Eastern and Southern Africa, as important in achieving their goals. These ties, and the work-sharing they facilitate, have been key in Tanzania, where the majority of local NGOs have a membership with considerable education, expertise and experience, yet few have a full-time staff complement which is large enough to cope with the demands made on the organisation. Even a premier women's issues NGO, relatively large by Tanzanian standards, runs with only six full-time project staff and three support staff. A programme officer there explained succinctly how other NGOs have played an important role in the work of her organisation: 'We couldn't have managed to work without the networking and the coalition' (Interview with Programme Officer, Local NGO #37, Dar es Salaam, 8 December 1999).

By working together, pooling resources, distributing areas of responsibility and (perhaps most importantly) sharing the credit for their successes, women's NGOs have been able to stage successful and innovative campaigns and develop a reputation for excellence with both government and donors. The collective gender budget initiative organised by this group of local NGOs to address allocative inequalities was one such high quality campaign. It was so successful that gender budgeting has now been permanently incorporated into the Government of Tanzania's financial planning and is in the process of being adopted in several other countries in the region.

While networking has helped women's NGOs to achieve together what none of them could have done individually, it has also helped them to prevent the overlap that inevitably occurs when NGOs work in isolation. This has been a considerable problem among Tanzanian NGOs working in legal and human rights, where networking has been much less ingrained. The degree of duplication and competition for funds and projects in this sector led one donor agency to create an NGO explicitly mandated to co-ordinate NGO activity to provide better geographic coverage of the country and to encourage co-ordinated large-scale lobbying efforts around legal and human rights issues. So while local NGO competition for space in certain sectors does exist, efforts are already being made to reduce its negative impact. In the majority of sectors, NGO relationships are more likely to mirror the strong and close ties between NGOs working in gender issues. NGO relationships across sectors of development are also strong, as was illustrated by NGO mobilisation around the development of a government policy on NGOs.

Although the government invited only a few mainstream local NGOs to participate in designing the policy when the process started in 1996, local NGOs co-ordinated a powerful lobby and exerted their influence to make drastic changes to the government-proposed versions of the policy before its acceptance in 2001. The strong and collective lobbying by all sectors of local NGOs in Tanzania is one reason why the new policy remained in discussion for several years, with NGOs gaining additional powers and freedoms with each new draft. By 1999, drafts of the policy began with the government recognising 'the need to work together with NGOs' because they are 'potent forces for social and economic development, important partners in nation building and national development, valuable forces in promoting the qualitative development of democracy and, not least, important contributors to GDP' (Office of the Vice President 1999). These few words represent a significant change in the government's attitude towards NGOs from the beginning of the process. The voice of local NGOs as a whole has also been gaining prominence in the growing national debates over land issues and constitutional reform. In contrast to Zimbabwe, the government of Tanzania has seen and recognised the importance of NGOs in both these processes. More significantly, it has also begun to create the political space to enable NGOs to carry out these roles.

Somewhat counter-intuitively, one of the reasons that the NGO sector has developed such a strong voice as a whole is because its umbrella body has been relatively weak. The Tanzania Association of Non-Governmental Organizations (TANGO) was created in 1985 to help co-ordinate activity around that year's UN World Conference on Women in Nairobi, but has since been consistently perceived as a less effective leader than many of the local women's NGOs it was originally created to bring together (Angwazi 1993). Local NGOs often complain of TANGO's inability to represent adequately their interests and of its overly close relationship with government. This was especially true around the NGO Policy discussions, where TANGO, as the invited representative of the NGO sector, agreed to early government proposals which severely restricted NGO freedom. Local NGOs are not the only development actors that lack confidence in TANGO. Both donors and Tanzanian government officials also recognise TANGO's inability to draw its members together and to address many of the challenges that face the NGO sector. The weakness of the NGO-co-ordinating body in Tanzania mirrors that of NANGO, its counterpart in Zimbabwe. This raises the question of what the role of an NGO umbrella body should be and whether strong umbrella bodies encourage strong NGOs.

What the role of international NGOs should be in African development is also a crucial question to be addressed in this book. In Tanzania, as in Zimbabwe, there is very little contact between indigenous NGOs and the international NGOs present in the country. Only one of the local NGOs I encountered cited an INGO among the organisations that supported it. Those INGOs which do choose to work with local partners tend to work not with NGOs, but with Tanzania's many community-based organisa-tions (CBOs), such as village development associations and district development trusts (TANGO 1994, Gibbon 1995, Kelsall 2001). INGOs also rarely work alongside local NGOs in policy discussions, whether in terms of the NGO Policy, constitutional change or land distribution. This trend is heavily contrasted with the very strong relationships that many Tanzanian NGOs have developed with non-operational northern NGOs resident abroad – relationships that many local NGOs see as key factors in their success and survival.

Civil society organisations
Civil society has far fewer players in Tanzania than in many other African countries. In post-independence Tanzania, the role of labour movements and religious organisations, (each of which continues to mobilise signifi-cant proportions of the Zimbabwean population, for example) has been circumscribed by government and is now modest (Qorro 1993, Meena 1997). Links between local NGOs and all of these groups are therefore predictably weak.

However, local NGOs have built several sets of important relationships with other actors in civil society, perhaps most notably with academics. The University of Dar es Salaam has a long-standing reputation as one of the best and oldest institutions of higher learning in East Africa and has long been associated with Tanzania's NGO sector. Academics and NGO personnel have therefore built strong bonds through the exchange of research and the undertaking of joint projects. A large number of NGO directors and members are also members of the staff or faculty at the university and regularly use their connections to assist their NGOs. The university administration itself has been generous with its resources, often providing support services and office space, and giving its employees time off to become involved in NGO work.

A second key relationship for local NGOs is with the local media. While a significant proportion of the media is state-controlled, the growing sector of independent media organisations has been called 'one of the most vital and critical forces for change in Tanzania' (Tripp 2000: 207). Their coverage of NGO issues is regular and generally favourable and has helped local NGOs to develop a higher profile (Lange *et al.* 2000). It is common to see newspaper articles on workshops and training sessions being held by NGOs – events that are rarely considered newsworthy in Zimbabwe or in many other African countries. NGOs also feature regularly on the radio, broadcasting their own scheduled programmes and, for example, offering advice on legal issues. The partnership between radio stations and development organisations is especially important to many local NGOs as it allows them to reach communities which are too remote to reach in person. This relationship between local NGOs and the media has been difficult to build in many countries; in Tanzania, it is facilitated by the large number of media professionals who are also NGO members.

The relationships between local NGOs and small community-based development organisations throughout the country are also significant to the local NGO sector. These ties were uniquely observed in Tanzania among the African case study countries, and can be traced back to the country's post-independence history of local organisation for self-sufficiency. In many parts of the country, present-day village development committees and district development trusts – echoes of socialist-era communal structures – continue to be the main providers of services and focal points for communal development planning (Ndaro 1992, Urban and Rural Planning Department 1999). They are, therefore, crucial partners for local NGOs wishing to work in more rural and isolated parts of the country, where they are numerous. In 1993, for example, there were around 1,000 local development associations in Tanzania compared with only 224 local and international NGOs (Kiondo 1995). Even in contexts where CBOs and NGOs rarely work together, NGOs have continued to maintain good relationships with these organisations, which can often act as gate-keepers to external participation in community life.

It is important to distinguish these community development associations in Tanzania from the local government structures to which responsibility for development has formally been devolved from the federal government. Many CBOs in Tanzania are tacitly linked to local politicians and government officials and, more likely than not, work with some level of local government (Lange *et al.* 2000, Kelsall 2001). But they are civil society organisations nonetheless, created by communities to organise social service provision and to search for donor funds. And given the inability of formal government structures to provide these services they are increasingly important (Havnevik 1993, Qorro 1993).

Donor agencies

With few opportunities for internal income generation, Tanzanian NGOs look to donor agencies to secure funding for their projects. Official sources account for the greatest proportion of funding to NGOs, with the Nordic and Dutch embassies and official development agencies providing a significant proportion of that funding. These donors tend to be well respected. Denmark and the Netherlands, in particular, have been singled out for their NGO-friendly funding policies. These countries give considerable decision-making power to their local embassies or agency offices and are therefore better able to respond to their partners' needs. Private funding agencies, especially the Ford Foundation, are also important funders for many local NGOs, and the more so because of their less rigid and restrictive approach to funding.

A key type of financial partner for local NGOs in Tanzania is one which is not often observed in Zimbabwe: the non-resident northern NGO. These northern NGOs are most often from Europe or North America and are generally specialists in the same field as their local partners. They are not only significant for the financial support they offer but also for their co-operative approach – which includes more flexible funding contracts and support for equipment and overheads. This support comes with various types of non-material benefits, such as moral support and opportunities to attend conferences and training courses abroad, which can make as big a difference to local NGOs as financial support.

Funding from non-resident, northern NGOs for local Tanzanian NGOs is directly contrasted by the lack of funding they receive from international NGOs working in the country. Most INGOs in Tanzania are operational and act as recipients to donor agencies rather than as donor agencies to local bodies. These country offices of INGOs often find it more lucrative to raise money locally than to depend on their headquarters to organise larger-scale multilateral or bilateral projects. The general perception of low capacity within the local NGO sector by donors helps international NGOs to tap into local sources of funding, since donors have greater confidence in INGOs and often prefer to fund them over local alternatives.

The representative of one donor organisation that funds both local and international NGOs in Tanzania, spoke of having to 'water down' his organisation's selection criteria because very few local NGOs can meet them (Interview with Representative, International Donor Agency, Dar es Salaam, 4 November 1999). Tim Kelsall (2001) reports that DFID fails to fund any Tanzanian NGOs because they have been unable to find suitable partners. This perceived weakness of local NGOs, combined with the reluctance of donors to become involved in managing projects, has also favoured INGOs, which require little donor support beyond the financial to make their projects successful. Those donor agencies which do see a direct role for themselves in building local capacity often focus their efforts on CBOs, which are attractive because they have strong connections to rural grass-roots communities and generally require only small amounts of funding for their projects.

So local Tanzanian NGOs, while receiving good financial support from northern NGOs abroad and from a certain cadre of official development agencies, also face several obstacles in their search for funds. Negative donor perceptions and competition for donor funds from international NGOs and CBOs have serious implications for the power that they have been able to gain. Yet despite the difficulties which the majority of local NGOs face in their relationships with donors, a handful of the local NGOs I met in Tanzania exhibit characteristics which we would associate with local NGO power. One NGO has negotiated full core funding from a donor because of its strong reputation. Another has been able to retain funding despite being officially deregistered by the government. Two other NGOs, both of which are leaders in their fields with growing international reputations, have decided to only accept common pool funding from their donors. This gives these NGOs a rare financial strength and an ability to target funding towards their own priorities.

Government bodies

> Government has realised that NGOs have a very important role to play (Interview with Director, NGO Division, Office of the Vice-President, Republic of Tanzania, Dar es Salaam, 9 December 1999).

For many local NGOs in Tanzania, this most basic statement from the government officer in charge of NGO affairs represents the success of years of struggling for recognition. In the early post-independence era, NGOs and most forms of extra-state formal social organisation were outlawed and social groups focussing on women's issues or youth issues were created under the auspices of the ruling party (Kiondo 1995, Meena 1997). Andrew Kiondo, an expert on this period of Tanzania's history, considers the state of that era as a tensile institution which fulfilled the people's need for fora in which to organise by creating party associations through which meeting and mobilisation were made possible (Interview, Dar es Salaam, 1 December 1999). 'There wasn't very much room for NGOs under ujamaa', they were 'seen as a threat' is how a government source described this early conflict between the state and civil society actors like NGOs in Tanzania (Interview with Government Official, NGO Division, Dar es Salaam, 9 December 1999).

As the government liberalised both its economic and social policies in the mid-1980s, space was created for NGOs and other civil society actors in Tanzania – though not without restrictions. Registration was the first major hurdle set up by government. It created several ways for NGOs to register, all involving different amounts of bureaucracy, waiting periods (some of up to two years), and likelihoods of being turned down (Mtatifikolo 1997, Kelsall 2001). NGOs whose mission or target group paralleled those of existing party or state structures had a particularly difficult time being registered (Tripp 2000). In many cases, NGOs avoided applying for their registration through the two most logical ministries – Home Affairs, and Community Development, Women and Children, because of the difficulty of being registered by them. Once registered, local NGOs still faced an assortment of direct and indirect difficulties in their relationships with government as described by these local NGOs:

> Our relationship with the government has been conflictual, a bit conflictual. It has been a tense relationship. We even reached a point of rallying, joining some people to push for an agenda, and the government sent police forces (Interview with Programme Officer, Local NGO #40, Dar es Salaam, 13 December 1999).

> They [government] get very angry at times, they would do without us if they could. But then they also want to be seen to engage civil society in policy dialogues and policy debates, and because of that they have to contend with our presence. They would want to control us by remote control, sort of 'we give you this, but we want you to know which side your bread is buttered' (Interview with Director, Local NGO #31, Dar es Salaam, 2 December 1999).

These remarks illustrate that despite the government's post-liberalisation willingness to allow local NGOs to exist, its fear of political opposition has constrained the space available to local NGOs in the country. This fear, and the conflict over political space, was most exposed in late 1996 and early 1997, when one of the country's largest NGOs, BAWATA[4] – the Tanzania National Women's Council – was deregistered and banned by the government, which claimed that it had been acting 'as a political party' (*Sunday News*, 5 January 1997, Peter 1999). According to BAWATA's administrator, 'our success was our failure' (Interview with BAWATA Administrator, Dar es Salaam, 13 December 1999). The strength of BAWATA's voter education campaign and election publication during the run-up to the 1995 Presidential Elections – said to have 'heralded in a new era in the Tanzanian political scene' – was the cause of this 'failure' (Peter 1997: 732). It won BAWATA threats from the ruling party during the elections and intimidation, death threats and the demotion of relatives of BAWATA leaders from government jobs thereafter (Tripp 2000). In 1997, BAWATA was dissolved by government. Later that year, however, it won an appeal against its deregistration and the constitutionality of the law which was used to deregister it. The deregistration was officially reclassified as a suspension of activities. Yet even today BAWATA remains uncertain of its future.

---

[4] Baraza la Wanawake Tanzania.

Government suspicion of local NGOs challenging for political space in Tanzania is also expressed in less overt ways. A senior government official admits that 'advocacy NGOs could have been very much effective but the government is always taking them to be too much involved in politics,' and that, 'we have some very good [advocacy] NGOs, but all that they have been saying has been swallowed by the government, not taken seriously' (Interview with Government Official, NGO Division, Dar es Salaam, 9 December 1999). This government reticence around NGOs involved in lobbying and advocacy presents a major challenge for local NGOs in all sectors, since issues from HIV/AIDS awareness to women's education or environmental stewardship can all become highly politicised. As one writer on the BAWATA crisis asked:

> What is politics? Is it making public speeches? Politics is everyday life. How one earns his life, whether there are medicine[s] in hospitals, whether teachers are teaching in schools, are bureaucrats corrupt or not, how much one is paid as wages, what one listens [to] in the radio or reads in newspapers, who owns what in the country – all these are political issues. Should BAWATA keep quiet on these everyday issues and go back to cooking, knitting and running kindergartens? (Peter 1997: 732).

With the growing political power of local NGOs, the Government of Tanzania began to formulate a comprehensive National NGO Policy around the time of the BAWATA deregistration. While the government saw this policy as beneficial in helping to develop the proper enabling environment for NGOs in Tanzania, many local NGOs and donors saw it as a government attempt to control the sector (Meena 1997, Embassy of Sweden 12 October 1999, TANGO 1999). Local NGOs, with the backing of several donors, managed to force the government to involve them in the process in greater numbers and in greater variety, including more radical groups in addition to the mainstream ones which had thus far been favoured. But while it took almost five years to produce an NGO Policy satisfactory to both government and NGOs, while an NGO Bill currently in discussion threatens to replace the many gains made by NGOs in the NGO Policy with additional controls and restrictions, and while NGOs like BAWATA still face the pressure to avoid stepping into areas which could be deemed political, Tanzania has been able to avoid heightened levels of open antagonism between the government and local NGOs.

The close relationships between NGO and government personnel in Tanzania could be one explanation for the absence of these tensions. A large number of NGO directors hold, or are on leave from, government jobs, are retired or ex-government employees. This is a significant trend, especially considering the traditional perspective of NGOs as positioned in opposition to government, and of clear boundaries between the state and civil society. Understandably, then, the strong personal ties between individuals in the NGO sector and their present or past colleagues in government reduce animosity between the two groups. They also facilitate the work of both parties. In the words of one NGO director, 'the bureaucratic system in the government causes a bit of problem on our side. But having worked in government for so many years, that has been one of our strengths here. Because it's easy for me to contact people who are in the government, and to talk on friendly [terms]' (Interview with Executive Director, Local NGO #34, Dar es Salaam, 7 December 1999). If the contrast in Zimbabwe between central government animosity towards NGOs and local government co-operation with NGOs could be explained in terms of the support provided by NGOs to local levels of government, in Tanzania it is these strong personalistic ties which seem to have encouraged local levels of co-operation between government and the NGO sector.

Indeed, these formal and informal contacts not only promote cordial relationships between local NGOs and government, but also result in more tangible material benefits. Several local NGOs in Dar es Salaam have been given rent-free or reduced-rent office space from government agencies and several government bodies allow their employees to miss time at work when they are needed at their NGO. Some government departments go even further, providing funds for NGO office and travel expenses or allowing their workers to do NGO work while on government business trips in remote regions of the country. Relationships between local NGOs and local government bodies are generally also positive. While several NGOs have experienced the challenge of dealing with local village or district government bodies which stationed themselves between the NGO and the community, these relationships have generally evolved positively over time (Institute of Development Studies 1999). It seems fair, then, to say that no matter what the relationship of local NGOs to central or national government, relationships at more intimate levels seem to work successfully.

International development community
The most important set of international relationships built by Tanzanian NGOs is with northern NGOs, resident abroad and not locally active. These links are more visible in Tanzania than in Zimbabwe or Senegal and approach the ideal notion of 'partnership' to which so many NGOs aspire. Local NGOs in two sectors – human rights, and natural resources and the environment – benefit most from strong relationships with northern partner NGOs, which include the Royal Society for the Protection of Birds, the Swedish Nature Conservation Society, the World Resources Institute and the Danish Centre for Human Rights. These groups support NGOs in several ways.

Firstly, northern NGOs offer financial support to their Tanzanian counterparts. This funding is significant since it tends to be untargeted and allows local NGOs to invest in the capital purchases and core expenditures which other donors rarely contribute towards. It is also especially significant to local NGOs with highly specialised or multi-sectoral projects. These NGOs often find it difficult to attract funding from traditional donor organisations, whose target funding areas are narrowly defined and inflexible. Secondly, these northern NGOs offer a diverse range of professional development and capacity-building opportunities to their local partners, inviting them to conferences and colloquia and providing funds and opportunities to attend workshops and training courses. Thirdly, non-operational northern NGOs help local NGOs to increase their connections abroad. The International Institute for Environment and Development, for example, widely disseminates the research of one of its local partners.

Significantly, non-resident northern NGOs also help their Tanzanian NGO partners to forge connections to international media bodies, which help them to enlarge their international reputations. While the relationship between local NGOs and the local media is strong and has benefited local NGOs, links to the international media help to focus global attention on development issues and organisations in Tanzania. The impact of this international attention was perhaps most evident in 1998, during national debates on the controversial Rufiji dam project. After the government approved the establishment of a massive prawn processing plant, which was to eliminate 30,000 hectares of land containing the world's highest concentration of mangroves, local NGOs started a countrywide debate over the project and the consultation process which was used to approve it. As this campaign grew, local NGOs called on their NGO partners in the North for support. These northern partners, in turn, mobilised interest groups and the media in their own countries to create a powerful international campaign against the project. Under this intense international pressure and scrutiny, the government eventually cancelled the Rufiji dam project.

While this victory was not the result of the power of any one local NGO, it does highlight the importance of international linkages to the collective power of the NGO movement in Tanzania. Political support for local NGOs is key to their success and is a unique benefit offered by NGOs in the North with similar mandates and areas of specialisation. Because they are resident abroad, and have no operations in their local partners' countries, these northern groups can openly lobby or disagree with local governments.

Donors and resident international NGOs on the other hand (which were not cited by NGOs as having been relevant to the campaign over the Rufiji delta), must refrain from engaging in conflict with the Government of Tanzania. International NGOs need to maintain cordial government relationships in order to remain in the country and continue their work. Official development agencies and embassies, for their part, shy away from political activity that could cause friction between their home government and their host government. As this example illustrates, then, strong connections to the outer world are essential to building the strength and power of local NGOs, and non-resident organisations in the North have played an important role in Tanzania in facilitating these connections.

Power

One of the most striking characteristics of the local NGO sector in Tanzania is that its NGOs are awash with apparent contradictions. They have few full-time employees, but highly skilled and experienced volunteers. They are outcompeted by international NGOs and overlooked by donors in the country, but have built strong funding relationships with northern NGOs abroad. They have historically found themselves in regular conflict with government, yet the government now provides many of them with travel funds and office space. How have all of these trends affected their power?

Space
The Government of Tanzania has had a considerable impact on the space available to local NGOs, at times helping to widen that space and at times working to restrict it. In recent years, the government has committed itself to creating a better environment for NGO activity. It has invited an NGO working on women's issues to sit on government committees across several ministries. It has hired NGOs working on gender and the environment to undertake research and produce reports and it has provided office space to NGOs working in the fields of credit, agriculture, legal rights and the environment. At the same time, however, the government has gone to great lengths (as in the example of BAWATA) to stop local NGOs gaining political space. Many local NGOs plan to increase their involvement with political issues in development in the future. This should both help local NGOs to secure greater political space as a group, and encourage the government to accept their role in all aspects of development. Given the increasing commitment of the government to accepting and aiding high quality local NGOs and the decreasing government animosity towards NGOs over the last few years, we might, therefore, expect to see local NGOs gaining greater space in Tanzania over the coming years.

Yet despite the increased space made available to Tanzanian NGOs by the government, local NGOs still face stiff competition from INGOs and CBOs for both space and the funding that can help to secure it. As part-time organisations, a majority of Tanzanian NGOs lack permanent project staff and their activities tend to be constrained by the expertise and availability of their members. While a few days with certain local NGOs in Tanzania would be more than enough to dispel the notion that their members lack a wholehearted commitment to voluntarism and development, the absence of full-time personnel within these NGOs has affected their ability to implement projects and to undertake those which require long-term or on-site resources. Many donors see this phenomenon as reflecting a lack of capacity and professionalism on the part of all but the most vocal and well-known of NGOs and, as a result, channel a significant proportion of their funding through other civil society organisations in the country.

These other civil society organisations tend to fall into two categories: operational international NGOs, known for their capacity and professionalism, which are a low-risk choice for donors and often from their own home countries; and very small-scale CBOs, whose lack of professionalism is less important than their immediate connections to the grass-roots level. They generally require so little money that they too become low-risk investments for donors. These two types of groups also allow donors to reach beyond the urban centres where the majority of local NGOs are located. CBOs are generally located within rural villages and districts and INGOs have the resources to reach these areas. These trends have resulted in almost a crowding out of indigenous NGOs, particularly in welfare sectors of development.

The degree to which local NGOs have been affected by this trend cannot be overstated. When considering space as a key element of power, the competition that local Tanzanian NGOs face for development space, especially from INGOs, is the most obvious explanation for the absence of power among high quality local NGOs. Local NGOs see geographic expansion throughout Tanzania as one of their goals for the future, and the coming years will tell whether this increased physical presence in the rural areas of greatest need will help them to gain space and power, or whether they will continue to lose space to their better resourced and better connected INGO counterparts.

Financial independence from donors
A local NGOs' financial independence from its donors is perhaps most linked to its ability to generate revenue internally. Most local Tanzanian NGOs have few sustainable opportunities for income generation, with the majority counting membership fees as their only source of this kind of revenue. As such, these local NGOs would be expected to be heavily dependent on their donors for funding and, consequently, lacking power *vis-à-vis* these donors.

Interestingly, however, local NGOs in Tanzania maintain their independence from donors, while still lacking power. As part-time organisations, many forego the standard accoutrements of the NGO sector: permanent staff, office space, vehicles and publications. They require only small sums of funding to run their projects, funds that they can often access on relatively good terms from northern NGOs abroad. But while these NGOs rely much less heavily than most on donor organisations, they have not actually increased their power *vis-à-vis* donors at all. None of the NGOs I interviewed in Tanzania spoke of having turned donors down in the past and few had secured levels of core funding from which they were consistently able to set their own priorities and define their own agenda irrespective of donor interests.

Links to the international development community
This is the one element of power in which Tanzanian NGOs overshadow their counterparts in Zimbabwe and Senegal. Local NGOs have cultivated strong ties throughout their region, and gender and environmental NGOs, for example, work on projects with development organisations across the continent. Tanzanian NGOs have also built lasting ties to a broad range of development organisations in other parts of the developing world and throughout the North. Non-resident northern NGOs and the international media are two types of organisation which local NGOs highlight as being key to the success of their projects and campaigns. If Tanzanian NGOs begin to gain additional space in their country's development programme and additional financial independence, these strong ties to the international community will prove crucial in publicising their accomplishments and disseminating their research. This will enable them to develop an international reputation and to gain power in the wider international development community.

Engagement with the political aspects of development work
The engagement of local NGOs in Tanzania with political issues in development mirrors the experience of their counterparts in Zimbabwe, and seems to reflect the increasing movement of local African NGOs towards institutional and policy debates, or, after Korten, towards 'third-generation' development activities. Tanzanian NGOs are increasingly incorporating empowerment, lobbying and advocacy activities into their work and highlight the role that these activities will play in the future. This engagement with the political also helps their financial situation. Where Zimbabwean NGOs benefit from high levels of donor funding because of their political approach, an engagement with political issues within development is often the only factor which sets Tanzanian NGOs apart from their INGO and CBO counterparts, helping them to gain space and funding. Moreover, it has helped local NGOs to gain coverage in an international press which has become increasingly concerned with issues of civil society and democratisation, and interested in supporting local NGOs involved in lobbying and advocacy activities.

Tanzanian NGOs have endured conflict with a government trying to contain their influence on political issues. But aside from the BAWATA deregistration,[5] the government has generally allowed NGOs to speak freely and has refrained from vitriolic assaults against the NGO sector as a

[5] This is sometimes rumoured to be more complicated than I have represented. Generally considered a question of government wanting to circumscribe the voice of NGOs, allegations also exist that, as the head of BAWATA was married to an opposition candidate in the 1995 Tanzanian national elections, the NGO was not always impartial in its voter education programmes.

whole. In contrast to countries like Zimbabwe and Kenya, conflict between the two groups in Tanzania has rarely developed into full-blown antagonism or prevented them from building strong relationships at local levels. Given the levels of poverty in the country, the need for NGO services and the international pressure on government to include NGOs in its programmes, we would increasingly expect government to respect the voice of local NGOs in all aspects of development. As Tanzanian NGOs find greater political space and enlarge the political content of their work, we might, therefore, anticipate that they will also find a funding niche of their own, develop a wider international reputation, and be able to turn all of these into increased power.

Conclusion

Despite their strong links to the international development community, their unusual strategy of making do without funding as a means of reducing donor dependency, and the much less restrictive political climate which Tanzanian NGOs enjoy (as compared to their counterparts in many other African countries), none of the local NGOs I encountered in Tanzania can be considered powerful. Many well-regarded local NGOs are regularly outcompeted for funding by INGOs in their fields, and few donors are willing to take a chance on funding local NGOs when so many more professional INGOs are operational in Tanzania. Other local NGOs, which have secured space, funding, and a reputation for quality, are woefully short of full-time employees and see their potential impact limited by a lack of human resources – not because of the weakness of human resources in Africa as some might suggest, but because these resources are employed elsewhere. Despite noble intentions, large numbers of volunteers, and high-quality work, Tanzanian NGOs have not been able to develop the kind of power wielded by the SEWAs and IBASEs of the world.

5
The Power of Local NGOs in Senegal

The citizens of Senegal take great pride in the fact that Senegal is one of sub-Saharan Africa's longest-standing pluralist democracies (Young and Kante 1992). While the Socialist Party, formerly known as the Senegalese Democratic Block,[1] held office from independence in 1960 until 2000, when it was voted out of power, government in the country has been relatively benign, nonauthoritarian and stable. In 1981, Léopold Senghor, Senegal's first president, illustrated the country's early commitment to democracy when he became the first African head of state to retire voluntarily and relinquish power (Sklar 1986).

One of the reasons for Senegal's relative political stability is the strength of religious structures in the country and the close ties between religious elites and government officials. With a population that is over 90 per cent Muslim, Islamic religious organisations are a powerful force in Senegal, forming a sort of 'religiously based civil society' (Villalón 1995: 12). In many areas, Islamic social structures supersede the development structures of government and NGOs. Adherents turn to the leaders of their brotherhood for their social and economic needs, in addition to their spiritual ones. Able to commend to their faithful the candidate they should support in government elections, these Islamic brotherhoods wield considerable influence in the political arena. In return for their political support, they have been able to secure regular concessions, freedoms and funding from government (Behrman 1970, Coulon 1981, Creevey 1985, Patterson 1999). These mutually beneficial arrangements have helped to increase the attention paid by government to all civil society organisations in the country and have made the brotherhoods a key force in Senegal's social, economic and political processes (O'Brien 1971, Gellar 1995, Clark 1999, Devey 2000).

[1] Parti Socialiste and Bloc Démocratique Sénégalais, respectively.

91

Historical setting

While the Islamic brotherhoods, along with student movements and trade unions, have been active throughout Senegal's history, it was only amidst the droughts and fiscal crises of the 1970s that NGOs also began to grow in number and influence. In the early 1970s a major three-year drought hit the entire Sahel region of West Africa, sending many countries into food crisis (Gueye-Tall 1989). With weak human resource capacity and a financial deficit which would worsen in coming years with global oil shocks, the government was unable to meet the food and income needs of starving communities and agricultural producers, and encouraged local NGOs to work with these populations (Concept 1997, Bâ 1999). The newly emerging Senegalese NGO sector was initially involved in relief activities until the scaling back of the state propelled NGOs into the diverse range of development sectors in which they now work (CONGAD 1999).

The disengagement of the state from many sectors of development activity over the last decade, as the politics of structural adjustment and decentralisation have gripped the continent, has been a major driving force behind the growth of local NGOs in the country. Senegal's decentralisation policies date back to 1972 when rural government community structures were created, but were only seriously advanced in the early 1990s (CONGAD 1997). By 1996, Senegal had been divided into three layers of local-level government and its ten regions had been granted both legal status and financial autonomy (Nzouankeu 1997, Ndiaye 1999). In return, these regions assumed responsibility for environment and natural resources management, health and social action, youth, sport and recreation, culture, education, and local area planning (CONGAD 1997). In the face of this decentralisation, NGOs have been propelled to the fore of national development processes, a role which they have been called on to play by local communities, donors and the state alike. With the country's worsening levels of poverty and human development, the role of Senegalese NGOs seems likely to continue to grow in the future.

The local NGO sector in Senegal

The local NGO sector in Senegal is the oldest in the case study countries. This reflects both the great need for NGO services in Senegal and the relatively early acceptance and support of NGO activity by the government. The sector differs from its counterparts in Zimbabwe and Tanzania in terms of its French colonial history and the unique predominantly religiously based civil society of which it is a part. All of these aspects contribute to a development space which is quite unlike those which I have examined to this point. In 1999, over a hundred NGOs were registered with the country's main umbrella body. What role do these Senegalese NGOs play in their unusual environment, and does it provide them with any advantages in terms of developing power? To answer this question, I conducted interviews with local NGOs, INGOs, donors, government representatives and other relevant development actors during 2000. The local NGOs I sampled had an average age of fourteen.

In what sectors are Senegalese NGOs most active?

Local Zimbabwean and Tanzanian NGOs seem to dispel the perception often held of local NGOs as lacking focus and specialisation. NGOs in Senegal both fulfil and reinforce this stereotype. An overwhelming majority of Senegalese NGOs are generalists, working across a variety of fields, rather than specialising in one. Most count some form of credit, health awareness, education and natural resources management among their activities. Over half of the NGOs I met were active in three or more sectors. Trying to categorise NGOs on the basis of the sectors in which they work may be an arbitrary oversimplification of development work and of the multifaceted roles that NGOs play in communities; nonetheless, the majority of local NGOs in Tanzania and Zimbabwe concentrated their activities around the one area in which they had the greatest expertise. Some of the NGOs in these countries straddled two related sectors of development, gender and credit, for example, but they rarely extended their activity into other sectors in which they lacked specialised resources.

With very few specialist NGOs in Senegal, a high degree of duplication of activities within the NGO sector would seem likely. This is indeed the case, and the director of a well-respected international NGO that works very closely with local NGO partners highlighted that 'the problem of overlap is a serious one' (Interview with Director, International NGO, Dakar, 8 February 2000). Strangely, this overlap of mission and activity has not resulted in heightened competition between individual local NGOs.

On the one hand, the population's need for development services could be so great that each NGO has enough development space in which to work and enough clients with which to work. A more likely explanation, however, seems to lie in the geographic specialisation of local NGOs. If each one is drawn, or pushed, to a different part of the country, then despite their duplication of services, they will never be in direct competition with each other. Individual Senegalese NGOs are generally active in only a small part of the country, and one in which there is little other development activity. In Tanzania, the difficulties and costs of being represented in the country's interior regions meant that local NGO activity tended to be centred around Dar es Salaam and nearby rural regions. These costs are not as prohibitive in Senegal, however, the smallest of the field-work countries and one in which transportation around the regions is not especially difficult or costly. Here, it is personal connections and economic opportunities, rather than economic restrictions, which have resulted in the narrowly specialised geographic focus of Senegalese NGOs. Donor agencies in Senegal have, in essence, 'balkanised the country', with different donors taking different regions as their area of focus (Interview with Director, International NGO, Dakar, 8 February 2000). When AIDS interventions became a funding priority for donors, for example, they split up the country, each taking a block of regions in which to work. As such, most of them only offer funding to NGOs working in those areas. In response, local NGOs have specialised geographically, focussing their work in specific regions in order to find stable funding and to escape competition from other local NGOs and development agencies. One local NGO director explained how their main donor has influenced their region of activity: 'USAID works a lot with Casamance. So as we are partners of USAID, who funds our projects, so we have started a lot of work in Casamance' (Interview with President, Local NGO #59, Dakar, 27 March 2000).

In Zimbabwe, a developed travel and communications infrastructure, combined with important issues of ethnic and linguistic representation, has encouraged local NGOs to expand their work geographically while keeping it narrowly focussed on the expertise of their staff. In Tanzania, local NGOs have made effective use of the specialist skills of their volunteers in developing a specialised mandate for their work, but their organisational structure and resource shortages have handicapped their prospects for national expansion. In Senegal, local NGOs are a sectorally diffuse, but geographically specialised group. The search for donor funds drives them to specialise according to donors' geographic areas of focus while diversifying their activities to fulfil as many sectors of interest to donors as possible. Each of these strategies has developed in response to the particular amount of development space available to local NGOs in each country. Driven by the need to find, create or guard a development space, local NGOs in Zimbabwe, Tanzania and Senegal have evolved their own combination of strategies to survive and succeed.

In addition to the number of sectors in which they are active, Senegalese NGOs also provide quite a contrast to their counterparts in Zimbabwe and Tanzania in terms of the kinds of sectors in which they are active. While NGO activity tended away from the more traditional welfare sectors in those countries, the majority of Senegalese NGOs in Dakar are involved in promoting welfare in the fields of education, health care and children's services, with a significant proportion working in the field of education alone. Senegal also has the smallest number of local NGOs focussed in the areas of human rights, legal issues and democracy-building. Many people attribute this to the long-standing cordial relationship between the state and civil society organisations in the country, and to the generally democratic nature of post-independence government. Both of these factors have made the proactive lobbying role of local NGOs less important than in other countries, and NGOs have focussed instead on creating access to politics through civic education and literacy.

How strong are the human resources of Senegalese NGOs?

The generalist strategy of local NGOs is partly a result of their non-specialist human resource bases, starting at the level of their directors. The great majority of local NGO directors arrived at their present job from a position with another NGO, or directly after completing their education. This certainly reflects their commitment to development issues and illustrates that the majority of them are very familiar, experienced and interested in the workings of the development sector.[2] It also, however, indicates that in most cases, familiarity with the NGO sector is their only specialist development knowledge. Moreover, while all of the Zimbabwean NGO directors in the case study sample were employed on a full-time, salaried basis, nearly one half of their counterparts in Senegal derive their livelihood elsewhere. This includes both the Senegalese NGO directors who have other full-time jobs, and those who work full-time at their NGO, but as volunteers. As in Tanzania, the need for a significant number of these NGO directors to concern themselves with a job elsewhere or with the search for income, has affected the ability of local NGOs in Senegal to act quickly and flexibly and to undertake demanding large-scale projects.

The lack of highly skilled and full-time staff among Senegalese NGOs is similarly related to their generalism. Most NGOs have only small numbers of permanent staff and rely heavily on the efforts of volunteers. Some NGOs in the capital city Dakar, including two working in health, two in education, one in human rights and one in child welfare, have no paid staff at all. And while local NGOs in Tanzania also rely heavily on voluntarism in their programming, most of their volunteers are highly skilled and experienced in the NGO's field of activity. It is perhaps important at this juncture to recognise that voluntarism lies at the heart of development work and NGO work, in particular, and can be as important to NGO success as economic considerations. However, what this example serves to illustrate is that NGO reliance on voluntarism, in the absence of more formalised human resource structures, can impair the ability of local NGOs to grow and to perform to the standards demanded by their donors and hoped for by their clients.

The majority of the local NGO directors in Senegal who are not being paid by their NGOs or by full-time jobs elsewhere are general development consultants and derive their income from short-term contract employment that they undertake for donor and multilateral agencies. The variety of jobs that these directors take on is great, and most of them are not in the financial position to turn down consulting contracts that draw them out of their immediate field of expertise. Such consultancies often also lead to larger contracts for their NGOs, which further draws these

---

[2] Even those directors with no prior NGO experience had been active participants and organisers of various social movements in the country, most particularly the strong student movement of the late 1960s.

organisations away from their professed mandates and towards a generalist approach to development. This trend might make us ask whether it is preferable, in terms of the interests of an NGO, to have a director who is a full-time employee elsewhere, as was observed in a great number of cases in Tanzania, or to have one who is a full-time volunteer with the NGO, but constantly searching for income on the side. It is a difficult and subjective question to answer. One obvious response however, is that the full-time, salaried local NGO directors in Zimbabwe certainly seem to provide the greatest amount of stability and guidance for their organisations and as such, are preferable to either of the other options presented in Tanzania or Senegal.

How are Senegalese NGOs financed?
One characteristic of NGO power is financial independence from donors. Rather surprisingly, it is in Senegal that local NGOs seem to have achieved one element of this independence from donors, namely the ability to turn down donor funding. A third of these NGOs had refused to work with a particular donor or called an end to an existing funding contract because they were unhappy with the terms of that funding, or with their relationship to that donor. This is surprising when compared to local NGOs in Tanzania, none of whom mentioned having refused to work with a particular donor and even more surprising compared to the local NGOs in Zimbabwe. There, only a very small number of well-reputed and busy organisations had the ability to turn down funds, which they used only when their NGO was so stretched that it did not have the internal capacity left to deal with additional funds. In Senegal, by contrast, the NGOs which had refused funds were not necessarily the best known and most sought-after, the most stable, or grouped in any one specific sector.

How are local NGOs in Senegal, which would not otherwise be described as powerful, able to turn down funding opportunities? One possible explanation is that these NGOs, like those in Tanzania, have very low overheads because of their informal structures and their reliance on voluntarism, and so are not in need of additional funds. This is simply not the case, however, and Senegalese NGOs often highlighted their specific financial needs, most often for core funding. Even where wage bills are small, NGOs still require funds to pay for their office and vehicle expenses. Moreover, many NGOs able to cover their core or basic survival expenses, are unable to invest in growth expenditures – those costs involved in undertaking publicity, publishing papers, networking and promoting staff development. These expenditures, which help an NGO to gain an international reputation and to create and protect space, are key to their power and sustainability.

Perhaps local NGOs in Senegal are able to refuse opportunities for donor funds because they are able to generate adequate internal financing for their programmes. Again, however, this seems not to be the case.

Whereas several local NGOs in Zimbabwe generate income from their publishing, consulting and training work, and many Tanzanian NGOs regularly collect fees from their members, few local NGOs in Senegal have identified regular opportunities for internal income generation. Indeed, the few such opportunities that were discussed with me tended to be opportunities for the volunteer director, as an individual, to gain personal income. Moreover, with the majority of Senegalese NGOs firmly grounded in welfare activities, few of them have the potential for future private sector partnerships, or even opportunities for significant income generation through cost recovery. Internal revenue generation is also, therefore, an unlikely explanation for this unusual trend.

If local NGOs are able to turn down donor funds, not because they do not require them, nor because they are able to generate the required funds themselves, then perhaps they are easily able to find funds elsewhere. This seems to be the most likely explanation. Senegal receives one and a quarter times and more than triple the ODA per capita that Tanzania and Zimbabwe receive, respectively (UNDP 2003). Not only are there large numbers of donor agencies at work, but unusually, there are also a large number of INGOs investing in local NGOs. It follows that local NGOs are able to turn down donor funds offered on unfavourable terms because they know that there are many more sources of funding available. But this is only half of the picture.

Large amounts of funding may be available throughout Senegal, but for specialised NGOs, the majority of this funding would be inaccessible to them, targeted as it is at activities outside their realm of speciality. This, then, is where the generalist strategy of Senegalese NGOs pays off, for it is only in being able to adapt equally to the priorities of different funders that local NGOs can minimise the competition between them and pick and choose among donors. This contrasts with the generally held notion that NGOs will specialise as the competition they face increases; in Senegal, competition in the development sector has instead produced a sector of generalist NGOs (Garilao 1987). This strategy has been very successful for Senegalese NGOs – but does it confer power? Financial independence from any one donor is not as meaningful to the development of power as financial independence from the donor sector as a whole. Moreover, there is a trade-off between what generalist NGOs gain in financial opportunity by pursuing a generalist strategy and what they lose in terms of the reputation and space that come with being a recognised leader in a particular field of development.

With whom do local Senegalese NGOs form relationships?
To this point in our discussion I have alluded to several ways in which Senegalese NGOs differ from their counterparts in Tanzania and Zimbabwe, including through their unusual relationship to donor organisations, INGOs and government. What do these relationships look like and how have they affected the power of local NGOs in Senegal?

Other local NGOs

As in Zimbabwe and Tanzania, relationships within the local NGO sector in Senegal are strong and fruitful. In many NGOs, these ties are as old as the organisation itself. One director highlighted the importance of these strong links to other local NGOs, saying: 'There are many NGOs who have supported us. We have sister organisations, many. Which makes me very happy. When we have financial difficulties, we borrow money from them. [...] We have been able to survive solely because of the solidarity within the [NGO] network' (Interview with President, Local NGO #43, Dakar, 10 February 2000). These sorts of ties between local NGOs, which have facilitated loans, the sharing of office space and, more regularly, the co-ordination and planning of shared activities, are largely due to the amount of NGO networking that takes place in Senegal. While the greatest amount of inter-NGO networking in Tanzania and Zimbabwe was ascribed to women's NGOs, even in the absence of a gender-based NGO sector in Senegal, networking is key and cuts across all sectors of NGO activity.

To anyone familiar with the NGO sector in Senegal, this close contact among local NGOs in the country is a result of the work of CONGAD (the Council of Development NGOs),[3] Senegal's NGO co-ordinating committee. Almost every single Senegalese NGO director I met cited CONGAD as one of the groups that supports their work and many went so far as to cite the strength of NGO relationships facilitated through CONGAD as one of the primary reasons for their success. This is an obvious, drastic and important contrast with the place that NGO umbrella bodies seem to occupy in Zimbabwe and Tanzania. While NANGO and TANGO are variously ignored and criticised by the NGOs they are meant to represent, Senegalese NGOs see CONGAD as an organisation which benefits the whole NGO sector and one of which they all want to be members.

This respect for CONGAD is not limited to local NGOs, and both the government and donors recognise the position of CONGAD as a legitimate representative for Senegalese NGOs. CONGAD acts as the delegate for NGOs on several government committees, one of which is the committee responsible for registering NGOs in the country. While Tanzania's NGO policy also calls for substantial NGO representation in the official NGO registration process, Senegal is the only one of the case study countries in which an NGO co-ordinating committee is both sought after for their opinion on the matter by government and trusted by NGOs to offer that opinion. Donors regularly work through CONGAD to offer capacity-building workshops and seminars for the NGO sector and many regard it so highly that they will only fund local NGOs which are members. CONGAD's reputation is also rapidly growing beyond the confines of Senegal. As the first NGO collective in West Africa, it has long played a guiding role in the region, supporting the establishment of other umbrella organisations and of networking links between them. And

---

[3] Conseil des Organisations Non-Gouvernementales d'Appui au Développement.

CONGAD has become the first point of contact for anyone, the world over, interested in the Senegalese NGO sector.

What is it about CONGAD that makes it so successful and so rare among NGO umbrella bodies? First, there is its approach. CONGAD has sought to include NGOs, not just as members, but also as its executive and governing body. While most other NGO umbrella bodies were designed to operate in the same way as CONGAD, NGOs in other countries are often only nominally in control of their governing body. In Senegal, by contrast, the election of local and international NGO members to CONGAD's board, their regular and transparent replacement and their very real influence on its work, have resulted in an umbrella body which, its members feel, is truly accountable to them.

A second reason for CONGAD's success is the variety of services that it offers to its members. These include a bulk purchasing centre, a monthly newsletter, meeting space and a very current resource library, all of which are regularly used by a great number of NGOs. The CONGAD building, nicknamed the 'House of NGOs' is never quiet; it is crowded daily and considered a meeting place for all NGOs. While the NGO umbrella bodies in both Zimbabwe and Tanzania also produce newsletters and hold training sessions for their members, their services are never as well thought of by the NGOs themselves. These factors have led to a rare trust between Senegalese NGOs and CONGAD.

Many years of hard work, focussed representation of NGOs to government and carefully chosen battles with its agencies are a third reason for CONGAD's success. CONGAD was established in 1981, long before NGO activity in Tanzania was legalised, and just as the state of Zimbabwe was itself being created. As such, it has been able to promote a sustained trust between the NGO sector and the Government of Senegal for over twenty years. Despite sometimes acrimonious battles between CONGAD and government, an example of which will be examined in a later section, CONGAD has nonetheless built strong personal relationships with government officials and has remained aware of the fact that without the strong support of government, even if only in principle, its work would be considerably harder to do.

One last reason for CONGAD's success is its ability to incorporate international NGOs into its network. This has made the collective voice of NGOs in Senegal stronger and has increased the interaction between local and international NGOs. While local NGO–INGO partnerships are still not widespread, there are a significant number of NGOs in Senegal that receive both non-material and financial support from INGOs in the country. This could be attributed to several factors. While the vast majority of INGOs resident in Zimbabwe or Tanzania are operational, there are several within Dakar alone that exist solely to build the capacity of local partners. In the HIV/AIDS sector, for instance, INGOs are instrumental in providing training and technical support to local NGOs.

Moreover, of the group of international NGOs that are operational, many work in partnership with local NGOs. This is surprising given that many of these INGOs are also represented in Tanzania and Zimbabwe, where they have no record of involving local NGOs in their projects. Part of the impetus for this trend, as suggested by the local NGO directors I interviewed, is that CONGAD and donor agencies in Senegal pressure INGOs to incorporate local NGOs into their work. The benefits to local NGOs of these links with international NGOs are not limited to capacity-building support or to the opportunity to work with INGOs on their projects. Several local NGOs also benefit from direct funding from INGOs. Although small in absolute numbers, it is a promising trend, and one that may become more widespread in the future. Local NGOs in the country are currently beginning to lobby against the competition they face from larger international NGOs, especially in the welfare sectors of development, and to call for a re-evaluation of the operational mandates of INGOs. If this campaign is a success it may see more INGOs in Senegal re-evaluate their mandates and switch their focus from providing services directly to the public to providing capacity-building support and funding to local NGOs.

Will it fall to CONGAD to spearhead this local NGO campaign for greater development space? Is this even the role of an NGO umbrella body? It is a difficult question to answer. NANGO in Zimbabwe, TANGO in Tanzania and CONGAD in Senegal share many roles in common, roles which we might consider to be part of the responsibility of any NGO-co-ordinating body. These include facilitating networking and information sharing throughout the NGO sector, providing training and capacity-building support to interested NGOs and representing NGOs when government and donors require input from the NGO sector (Stremlau 1987). NGO umbrella bodies have developed great skill at fulfilling these roles and the majority of these organisations continue to focus their attentions on this range of activities.

But CONGAD, the most respected of the NGO umbrella bodies considered, has achieved its success by creating innovative roles for itself, in higher-level policy debates across the country, the West African region, and internationally. Its history of enhancing the reputation of the local NGO sector, while continuing to provide the everyday support that many NGOs have come to rely on, provides one example of what local NGOs should expect from their governing body. It may not be possible for all NGO umbrella bodies, particularly those created or funded by national government, to play similar roles in their communities. But CONGAD's example illustrates that these bodies have many more potential roles to play in their countries than the standard ones on which the majority have, to date, been focussing. Capitalising on opportunities to create new roles for themselves may prove to be the key to survival and success for NGO umbrella bodies and the local NGOs they serve, as the space for development in Africa becomes ever more crowded.

Civil society organisations

The CONGAD-facilitated cohesiveness of the local NGO sector in Senegal has encouraged strong ties between NGOs and other civil society actors. NGOs often take part in campaigns and projects with political parties, unions and labour movements, and university groups. This spirit of community among the various organisations working in social, economic and political development serves to greatly strengthen all of their reputations, *vis-à-vis* both government and donors. The local media also play a prominent role in gaining recognition and publicity for local NGOs. Newspapers and television and radio stations provide regular and comprehensive coverage of NGO activities and the director of a human rights organisation which works closely with the media described their relationship in this way: 'We use the media a lot. As soon as something happens, we contact the media, so people get interested. [...] And that is what has made us a success today' (Interview with Executive Secretary, Local NGO #48, Dakar, 17 February 2000). The link between local NGOs and the media in Senegal mirrors the important link between the two groups which was observed in Tanzania. The local media can be similarly important in promoting and making accessible the work of NGOs in other countries across Africa and in helping them to seize power.

There are two other ways in which the links between local NGOs and civil society actors in Senegal parallel the relationships between the same groups in Tanzania. Firstly, links between local NGOs and the private sector in Senegal are very weak. Of the few local NGOs that are supported by the private sector, the majority receive only donations in kind – such as food and soap – from local corporations. This provides quite a contrast to the Zimbabwean case study where strong links between local NGOs and the private sector have yielded important long-term opportunities for internal income generation by local NGOs. Only one Senegalese NGO that I encountered was actually being sought after by local corporations for its consulting ability and few others looked poised to capitalise on such opportunities in the future.

The second set of NGO–civil society relationships which echo the experiences of Tanzanian NGOs are even more significant and widespread. These are the relationships between local NGOs and small local-level development groups such as women's groups and credit co-operatives – a trend which is likely evident in other African countries with strong histories of associative activity as well. In Senegal, these groups tend to involve a smaller sub-section of a village or district population than in Tanzania, where CBOs are commonly representative of a village as a whole and work on larger-scale projects. Moreover, where Tanzanian CBOs provide direct competition for local NGOs, in Senegal these community groups are important local project partners for NGOs. Not a single NGO director interviewed in Senegal spoke of having their donors prefer to work directly with such village-based collectives. Instead, local NGOs look at these village-level groups as key project partners, as gate-keepers to the community and also as local experts and long-term local managers for projects once the NGO has moved out of the community.

Interestingly, given the widespread presence and activity of Senegal's Muslim brotherhoods and the propensity of the country's local NGOs to work closely with other civil society organisations, there seem to be few formal relationships between NGOs and the brotherhoods. A number of NGO personnel and beneficiaries in urban centres like Dakar do belong to these religious communities. But most adherents actively participate in their orders' religious, social, economic and political activities and depend on their *marabout*, the leader of their brotherhood, and brotherhood social structures for their development needs. Brotherhood-based groupings called *daira*[4] – originally organised to further the religious education of followers – allow individuals join together to build mosques; address problems of youth unemployment or under-education; socialise with adherents who share their occupation, language or region of origin; ease the transition from rural to urban environments; and work together to address local community education, health care and sanitation needs (Diop 1981, Devey 2000, Gueye 2001). Few adherents engage with local NGOs and many of them have no option: there is very little development space available to local NGOs in the areas which surround the centres of Senegal's five Islamic brotherhoods. Slowly, however, independent Islamic associations and NGOs are beginning to develop, perhaps as a response to the declining political influence and economic prosperity of many of the brotherhoods (Villalón 1999). Across the country, a number of Islamic-based NGOs are now working to encourage youth and female education, to improve standards of health care and to reduce the number of street children in the country's urban centres.

Donor agencies

The relationship between local NGOs and donor organisations in Senegal contrasts with those in Tanzania and Zimbabwe in several important ways. A first contrast is in terms of the composition of the donor sector itself. Here, bilateral donors are much less prevalent funders for local NGOs. In Senegal, for example, I did not meet a single local NGO that received funding from DANIDA, NORAD or DFID, each of which is a very active funder in Zimbabwe and Tanzania. One fairly obvious explanation for this trend relates to the history of colonialism in Africa and explains why the British have a much greater presence in their former colonies of Zimbabwe and Tanzania. Colonial divisions also explain why the French government, the former colonial ruler of Senegal, funds local NGOs here, though not in the other case study countries. Language and culture also contribute to these trends, and INGOs and official donor agencies from France, Belgium, Switzerland

[4] Also known as *daara* in rural environments and *dahira* in urban centres (Diop 1981).

and Italy are similarly only notably active in funding Senegalese NGOs.

Despite these predictable geopolitical donor proclivities, there are two unexpected trends. Firstly, France seems not to fulfil the proposition that a colonial power will be the primary official donor for local NGOs in its former colonies. While it is the largest donor of ODA in Senegal, the bulk of France's official aid is channelled through government. Of the aid targeted at civil society, the most significant proportion is channelled through French NGOs working in Senegal, as opposed to directly through indigenous Senegalese NGOs. Secondly, and very surprisingly, USAID seems to be the largest donor to NGOs, and certainly the busiest. The reasons why the United States has chosen to focus its attentions on this French-speaking, very European enclave of Africa are not obvious, and yet it is firmly entrenched in its development.[5]

Perhaps even stranger is the fact that USAID is very well-respected, and one might go so far as to say, beloved, by Senegalese NGOs. While it was routinely named as the most difficult, least friendly, and all-round worst donor to work with by the NGO directors I met in Tanzania and Zimbabwe, USAID in Senegal is a well liked donor of over half of the NGOs I encountered. Nearly every one of them cited USAID as their preferred partner, echoing the words of these NGO directors:

> If we're talking of our favourite partner ... I'd lean towards USAID. They're a partner with whom we've had a lot of problems and a lot of disputes. [...] But also, I'd say that they're our best partners. [...] Financially they're the partner who has given us the most support. [...] They're also the partner who's given us the most institutional support (Interview with President, Local NGO #55, Dakar, 6 March 2000).

> Our best experience is with USAID, who is our principal donor. And the best part of what we retain from USAID is that they really taught us how to manage our projects. And to be strict in their management. [...] I have to say that really, our capacities, the improvement of these capacities, and in part, our success, are because of them (Interview with Director, Local NGO #57, Dakar, 15 March 2000).

These quotes highlight that USAID's approach in Senegal has been focussed on building the capacity of local NGOs. Its eleven million US dollar NGO Support Project,[6] through which the bulk of this funding came, lasted over eight years and touched local NGOs all over the country. It sent directors and financial officers on training courses, advocated

---

[5] I suspect that Senegal's historical importance in the African slave trade has increased its profile in the United States, and has made it politically important for the US to support through development assistance. This assistance is likely also linked to the US army presence in Senegal during World War II and the strong ties forged between the two countries at that time.

[6] Projet d'Appui aux ONG.

technology upgrades and linked local and northern NGOs through funding contracts. It would not be an exaggeration to say that this USAID NGO
Support Project has truly changed the face of the local NGO sector, a
thought that was echoed by many of the development actors I interviewed
in the country.

The contrast between this experience and that of local NGOs in the
other case study countries merits further discussion. While USAID in
Senegal focusses on building NGO institutional capacity, in Tanzania and
Zimbabwe it seems to be a more intrusive partner. It hired American
consultants to oversee the everyday direction of a local Zimbabwean
NGO and tried to restrict the political activity of one of its partners in
Tanzania. In fact, both of these local NGOs claimed to have come close to
collapse as a result of their relationship with USAID. NGOs often remark
on how a change of donor personnel within a country office can transform
their relationship to a donor agency. This example also illustrates the
importance of individual country contexts, and how the nature of the
same donor agency can differ across the countries in which it works,
depending on the attitudes and policies of individual country directors
and staff.

While Senegalese NGOs have benefited from USAID's funding strategy,
the majority of them have also capitalised on close ties to non-resident
northern NGOs. As in Tanzania, these NNGOs offer funding and other
resources to local NGOs, while, as foreign-based organisations, providing
little competition for funds or development space. As NGOs themselves,
these groups also tend to have an attitude towards development which
coincides more closely with that of local NGOs, as this Senegalese NGO
director expressed: 'Most of our donors are essentially NGOs, [...] because
most often we have the same visions, we understand [each other ... and]
the relationship is much easier' (Interview with Secretary General, Local
NGO #54, Dakar, 10 February 2000). Moreover, the relationship between
NNGOs and local NGOs tends to be a more equal partnership, where
common aims serve to reinforce the ties between them. Another of the
NGO directors I interviewed described one such partnership in this way:
'We share a lot of things. For example, they sent us their last strategic plan
for 2000–2004 so that we could add our input, make suggestions etc. [...]
So there's a certain interaction beyond the financial' (Interview with
Secretary General, Local NGO #52, Dakar, 1 March 2000).

Local NGOs in Senegal are also the only ones in the case study
countries to receive funds from operational international NGOs. While
the majority of these INGOs compete with local NGOs for funding,[7] some
do extend grants to local NGOs or fund their involvement in INGO
programmes. In Senegal, large operational international NGOs, often
notorious for their weak links to local NGOs in other countries, work on

---

[7] USAID's NGO Support Project, for example, funded both local NGOs and a number of
American NGOs working in Senegal.

projects in co-operation with local NGOs, with which they share a proportion of their funding. The strong links between these two groups of NGOs, reinforced by CONGAD, are a sign that increased co-operation between local and international NGOs seems likely in the future.

All of these trends signal that local NGOs in Senegal occupy a very fortunate position compared to the majority of their counterparts in Zimbabwe and Tanzania. They benefit from funding from non-resident and resident international NGOs, and receive large amounts of capacity building and core funding from an official donor that is widely disliked in other countries. This glut of donor funds is one reason why such a large proportion of local NGOs are able to pick and choose among donors and turn down donor funds. But as discussed earlier, the availability of large amounts of donor funding alone does not make local NGOs confident enough in their ability to access funds from other donors that they will turn down offers of funding. This confidence comes from the generalist strategy pursued by the majority of Senegalese NGOs, which realise that because there are so many donors available, and because they can adapt to the priority areas of any of these donors, they can therefore choose from whom to accept funds. This strategy of working in several sectors increases a local NGO's chance of having continuous funding in Senegal and has become a viable local NGO strategy for survival.

The generalist strategy does have drawbacks, however, particularly as it frames an NGO's mandate as reactive to donor priorities. The focus of local NGOs, like the one described below, are decided, or at least heavily influenced, by donors.

> [Donors], sometimes you don't find them [focussed] on your needs. They also have their own objectives. At times, they say it's women that they're working on, you must help women. At times they say there are problems with the environment, someone must take care of the environment. At times they say there are diseases, sexually transmitted diseases, AIDS, someone must [work on these]. So if you want your structure to endure, because there are costs – your office, secretaries, there are these things which arise, you have to at least manage these programmes. You have to have programmes to run. If you say, [you only work on] employment, but employment is not financed, you risk not working on employment and you risk closing. [...] Which has meant that [we] have worked on many varied programmes. Which has maybe, it hasn't distracted us, but it has splintered us a bit from our objectives (Interview with President, Local NGO #55, 6 March 2000).

Another example of this phenomenon is the geographic specialisation of local NGOs according to areas of donor activity. This indicates that NGOs look at generalism as a necessary survival strategy, and as evidenced throughout this chapter, it certainly has contributed to the survival of local NGOs. But what the NGO director above saw as an easy choice between subscribing to donor preferences and failing to survive is not as clear cut, and an important consideration is whether in surviving by generalising and following donor priorities, Senegalese NGOs sacrifice their potential to develop power in the long term. Financial security and an ability to turn down donor funds are important manifestations of power, but they are likely to be meaningless if an NGO has lost sight of its objectives and is following someone else's priorities.

Government bodies
Early government–NGO relationships in Senegal were fraught with confusion, mistrust and conflict. Many local NGOs saw their paths blocked at each step by government agencies and found themselves working in a hostile political climate. Several had more serious run-ins with government as these directors recounted:

> In the beginning, we had so many problems that at a particular moment, our [NGO] agreement was suspended. [...] Because the state said that we were working for an opposition party, the PDS [Parti Démocratique Socialist]. And Lord knows, we were far from the PDS (Interview with Executive Secretary, Local NGO #60, Dakar, 31 March 2000).

> We were not at all accepted by the Minister of National Education. On the contrary. We were fought, we were chased. [...] It was a fight with civil servants, Ministers, up until the day the governor of Dakar sent in the police to remove us from our training centre (Interview with Secretary General, Local NGO #54, Dakar, 6 March 2000).

Even CONGAD faced a fierce battle with the Senegalese government when a draft protocol on NGO registration that it had worked on was changed by government without their input and presented to the NGO sector as *fait accompli*. This controversy lasted from 1993 to the end of 1995; involved much conflict between CONGAD, local NGOs and government ministers; saw both heated exchanges and allegations in the local media; and resulted in the replacement of the government minister overseeing NGO affairs (CONGAD 1995). Eventually, however, the protocol was made acceptable to both groups. Since then, relationships between both CONGAD and government, and government and the NGO sector at large, have been cordial.

These relationships are reinforced by close ties between civil servants and NGO workers. Government colleagues of NGO employees, for example, often supply NGOs with project supplies and offer them lucrative government contracts within the development sector. Even those NGOs without personal ties to government now seem to enjoy close relationships with individual Ministries, government divisions – such as the police and justice system – and the government technical services which are present in most rural areas. These teams of local specialists, which have technical knowledge in fields such as engineering or forestry, and an in-depth understanding of the community with which they work, are important local partners for NGOs and are often an NGO's first point of contact in a community.

In Senegal the distinction between local level and national government seems to be of little importance when discussing positive NGO–government relationships. The federal government has, for the most part, shied away from Zimbabwe-style histrionics against the NGO sector, allowed tax and duty concessions and, through CONGAD, encouraged NGO representation on ministry committees and national commissions. So with the exception of their early years, none of the local NGOs I met in Senegal had significantly more difficulty working with national government than with local government.

International development community
The last set of links built by local NGOs which merit consideration are those to the wider international development community. With their strong ties to northern NGOs, Senegalese NGOs including CONGAD benefit from the same kind of international exposure as Tanzanian NGOs. This includes opportunities for travel to Europe and America and the forging of bonds to like-minded organisations in those countries. For human rights organisations, these relationships provide much needed moral support. They also help to raise the profile of both NGO work and the response that NGOs require from the international community to prevent or redress human rights abuses. These links can be prolific. For a local NGO working in health care which gathers and disseminates knowledge on traditional medicine, international ties surpass the usual links to universities, research institutions and like-minded local NGOs in other countries, to also include voodoo societies and traditional healers across the globe.

As illustrated by these examples, a striking majority of Senegalese NGOs take part in regional or international networks. These organisations not only benefit from their membership in such networks, but also from their active participation in their meetings, workshops and campaigns. Such activity requires substantial funding, and the cost of travelling to neighbouring countries for participation in network activities would have been prohibitive for the majority of local NGOs in Tanzania and all but the most successful in Zimbabwe. In Senegal, the financing to attend these meetings comes from donors, CONGAD and often from NNGOs. This makes local NGO–NNGO links even more critical than previously illustrated. Given the importance of forging links to international development actors, as demonstrated throughout these last three chapters, funders need to find better ways to facilitate increased and more strategic networking for local African NGOs. More attention will have to be given to the high costs of networking in Africa, where the communications infrastructure can be poor and travel expensive. Without better access to international networking it is unlikely that many local NGOs in Africa will have the chance to profit from the potentially power-enhancing links with international organisations that have so benefited Senegalese NGOs.

The last important international link observed in Senegal is one that is unique to its local NGOs. These links are between NGOs and their own 'antennae' or field offices in other countries. Surprisingly, it was in Senegal that all but one example of this trend of case study NGOs expanding their activity outside their own country were observed. The numbers in which this phenomenon occurred are substantial; a quarter of the local NGOs sampled had developed offshoots in other countries. Antennae organisations were predominantly found in countries in the sub-region, though two NGOs had offshoots reaching as far as the US and Latin America. The presence of these country offices are remarkable: they could indicate both the potential of these NGOs to create considerable new development space for themselves and to exert their influence internationally, both key elements of power.

Power

This examination of local NGOs has attempted to do justice to the enigma that is the local NGO sector in Senegal. As in Tanzania, it is filled with puzzling contradictions: donor agencies seem to throw vast sums of money at unremarkable and inexperienced NGOs; local NGOs are at once independent from, and beholden to, donor organisations; few NGOs wield individual power, yet collectively they have tremendous strength. It is Senegalese NGOs, with their generalist approach and weak human resources, and not their counterparts in Zimbabwe and Tanzania, which are able to turn down donors, work closely with high-level government committees, and spawn off-shoots in other countries. Is this an indication that Senegalese NGOs have achieved power?

Space
Unlike their counterparts in Zimbabwe and Tanzania, local NGOs in Senegal face little competition for space from INGOs and government. Many international NGOs in the country pursue non-operational mandates: training, supporting and often funding local NGOs, while local NGOs concentrate on delivering development services to the population. Even those INGOs that are operational have been encouraged by CONGAD and donors to incorporate local NGOs into their programmes, helping to reduce conflict for space between the two groups. Local NGOs have similarly faced little competition for space from government in recent years. While some tensions existed between the two groups earlier in their history, relations are now cordial, and the two groups rarely find themselves in conflict, even over political space.

The unusual survival strategy pursued by local NGOs in Senegal has, however, been detrimental to their ability to innovate and to seize space within development. By specialising geographically, local NGOs have been able to position themselves in regions in which they face little competition from other development actors, and in which donor funding is strong. Moreover, by approaching development from a generalist perspective, they have been able to respond to the ever-changing funding priorities of donor agencies and find themselves a niche regardless of the development trend of the moment. But while this strategy has meant that Senegalese NGOs have been able continually to find space, as offered to them by donors, they have been unable to guard or reinforce it. This has had a severe impact on power among local NGOs in the country.

The strength of the NGO umbrella association CONGAD has perhaps also reduced the impetus for, or ability of, individual NGOs to seek space and power in Senegal. Thus far, it is the Senegalese NGO sector as a whole that is gaining power and not individual organisations within it. When government and donors seek NGO input, they contact CONGAD first. When an international conference is looking for Senegalese representation, it contacts CONGAD. It is CONGAD that has an international reputation, that publishes and publicises the work of the NGO sector, and that is most often the focus of donor capacity-building efforts. Nevertheless, there are several benefits to local NGOs of a strong NGO coordinating body, especially in terms of enlarging the space available to NGOs and providing opportunities for international linkages. Over time it is likely that individual NGOs will begin to capitalise on the many resources provided by CONGAD and the collective strength of the Senegalese NGO sector, and parlay these resources into their own space and power.

Financial independence from donors
The glut of funding available in Senegal from donors far outweighs the funding that most local NGOs in Zimbabwe and, especially Tanzania, have at their disposal. In order to capture any of it, however, local NGOs must adapt to donor priorities, whether in terms of conceptual or geographic areas of activity. So while a great many local NGOs are able to refuse funds from donors that they do not like – a sign which should signal their financial independence from donors – in this case it seems to be more an indication of the availability of large sums of funding from alternative donors, than an indication that these NGOs could survive without donor funds. Moreover, none of the NGOs I encountered are able to insist on basket funding, overhead funding or long-term funding contracts with their donors, all of which are elements of true financial independence from donors.

The ability to generate funds internally is also weak across local NGOs in Senegal. Few local NGOs in the country have developed regular means of generating revenue for their organisations, and in many cases, when such opportunities arise, they are used to help generate income for the unsalaried director of the NGO, rather than for the NGO itself. Only one of the Senegalese NGOs I interviewed was linked to the credit markets which are a regular source of revenue for both Zimbabwean NGOs and powerful NGOs like SEWA and Proshika. The majority work in welfare sectors like health and education in which there are few steady opportunities to raise funds. So despite local NGOs in Senegal being able to refuse donor funds, these NGOs are only financially independent from any one particular donor, as opposed to financially independent from all donor organisations as a group. With few opportunities to generate revenues internally, these NGOs lack the ability to set their own agendas and define their own priorities independent of donor interests.

Links to the international development community
Forging strong links to the international development community was the element of NGO power with which local NGOs in Senegal had the best success. While they had experienced difficulties in securing and protecting development space, and in gaining financial independence from donors, many local NGOs in the country enjoyed strong and bene-ficial ties to development organisations abroad. These ties are varied and individual NGOs at once cultivated links with a range of development groups across a wide range of countries. Within the field of education, for example, three local NGOs have between them developed links to development organisations in Finland, Great Britain, France, Belgium, Switzerland, Canada and the United States. Moreover, local NGOs in Senegal have the widest range of international partner organisations; while in Tanzania, the international partners of local NGOs are located in the United States and a small core of European countries, and Zim-babwean NGOs have mainly benefited from connections to development organisations in the UK.

The strength of CONGAD is one reason for this trend. CONGAD's international reputation has attracted international attention to the NGO sector and has helped its individual members to forge alliances abroad. The physical proximity of Senegal to Western Europe, as well as its cultural proximity and attractiveness as a place to live, have further attracted international development organisations to partner local NGOs. This is clearly illustrated by the ties between local NGOs and develop-ment organisations in France, Switzerland, Belgium, Italy and Germany. The legacy of slavery in the United States and the World War II connection between Senegal and America have also helped local NGOs to develop strong ties to American development organisations.

So local NGOs in Senegal have been able to develop solid links to the international development community. Yet these NGOs remain power-less since they, like their counterparts in Zimbabwe, remain reluctant to use their international connections to further their own reputations. In order to develop power, these local NGOs now need to build links to international partners in their fields, and to use their existing links to the international development community to publicise their work, build up their reputations, and generate increased attention and opportunities for funding.

Engagement with the political aspects of development
In Zimbabwe and Tanzania, an engagement with the political aspects of development is both a present strategy and a future goal for local NGOs. It has helped them to differentiate themselves from their INGO counterparts, create their own development space and, accordingly, to capture donor funds. In Senegal, however, very few local NGOs have incorporated regular lobbying and advocacy activities into their work. The generalist strategy employed by these NGOs discourages them from becoming involved in political development. Instead, they focus on adapting their activities to changing donor priorities and on capturing the space that is created whenever a donor targets its funds at a particular issue. Since donors have rarely been interested in specifically funding political development activities, and since local NGOs rely almost exclusively on donor funds for survival, they are uninterested or unable to engage with political issues in development to the same extent as their counterparts in Zimbabwe and Tanzania. This has hurt the power of individual local NGOs in Senegal.

Conclusion

There exists something of a cultural mismatch between the ethos of development in Senegal and that found in Zimbabwe and Tanzania, which makes it difficult to compare levels of NGO power across the three countries. It is clear from the analysis in this chapter, however, that Senegalese NGOs, like their other African counterparts, have been unable to gain power. Many of the remarkable characteristics of local NGOs in Senegal, such as their ability to refuse funds from donors, enjoy strong relationships with government and generate antennae organisations in other countries, suggest that there are local NGOs in Senegal which are moving closer to gaining power. Yet up to now, they have been unable to gain the space, financial independence from donors, links to the international development community and attention to political perspectives in their work which are necessary to parlay their many successes into actual power.

6

Why Power
is Crucial
to NGOs

The examination of local NGOs in Africa and around the world in the
past four chapters illustrates the many ways in which local African NGOs
are excluded from power. It confirms that, despite the high quality of
many NGO projects and programmes in the case study countries, and the
many strengths and innovative strategies that their local NGOs have
developed, none of them have become powerful. It also confirms that this
is a phenomenon particular to Africa; while local African NGOs lack
power, their counterparts in other parts of the developing world do not.

Why do indigenous African NGOs lack power? Not for the reasons
usually given, whether in terms of weak financial accountability, low-
quality human resources or scarce funding. Even local African NGOs
which have overcome all of these shortcomings lack power. Power is,
similarly, not just a question of age or experience. Many of the world's
most powerful local NGOs are older than the groups studied in Zimbabwe, Tanzania and Senegal. But development space has been available
to many of these African NGOs for almost two decades. More than 15 per
cent of the NGOs I interviewed were over twenty years old, and in both
Zimbabwe and Tanzania, several were older than SEWA, BRAC and
IBASE. Yet none of them were as powerful as their younger counterparts
in India, Bangladesh or Brazil. While many might be tempted to point to
authoritarian African states as the main cause for the powerlessness of
local NGOs on the continent, studies have shown that there is no
'minimum degree of democracy' that is necessary for NGOs to achieve
influence (Thomas et al. 2001: 172). The successes of local NGOs like
FASE, DESCO and the Madres, each of which was started under in-
auspicious political climates, illustrate that NGOs can survive and gain
power in a number of different political contexts. Moreover, the absence
of power among local African NGOs cannot simply be explained by size
differences between African countries and those in Latin America or
South Asia. The millions of clients with which NGOs in Bangladesh,
India and Brazil work clearly make the stories of these NGOs compelling

for the development world at large. But by that argument, the size and regional importance of countries like Nigeria and South Africa would have resulted in local NGOs in those countries gaining power and rising to international prominence.

In fact, the lack of power observed among local NGOs in Zimbabwe, Tanzania and Senegal is not limited to local NGOs in these few countries; it seems to be the rule, rather than the exception among African NGOs. Despite differences in the age, size, wealth and stability of African countries; levels of aid availability; the activity and roles of INGOs and church movements; government responses to civil society; and the strength of NGO representatives and umbrella bodies, indigenous NGOs across the continent have the same experience of exclusion from power. In war-torn countries like the Democratic Republic of Congo and Sierra Leone, local NGOs, where they exist, have limited staff and means, and little impact on national development, which itself rarely extends beyond the most basic relief and welfare services. Even in African countries with relatively stable political structures and substantial local NGO sectors, the story is much the same.

Ghanaian NGOs, a relatively recent phenomenon, suffer from many of the weaknesses regularly present in local African NGO sectors. They tend to be unco-ordinated and largely focussed around welfare activities as a group, and small, isolated and only questionably sustainable as individual organisations (Smillie 1995, Gary 1996). And NGOs affiliated with government or government officials dominate much of the Ghanaian NGO sector (Oquaye 1996). A similar picture can be found in Malawi. Only eleven NGOs were registered in the country in 1990, and the majority of the 300 or so active today originated only after the UDF government came to power in 1994 (Lawson 2000). These very young NGOs continue to be dependent on donors, both in terms of funding and sectoral focus and lack a unified and influential voice on national debates. Moreover, tensions between the government and NGOs persist, particularly around political issues within development. Somalian NGOs face similar difficulties in their search for power. They too are relatively young, only emerging after recent civil war and famine in the country. Local NGOs across sectors compete with government for development space and scarce resources, and have only the most limited access to the international development community (Abdillahi 1998).

In other African countries, where NGOs are a more entrenched part of society, NGOs face a more direct and potent challenge for power from their national governments. In Nigeria, NGOs and most civil society organisations, whether the independent press, student movements or labour groups, have been dominated or co-opted by successive military and authoritarian governments, and alienated from the state to the point that today 'there are many who might even argue that there is no civil society worth talking about in Nigeria' (Kukah 1999: 58). Competing ethnic groups and regional interests have also splintered civil society and increased government suspicion of its aims, making NGO co-ordination and co-operation difficult and further reducing the space available to civil society organisations (Ikelegbe 2001a & 2001b).

In Kenya, on the other hand, civil society is strong and vibrant and has been an important part of the country's historical development through very active church organisations and *harambee*, or 'self-help' movements. The Green Belt Movement, a grass-roots environmental and social movement that started with tree planting in the 1970s, for example, has been influential in the country and region, and has had widespread international acclaim for its approach and efforts (Maathai 1988). But the power of such groups has been curtailed by a government threatened by NGOs, human rights groups and other civil society organisations which challenge its monopoly on political space (Ndegwa 1996, Maina 1998, Kagwanja 2003). Since challenging the government on issues of both environmental protection and human rights, the Green Belt Movement organization has faced eviction, death threats and even the imprisonment of its leader (Tripp 2001). Despite the demise of the single-party regime and the rise of multi-partyism in Kenya, the state has continued to discredit and deregister local NGOs which speak out against the government, portraying them as agents of foreign governments and attempting to replace their leaders with individuals loyal to the central authority (Matanga 2000). It will be important to follow developments in the Kenyan NGO sector in the coming years: with the victory of Mwai Kibaki and the 'National Rainbow Coalition' in the 2002 presidential election, the trend of government antagonism towards NGOs in Kenya may well begin to change.

In South Africa, NGOs and social organisations have played many important roles in the country, not least in the anti-apartheid struggle and in providing crucial social services to disenfranchised populations under the apartheid government. The African National Congress (ANC) itself, just prior to its historic election win in 1994, recognised this critical role for NGOs in South African development, when it published its ideas for reconstruction and development in the country. It noted that 'mass organisations must be actively involved in democratic public policy-making' and that 'measures should be introduced to create an enabling environment for social movements, CBOs and NGOs' (ANC 1994: 131,132). Yet today, the situation is quite different. Local NGOs face increasing hostility from a national government suspicious of their motives and reluctant to relinquish political space to civil society (Cawthra *et al.* 2001). Many CBOs and local NGOs have lost large numbers of their staff to positions in the state apparatus (James 2000, Smit 2001). And the NGO sector is in 'dire financial crisis', as a significant proportion of the donor funding it had almost exclusive access to under apartheid is now targeted at the democratically elected government and its development initiatives (Gulati *et al.* 1996, Bornstein 2000: 194, Hearn 2000). In many cases, local NGOs are even less powerful now than they were under apartheid, when they had the ear of the international development community, as well as its trust and resources (Pieterse 1997).

There is, of course, no one reason why local African NGOs lack power and, accordingly, no universal panacea for solving the problem. In some countries, local NGOs are young, inexperienced and not yet at a stage in their development from which they can command power; in others, they are marginalised by the policies and practices of international development actors; in still others, power is only a far-off goal for local NGOs, preceded by working telephones and equipment, government officials who keep appointments, and reliable employees. In some African countries antagonism or co-optation by government interferes with the programmes and activities of strong and well supported local NGOs; in others competition from INGOs and CBOs for clients and funding impedes the development of power among even the best known and influential local NGOs. In still other countries, local NGOs take control for delivering the majority of development services in the country, and do so in both a timely and high quality fashion – yet they toil in obscurity, never publicising news of their work to the wider international development community and never developing an international reputation. At a fundamental level, all of these African NGOs, whatever their particular circumstances, lack power because they are unable to achieve the four elements that are central to its development: space, financial independence, strong links to the international community and an approach to development as a political issue. And because of their lack of power, development progress across Africa is hindered.

How does the absence of power among local African NGOs actually undermine development?

Many readers will ask why power matters. Why should the world be concerned that local NGOs across Africa lack power? Local NGOs are still a massive and growing presence on the continent and undertake critical work across all the main fields of development. Where they are unable or unqualified to provide development services, INGOs, governments, CBOs, church groups and a whole host of other actors all work to meet the development needs of different communities. As long as development work is undertaken on the continent and the plight of the poor and underprivileged is addressed, why does it matter that local NGOs, just one of the many groups of actors involved in development, seem unable to gain international power?

It matters because the social and political value of all providers of development services in the African development sector is not equal. Consider the variation in development service provision between local NGOs, INGOs and government agencies, the dual role of government as both a development service provider and client, and the very different levels of information and transaction costs facing the various suppliers of development services. It is not difficult to see that under these conditions, one actor may bear little resemblance to the next. For example, local NGOs can play a critical role in supporting and working with civil society actors and forces for democratisation in their countries, externalities not accounted for by a free market interpretation of the development sector, which sees all actors within it as substitutable. Local African NGOs also offer several other exclusive development benefits to the continent.

The first benefit that indigenous NGOs bring to development in Africa is perhaps the most obvious: that they are based locally. These groups have a level of local knowledge and experience that international counterparts can rarely match, whether in terms of speaking local languages, respecting social mores, or understanding local customs and traditions. Their familiarity with local contexts and closeness to local populations makes them better able to encourage community mobilisation, ensuring both that local actors are not marginalised by external forces and that a sense of local responsibility for local needs can be fostered. And perhaps most importantly, local NGOs are a longer-term vehicle for development activity in Africa – unlikely to disappear in years to come as geopolitical trends change and the political leanings and foreign policy considerations of Northern governments make it inexpedient or inopportune for international NGOs to work in particular African countries.

The second unique contribution of local African NGOs is an ability to engage with political issues within development and to stimulate a civil society voice capable of questioning government in national-level development debates and holding it accountable for its policy-making decisions. Another way to think of it is to consider the ability of local NGOs to act as 'consumer advocates' on social, political and economic issues, rather than commercial ones. This is a role that poor individuals and communities face several obstacles in playing. Based on their research, Engberg-Pedersen and Webster (2002: 6) write, 'from the perspective of the poor there are several problems with political endeavours: they tend not to deliver immediate material gains; they are often dangerous, in that they exacerbate the vulnerability of the poor; and they require resources that the poor seldom possess'. Small community-based organisations similarly often lack the national knowledge and contacts to play such a role on their own or to withstand government reprisals in times of conflict.

The ability of international NGOs, meanwhile, to play a key role in mobilising local civil society actors around development debates and political issues is constrained by their status as 'outsiders', their incomplete knowledge and understanding of local contexts and their lack of strong relationships to local actors (Marcussen 1996). The prospect of conflict with government is another reason why INGOs, donors and other foreign development groups have shied away from activities in potentially political sectors of development activity, such as environmental and natural resource management, gender issues, and human rights and democratisation (Clarke 1998). As guests in the country, raising the ire of national government would be both a financially and politically costly mistake for international development groups to make, and could spark a higher level diplomatic confrontation between their home and host nations. These trends were clearly visible in Zimbabwe where few CBOs or INGOs were active around issues of human rights, land reform, democracy and governance.

Some observers question whether NGOs merely perpetuate dominant political modalities and interests; others are sceptical of the extent to which NGOs are able to play such a political role on a regular basis and the actual impact of the influence that they do have (Chabal and Daloz 1999, Mercer 2002). In many countries across Africa, it was student and labour unions, churches, and opposition parties that led the struggle for democracy or development and were the catalysts for the growth of civil society organisations including local NGOs. Local NGOs do not alone create civil society or comprise its entire ranks in any country. And certain local NGOs do shy away from any work that could be deemed political, both for the sake of their relationship with government, donors and other partners, or their own beliefs and priorities. But empirically, in countries around the world, local NGOs add an often unheard voice to political debates and offer an opportunity for people to engage with wider political debates. Local NGO activities in Bangladesh, for example, have been instrumental in supporting poor people to run for office in unions and local government bodies (Westergaard and Hossain 2002). No matter how small, such opportunities and the opening of political space made possible by local NGOs should not be undervalued – especially in countries where political arenas are closely controlled by single party or virtual single party states.

A third externality which must be considered is that development work, in fields such as gender issues and democratisation, involves representing and mobilising local populations and, as a result, requires development organisations to gain legitimacy in the eyes of grass-roots populations (Atack 1999). Local organisations are the only appropriate groups to undertake such tasks and, perhaps, the only ones with the ability to succeed in work so dependent on understanding local social, cultural and religious contexts and on mobilising local populations. Local NGOs may not be quite as close to the people as CBOs, grass-roots organisations and social movements, but in employing country nationals, speaking local languages and having closer ties to local communities – through locally born workers, or employees whose families come from the area – they are far more aware and a part of local development contexts than their foreign-based counterparts. As large and well-experienced groups, with both strong ties to the grass-roots level and links to national-level actors such as government, the media and academics, indigenous NGOs are often also more able to mobilise and organise local populations than many of their CBO, religious and local government counterparts. The ability to encourage and secure the participation of local people in development projects and campaigns is an added advantage of local NGOs, and one which helps to cement their legitimacy as representatives of their beneficiaries (Riddell and Robinson 1995).

Further unique benefits of local NGOs in African development concern their freedom from some of the constraints under which their international counterparts labour. International NGOs in Africa are, to a great extent, beholden to the interests of their northern donating publics, and as the Georgetown or Islington agenda vacillates from saving the black rhino to educating the girl child to propagating the savings circle, the projects of INGOs must keep pace. As Tina Wallace writes:

> The public appears to want reassurance that their money has saved lives, has transformed the day-to-day experiences of the children of communities they sponsor and has been spent quickly and honestly. There is little recognition of the causes of poverty and distress, and the complexities of tackling these and of bringing about the kind of economic and social change that would prevent the perpetuation of conflict, poverty and exclusion in the future (2002: 233).

Local NGOs, meanwhile, rarely rely directly on the changing whims and short-term focus of Northern donating publics for their funding and are better able to remain focussed on demonstrated long-term local needs and priorities than their INGO counterparts.

The interests of the donating and voting public do undoubtedly influence the agendas of the bilateral donors on which many local NGOs depend for their funding (especially in this era of increased direct funding). These changing agendas have already been shown to have a detrimental impact on the freedom and flexibility of local NGOs in the case study countries. Yet there is some evidence that the distortion of SNGO agendas by direct funding from donors is less than the distortion of INGO agendas – an additional benefit of local African NGO activity to the needs and priorities of people on the continent (Wallace *et al.* 1997, Lewis and Sobhan 1999).

In addition to their accountability to donating publics, international NGOs are often confined by projects and programmes approved by head office. Local African NGOs are rarely tied to a similar hierarchical structure as smaller and less-diffuse organisations. This freedom has allowed local NGOs greater latitude in experimenting and innovating in their projects, without risking the overall reputation and goals of their head offices – an opportunity that local NGOs from India to Mexico have capitalised on, to the benefit of millions of people (Alvord *et al.* 2002). Whether in terms of developing or using new knowledge, equipment or communication tools, finding new ways of financing projects or creating new approaches to long-standing problems, local African NGOs are thus a more likely source of innovation benefiting development on the continent than their international counterparts. In the absence of rigidly defined financial planning, local NGOs are also able to treat the money they receive as fungible. They are often criticised for so treating their financing, and management tools supported by donors, whether log-frame analysis, budgeting or reporting, are all designed to reduce the ability of local NGOs to transfer funds, donated for one purpose, to another. But fungibility means that local NGOs are able to listen to their clients and better address the changing needs they demonstrate, by using what monies they receive for the up-to-date aims they find most important.

When considered in the light of all of these external benefits to development in Africa, it is clear that all development actors in Africa are not equal and that the worth of local African NGOs cannot solely be measured by their lack of power. These NGOs do not lack power because they are inferior development actors. While they all have their limitations, many indigenous African NGOs are able to engage with political issues within development, are not beholden to the interests of Northern donating publics, have legitimacy in the eyes of their clients and are able to use their funds fungibly; in these respects they are able to offer the continent what no other single development actor can. Yet as their exclusion from power has limited the extent to which they can play these roles, or has favoured alternative development actors unable to offer these benefits, it has had drastic ramifications for African communities in need and for African development at large. In the three case study countries and across the continent, local NGOs are thwarted in their efforts to achieve power by a small group of local and international organisations.

Whose activities have prevented local African NGOs from gaining power?

International NGOs

International NGOs have long been a presence on the African continent, playing an important role in social service provision through the colonial era and in humanitarian relief in more recent times (Mohammed 1992, Therkildsen and Semboja 1995, Van Rooy 2000, Suhrke 2003). Originally INGOs limited their work to those specific fields which local organisations had to forsake while busy fighting for independence, or in which local NGOs could not alone meet the sheer scale of need. Despite the continued need for relief services on the continent, however, the majority of INGOs in Africa have moved into mainstream and operational development activities. This has led to an increasing encroachment by INGOs on the space, funding resources and international links available to local African NGOs.

The number of new international NGOs present in Africa is on the rise. As their rate of growth has surpassed the growth of financial resources to support their development activities, these groups have increasingly turned to official sources for their funding (Fowler 1991). In their home countries, INGOs enjoy handsome direct financial support and indirect concessions from their governments, especially when working in Africa; many are even encouraged to take an operational role in the developing world (Smillie 1995, Campfens 1996, Adedeji 1997). Poverty and under-development were so pronounced in Bangladesh in the early 1970s that any donor organisation worth its salt targeted funding to development needs in the country; today sub-Saharan Africa is the new Bangladesh. With its civil wars, famines, high AIDS-related mortality and widespread poverty, donors need to be seen to be funding African development; and INGOs need to be seen to be undertaking development initiatives in Africa.

As they have increased their *in situ* operations in Africa, international NGOs have also increased their reliance on donor organisations at local levels, where many INGOs now find the majority of their funds. International NGO directors interviewed for this research explained how fund raising in the South tended to be much easier than competing for grants in their home countries. It also gave them, as individual offices within large, international organisations, more freedom and financial independence from their headquarters. These INGOs possess several advantages over their local NGO counterparts when it comes to fund-raising locally. They understand and are well-practised in the accounting, monitoring and evaluation procedures of Northern donors; they have research and analyses of the effectiveness of their projects and pro-grammes to recommend themselves to funders and; they have intimate knowledge of current donor trends in the North. With their relatively large organisations and wide geographic reach, INGOs are also able to absorb larger amounts of funding and capitalise on opportunities to 'scale-up' operations, yet another factor which recommends them to donor organisations in the South. In this light, the old argument for peaceful coexistence between local and operational international NGOs, founded on the belief that INGOs relied almost exclusively on their home governments and donating publics for financing, and as such, posed little threat to the funding sources of local NGOs, carries little weight.

International NGOs and their local counterparts in Africa compete not only for funding, but also, in many cases, for the very clients on which they will spend that funding. No NGO can survive without a clientele and local African NGOs can face stiff competition for clients. Outside urban settings, few communities will choose to work with more than one NGO at a time, which means that there are a finite number of clients, whether communities, individuals or grass-roots organisations, to be shared by all development organisations. As the number of development service pro-viders increases, the competition over clients intensifies. Senegalese NGO directors described how well-resourced INGOs were able to out-compete them, even in settings where they had considerable experience.

Because of their need to generate income, local NGOs often asked communities or individual clients to pay user fees for the services they received, or to contribute their time to the various projects from which they would benefit. INGOs, on the other hand, rarely asked for similar contributions from their clients, and moreover, at times offered both financial and non-financial incentives to clients to encourage their participation. Faced with the choice of working with local NGOs or international NGOs – with their fancy vehicles, large numbers of staff and financially ambitious projects – there are few communities which would not choose to work with the better-resourced international organisation.

In terms of financial resources, clients and development space, then, local African NGOs regularly find themselves in direct competition with international NGOs, which are usually older, larger and considerably better resourced. In a 1998 *Development Anthropologist* article, an INGO employee wrote that:

> Less than ten years ago, most Northern NGOs set up their own offices and extension services, celebrated their own successes, and largely ignored local NGOs or government agencies. Gradually, Northern NGOs have come to collaborate with host country organizations, first as sub-contractors, and later on as counterparts in longer-term, mutually beneficial arrangements (Perez 1998: 13).

This change in attitude among operational INGOs has not yet trickled down to the majority of those organisations interviewed in Zimbabwe, Tanzania and Senegal, however, where their co-operation with local NGOs is very limited. As Fowler (1998: 154) writes, 'northern NGDOs have not shown themselves to be skilled at building authentic partnerships, as opposed to project/product-based relationships, with similar organizations in the same field.' The INGOs present in the case study countries are inwardly focussed on their own projects and it is only in Senegal that local NGOs benefit from strong relationships with their operational counterparts. In Zimbabwe and Tanzania, on the other hand, the relationship between these two groups is characterised by the absence of any contact. Moreover, in all three countries, the flow of resources from international to local NGOs is rare. Local NGOs are certainly not receiving tangible benefits from INGOs to compensate for the competition they provide for local sources of funding.

This point bears repeating. In the case study countries and, I suspect, many other African countries, international NGOs are not donors to local NGOs, and most INGOs are themselves operational organisations at their core, undertaking a range of direct client services. While it is widely accepted that local and international NGOs are regular and the most common set of partners in development, few of the local NGOs I met had any direct interaction with, or financial ties to, an international NGO, and certainly nothing that could be called a partnership by even the most generous definition.

For example, while many international NGOs working in Africa are committed to 'collaboration' and 'partnership' with local NGOs and some do invest in nurturing them, the flow of resources and demands between the two groups is almost always unidirectional. In a study of 17 British NGOs, the authors found not only that 'enormous impositions' were placed on local partners by INGO project management methods and procedures, but also that there was 'an almost complete absence of changes being made or introduced into the [INGO] ways of programming and framing projects as a result of feedback or pressures from staff or partners in the South' (Wallace *et al.* 1997: 93, 90). And British NGOs are not remarkable among international NGOs for these trends in their relationships with Southern groups (Campfens 1996, Marcussen 1996, Mancuso Brehm 2001, Juma 2003, Mawdsley *et al.* 2002). In the words of one Malawian NGO official, with their continued reliance on donor funds and lack of commitment to building local capacity: 'INGOs are a terrible unsustainable model for local NGOs' (Lawson 2000).

Many international NGOs forego entirely the option of working with established local NGOs, instead funding or creating new CBOs. This trend may explain the absence of INGO–local NGO partnerships in the fieldwork countries. CBOs are set up to incorporate community input into INGO projects, but offer community members few opportunities to set their own priorities for development and undertake self-designed projects based on these priorities. With no full-time employees and no financial resources, these CBOs often only exist as an extension of INGO projects and fold when the INGO pulls out of the community. They are attractive to INGOs, however, because they offer the benefit of local community input and, frequently, unpaid labour, without the financial costs of involving local NGOs, with all of their expenses (Kleemeier 2000). Donors and government agencies often similarly bypass local NGOs in favour of working with CBOs, which demand little in the way of core or institutional costs, and are thought to represent more closely the needs of grass-roots people. The World Bank, for instance, noted in a 1999 review that Bank projects supported CBOs more often than local NGOs. In the 107 projects studied in this review, worth some 894 million US dollars, 80 per cent of funds, or 715 million dollars went to CBOs, compared to the 5 per cent, or 45 million dollars, that were used to support local NGOs (Gibbs *et al.* 1999).

International and local NGOs in Africa, with their overlapping aims, client bases, and funders, engage in a non-violent, but potent form of competition for space, financial resources and contacts. One of the priorities of Senegal's NGO umbrella body is to re-examine what the role of international NGOs should be in the South generally, and in Senegal more specifically. Based on feedback from the local Senegalese NGOs I encountered, it seems clear to me that this future role for INGOs will involve providing more support to local NGOs and engaging in less direct activity on the ground. Such a separation of roles and responsibilities between local and international NGOs, where local NGOs assume responsibility for direct service provision to clients, and INGOs focus on building capacity among local NGOs and working on publicising Southern development agendas in the North, would be one way to reduce existing levels of competition and increase 'authentic partnerships' between the different NGO groups at work in Africa (Fowler 1998, Fowler 2000a). In order to eliminate one of the major obstacles currently barring them from gaining power, local African NGOs now need to speak out against the competition that they face from INGOs and encourage foreign NGOs at work in Africa to rethink their operational mandates.

Government bodies
Governments can play very different roles in development, acting variously as the funders, suppliers and demanders of development services, and, as such, occupy a considerable proportion of a country's development space. Most branches of development activity could in fact be considered the responsibility of the state. And in many countries, the state is trying to meet this responsibility and to play a pivotal and uniquely placed role in development. While NGOs can have comparative advantages that they bring to their work, so too do governments. State-led economic development has set the stage for social and political development in countries across East Asia in recent years, and through history in much of the West (Wade 1990). The national, regional and local apparatus of governments and the national budgets they have at their disposal make it possible for governments to achieve economies of scale far beyond that which most NGOs, local or international, can reach. In the presence of democratic controls and free and fair elections, states can also be considered more directly accountable to the general populace than NGOs. It is obvious that state power is therefore of significant importance to African development. And as the power of government ensures state and human security and political stability, it further advances social stability and development, which are too often threatened by political instability and violent conflict.

Power is not a zero-sum game, however. And the goal of the development of power among local NGOs is not to weaken or supplant the state, to divert funding away from it, nor to absolve the state of its responsibilities to its citizens. To retain power and the potential to contribute positively to national development through its use, governments need not, therefore, seek to prevent NGOs in their countries from gaining power. Yet many African government officials continue to see a competition for development funding, in which funds that donors choose to invest in local NGOs are funds that government would have received in their absence. Because of these perceptions, government agencies will rarely suggest to donors that local NGOs are more experienced or better equipped than they to undertake a particular donor project. Most local NGOs see government as an apathetic, if not negative influence on their ability to secure a larger development space. And governments often continue to see local NGOs as their main competitors for funds.

The competition that local NGOs can potentially provide in the political arena is another significant reason why many governments have sought to restrict the power of local NGOs (Fisher 1998). Legislation on NGO registration through much of Africa limits the sanctioned activity of local NGOs to non-political arenas and, as such, attempts to keep NGOs out of African political space (World Bank 1997). In contrast, governments in the Philippines, Bolivia, Brazil and Colombia have all explicitly encouraged an expansion of the space available to NGOs, assuring NGOs the right to organise and to participate in 'all levels of decision-making in that country' in their constitutions (World Bank 1997: 12). As government antagonism towards human rights and good governance NGOs in Zimbabwe and the deregistration of BAWATA in Tanzania made clear, some governments are prepared to eliminate completely the space available to a local NGO, rather than allow that space to grow to encompass political issues. As African governments regularly impinge on the space available to local African NGOs and restrict their ability to be active around political issues in development – two key elements of NGO power – they also limit the power that these NGOs are able to develop.

Some may contend that it is, in fact, NGOs, local and international, which are encroaching on government's space and government's power. Sarah White makes this argument in her 1999 article, in which she speaks of the NGO challenge to the development activity of the state in Bangladesh in terms of the repercussions for the state's 'funding base, sovereignty and internal legitimacy' (White 1999: 312). Without conceiving of the debate as one about space and power, White appears to be making the opposite claim to my own: that in Bangladesh it is the encroachment of NGO activity into the government's development space which has resulted in the state's lack of power in development issues. In Africa, however, it is rarely the government which has suffered from a loss of power to local NGOs. Rather, the governments in each of the case study countries have, at one time or another, tried to circumscribe the amount of development space available to local NGOs. Michael Bratton (1989) cites examples from countries as diverse as Ethiopia, Togo and Kenya to illustrate the range of strategies employed by governments across sub-Saharan Africa to reduce the space for NGO activity in their countries.

Throughout Africa, governments have constrained the ability of local African NGOs to gain power. As a significant development actor across the developing world, and the one most able to affect the environment in which local NGOs work, governments must always figure in any examination of the power of indigenous NGOs. A World Bank study of the local NGO sector in Bangladesh concluded, 'NGOs need support and encouragement from the Government to facilitate their operations and extend their positive contributions' (World Bank 1996: xviii). But as the interactions between the state and local NGOs in Zimbabwe, Tanzania and Senegal illustrated, many government agencies compete directly and aggressively with local NGOs or seek to control or restrict their activities, and have been one of the main actors whose actions have prevented African NGOs from gaining power.

Donor agencies
The lack of local donors in Africa, whether in terms of a donating public, philanthropists or a commercial sector able to fund, endow or co-finance initiatives with local NGOs, has made indigenous African NGOs largely reliant on donor funds from the North. Bilateral and multilateral aid donor organisations are among the most powerful in international development today, and their relationship to African NGOs is an unequal one, as they can do to NGOs what NGOs cannot do to them (Elliott 1987). And despite the prevalent rhetoric of partnership within international development, there is a continued inequity of power between donors and NGOs in development. Donor agencies influence the organisational strategic planning and project development of their local NGO partners, dictate reporting, monitoring and evaluation procedures and performance measures, determine the size, scope and duration of funding contracts, and have the ability to bring an immediate end to their funding commitments to NGOs (Fowler 1998, Lister 2000, Townsend *et al.* 2002, Igoe 2003). Alarmingly for NGOs this trend is worsening, with donor demands by USAID, DFID and the EU mounting rather than diminishing over recent years (InterAction 2003a, InterAction 2003b, Wallace 2003).

Donor organisations also exert considerable control on the sectors in which the NGOs they fund are active, and on the kinds of projects and programmes they undertake in these areas. In Senegal, for instance, donor pressures have encouraged local NGOs to adopt a generalist strategy, incorporating each successive fad in donor funding into their work. One female NGO director interviewed there highlighted the donor pressures which caused the majority of local NGOs in Senegal to incorporate projects focussed on empowering women into their range of activities:

> It was after Mexico [1975 UN World Conference on Women] and everyone wanted to have women [involved], to talk about women. The donors became very demanding, they said if you don't have women's [projects], we're not interested. And I remember, my director said to me...if we don't, the donors won't give us any more funds (Interview with President, Local NGO #45, Dakar, 14 February 2000).

The experience of this director in Senegal is mirrored across Africa, as reflected in the words of this Malawian NGO official: 'I am in the environment planting trees and the donor comes to me and says 'it is a pity you are planting trees when I have all this money for giving credit.' Straight away I become a credit organisation' (Lawson 2000: 17). The international preoccupation with gender, environmental conservation and credit have since waned and been replaced by human rights or democratisation or HIV/AIDS education. But local NGOs are unable to predict what the next hot donor issue will be, and so remain spread across a wide range of development issues hoping to be able to capitalise on the next donor trend to come along, whatever it might be. More recently, donor influence has encouraged local NGOs across Africa to move back into welfare service provision, as the capacity of impoverished African governments to provide these services has declined. By pursuing a generalist welfare approach to development work, however, local African NGOs sacrifice space and a political impact on national development processes, two important building blocks of power.

By trying to encourage local NGOs to adopt what they see as sustainable behaviours, donors have also encouraged unsustainable NGO practices. The small size of donor funding contracts and their short duration, often of only one year, have meant that 'many NGOs find themselves scaling down projects to match funding patterns and abandoning more ambitious projects' (Moyo 2000b: 72). The reluctance of donors to fund non project-related or overhead expenses, whether salaries, rents or research, has further detracted from the ability of these groups to improve their sustainability by improving their level of financial independence. Donors, like their own financial supporters, want to see their money used by NGOs to provide immediate help to the greatest number of people possible (Wallace 2002). Yet many of the commodities that donors spurn as non-essential, such as property and equipment, can be used by local NGOs to generate income internally in the long-run and achieve a measure of financial security. BRAC's current financial independence from its donors, a cornerstone of its power, is largely tied to its money-making enterprises, many of which, like its printing press and building complex, were started with financial support from donors. Most local NGOs see the reluctance of their donors to fund overheads as an unfortunate idiosyncrasy of donor funding policy; given that donor organisations have overheads of their own which they seek to recoup from their contracts with governments or international institutions, their unwillingness to agree to support a standard percentage of their NGO partners' overheads is not just unfortunate, but exploitative and hypocritical.

Equally detrimental is the extent to which donor agencies in Africa regularly overlook indigenous NGOs in their funding programs. A brief anecdote about the experience of a donor agency looking for partner organisations in an African country should illustrate the point. This well known multilateral donor agency decided that microfinance projects could play a major role in economic development in this Southern African country, and so decided to invest considerable funds in such projects. Experts from the donor agency's head office were sent to the country on a two week mission. During this time, they had to both develop criteria for their funding and find NGOs who fit these criteria.

The donor mission first decided that it wanted to maximise the impact of its investments by funding NGOs that could provide maximum coverage of the country. This donor agency lacks the management capacity to look after many different NGOs and NGO projects at once, and so local NGOs – even where several of them could have collectively provided national coverage, with an in-depth knowledge and experience of each different region – are immediately at a disadvantage when compared to INGOs, which have their own core funds and both the financing and the personnel to be active throughout the country. As BRAC's management has said, when it comes to NGOs small may be beautiful, but not necessarily significant.

Secondly, this donor mission, quite appropriately, decided to fund only NGOs with good books and strong reputations in economic development. But asymmetries of information exist with respect to what donors can learn about urban-based international NGOs, with whom they've likely collaborated before, and what they can learn about local NGOs they may never have even heard of. It takes much less time to vet an international NGO than to learn about a local NGO, or a series of local NGOs, especially in this country with a poor communications and travel infrastructure and an official language which differs from the main language of the donor agency. Thirdly, the donor team developed a list of social and financial criteria on which they would evaluate prospective partners. These included the total number of borrowers, the number of female borrowers and the number of borrowers per income bracket, as well as repayment rates, delinquency and default rates, staff–client ratios, portfolios of risk and value of loans per capita. These are all statistics that INGOs, with strong research capacity and funding for research, can quickly provide and that they, with similar management philosophies to Northern donor agencies, are likely to invest in collecting.

In the case of microfinance NGOs, donors can actually develop measurable criteria on which to base their funding decisions. In other sectors of development, however, where measurable criteria of success do not exist, donors have to base their decision on the reputations of the organisations involved. With their organisational ties to the international development community and their personal ties to donor agents, INGOs usually enjoy much stronger reputations than indigenous African NGOs. In this example, the donor agency did decide to invest its funding in one large, international NGO, with both a foreign director and a majority of foreign staff. It felt that its funding would make the greatest impact in this way and be easiest to administer, given the agency's own management constraints. This push to reduce transactional costs by focussing funding on a small number of large contracts or NGOs is increasingly common to large donor agencies and is likely to fuel the support of international NGOs over smaller local NGOs (Wallace 2003). The donor agency in this example also felt that it was ethically inappropriate to spend its funds on small local NGOs whose reach could not match that of the INGO. As this example illustrates, there are many reasons why donors prefer to fund development work through international NGOs rather than local African

NGOs. In all of the African case study countries, and in many more across the continent, these donor preferences for INGOs, combined with the lack of donor funding specifically earmarked for local NGO projects, has meant that donor practices have seriously affected the space available to local NGOs in African development as well as their access to financial resources and linkages to the international development community.

Moreover, some donors, in addition to their more traditional role as external funders to other development organisations, choose not to work through local NGOs, or to fund them through their home INGOs, but to develop and run their own projects or create their own NGOs which compete directly with existing African NGOs. This often occurs when donors want to fund development in an area which has not been a priority for local NGOs, or when donors want to increase accountability for their funds. In these cases, donors act as international NGOs, providing a better resourced competition for local NGOs and reducing the space and funding available to them for their projects and activities. Even in sectors in which few local organisations exist or have proven experience, starting donor-run projects may result in greater coverage within a previously unserviced sector, but at the cost of local NGO participation in that sector. Local NGOs will be unlikely to enter a sector in which they face the direct competition of a well resourced donor-run project. And when donors decide to hand over the management of such projects, they will likely hand them over to operational INGOs from their home countries.

Of course donor organisations have also helped local NGOs to move closer to gaining elements of power. In Zimbabwe, for example, donor support of the NGO sector has helped local NGOs find political space and crucial links to the international development community. In other contexts, bilateral and multilateral donors create space for local NGOs in development, making some degree of government collaboration with NGOs a requirement in their official aid contracts. But at the level of individual African NGOs, these power enhancing benefits of donor policies are often cancelled out by the many ways in which these same policies and practices have made it difficult for African NGOs to gain space, financial independence, links to the international development community and a political approach to development issues.

Conclusion

Local NGOs across the African continent lack power and this absence of power is not always a result of their organisational or programmatic shortcomings. Many local NGOs in Africa do lack capacity and are woefully short of volunteers, experience and innovation. But contrary to common stereotypes, in each of the case study countries local NGOs with impressive capacity and a history of success are not difficult to find. Their internal strength as organisations is difficult to challenge. Yet none of them has developed power. If developing power were a straightforward issue of developing strengths and successes, then there would be as many powerful local NGOs in Zimbabwe, Tanzania and Senegal as we find in Bangladesh, India, Brazil or Colombia. But to date, powerful local NGOs in Africa are notably absent from the international development community because they have been unable to attain space, financial independence, international links and political mandates within development.

Across sub-Saharan Africa, the work of a host of international NGOs, governments and donor agencies has prevented local African NGOs from developing power. As these examples illustrate, some, like the government of Zimbabwe, act intentionally, and others, like donor agencies in Tanzania, act unintentionally, within their accepted policies and practices. But the result of all of these well-developed practices, solidly grounded in organisational management techniques and social action theory, is that African NGOs are excluded from power, even when they are talented, skilled and successful. And ultimately, less development progress is achieved for the millions of poor people across Africa than would be possible in the midst of powerful African NGOs.

This is an alarming trend and one worthy of the attention of NGOs, donors, governments and other groups interested in furthering development in Africa and across the South. Local African NGOs play a unique role in development: a role to which they, rather than the many other actors at work on the continent, are uniquely suited. They are able to engage with government on important political debates in development and have legitimacy in the eyes of the beneficiaries they represent in these debates. They can remain focussed on the needs of their beneficiaries, rather than on the priorities of Northern donating publics. And they are able to recognise and employ the fungibility of funding resources to benefit their clients. Without power, however, local NGOs will continue to be crowded out of African development by actors unable to provide these many crucial services and advantages to beneficiaries. But NGO power is not only an important end in itself – additionally, it is a key component of the sustainability of NGOs and their work.

7
Powerful ▌ Sustainable
NGOs ▌ NGOs

As aid monies from the North to South cycle through eras of feast and
of famine, wars and humanitarian crises arise and abate, and states gain
international support for adopting democratic governance or lose it for
failing to curb bureaucratic corruption, NGOs can also find their futures
assured at one moment, and in question the next. Undertaking development work can itself be inherently unsustainable: new government
leadership enacts different national development strategies, as demo-
graphics change NGOs adopt new priorities and move from one region to
another, donor contracts with NGOs end, long-serving project workers
leave to find new jobs, and even successful projects close. International
NGOs, among the most active groups in African development, are one of
its most unsustainable elements. By definition, successful development
in the South requires that international development agencies work
themselves out of their jobs; as they succeed in helping local groups to
develop their capacity and their development opportunities, the operational presence of INGOs on the continent should becomes less relevant
(Van Rooy 2000). Even local NGOs in the South recognise that their roles
are but temporary ones. In 1992, IBASE in Brazil wrote, 'Ideally, IBASE
will disappear when a democratic society is capable of democratizing
information' (IBASE 1992: 216). As Alan Fowler points out, 'to be
sustainable, development has ultimately to be controlled by those most
concerned and affected, that is primary stakeholders and Southern and
Eastern NGOs' (1997: 73). It is an important lesson for international NGOs
to learn.

Yet without sustainable local NGOs to assume the current development activities of INGOs, such international groups will remain an active
and powerful force on the continent and the goal of locally driven
advancement and empowerment will remain no more than a distant
ideal. Furthermore, without a cadre of sustainable local NGOs with
sustainable projects and programmes, the individuals and communities
they serve will fail to see the long-term benefits of development activities

130

and themselves be incorporated into positions of responsibility for meeting their own developmental needs. Providing long-term benefits to NGO beneficiaries must surely be at the heart of any effort to increase the power and sustainability of local NGOs in Africa. The sustainability of local NGOs is of particular concern in Africa today, as certain aid donors shift their aid monies away from NGOs and back towards governments, and others reduce their aid contributions outright. A 'beyond-aid' scenario therefore seems close at hand – and is something that African NGOs must start to prepare for.

What does sustainability mean for NGOs?

While the concept of sustainability has been rooted in several disciplines since the eighteenth and early nineteenth centuries, it was only with the release of *Our Common Future* in 1987 that sustainability was raised to the level of a widely accepted development policy objective (Tijmes and Luijf 1995). The World Commission on Environment and Development (WCED) was set up by the United Nations in 1983 to consider problems of environment and development and to distil from these discussions a 'global agenda for change' (WCED 1987: ix). *Our Common Future*, its final report, focussed heavily on a concept of sustainable development, which was defined as 'development that meets the needs of the present without compromising the ability of future generations to meet their own needs' (WCED 1987: 43). Situating sustainability at the nexus of the disciplines of economics, ecology and development, the Commission linked the drive for economic growth with the need for environmental management and highlighted the trade-off between the needs and rights of present and future populations.

Despite its widespread dissemination, however, the report failed to establish an unambiguous common ground between the many disciplines to which sustainability is a relevant concept. Each of these fields has therefore tended towards a self-contained view of sustainability which fits neatly into its particular discourse. For economists, this means that sustainability, concerned with preserving 'acceptable levels of human well-being over time', is a supply-side concept focussing on intergenerational fairness and maintaining levels of capital stocks, utility and welfare (Howe 1997, Norton and Toman 1997: 555). For environmentalists and ecologists, meanwhile, sustainability centres on mitigating the impact of human beings on the environment. They focus on measuring and valuing changes in environmental quality as a means of protecting the resilience of ecosystems and conserving depletable resources (Club of Rome 1972, Van Pelt 1993, Norton and Toman 1997).

Sustainability has also been integrated wholesale into the development canon. One author examining the sustainability of development projects writes, 'for all concepts of self-help and all forms of technical,

personnel-based, or financial assistance, sustainability is, at least impli-
citly, an objective of overriding importance' (Stockmann 1997: 1767). One
would be hard-pressed to find any development initiative today which
did not find its approval, renewal or success rating related to its sustainability. Accordingly, definitions of sustainability specifically adapted to
the field of development have emerged. These definitions mirror those
used in the fields of economics and ecology in entailing the preservation of
the benefits of, and commitment to, development activities over time.

When specifically applied to development NGOs, sustainability has
both an internal and an external component. Internally, NGOs seek, and
are pressured by their donors to seek, greater organisational sustainability
within the structure of their NGO. This quest has spawned a large and
growing interest and literature on the elements of NGO sustainability, and
'capacity building' in particular (Eade 1997, James 1998, Fowler 2000c,
Kaplan 2000, James 2001). Instructing NGOs on how to improve their
skills and address issues from planning to financing within their organizations, this movement has addressed a fundamental question about the
long-term future of NGOs as organizations, and of the long-term benefits
of NGO activity. Despite the current popularity of capacity-building as a
concept, its definition, too, varies widely and tends to be focussed at
different levels of an NGO. Capacity-building interventions can be
targeted at individuals, as in staff or leadership training, at the organisation as a whole, as in financial management or strategic planning, or at the
inter-organisational level, as in support for networking or publicity
(James 2001). All of these levels of capacity-building are relevant to
building internal NGO sustainability.

Externally, NGOs seek to achieve the sustainability of their projects,
and of the benefits of these projects to the communities with which they
work. NGOs are therefore both an object of sustainability and a trans-
mitter of sustainability (Stockmann 1997). An NGO achieves external
sustainability where the lessons, impacts and benefits of its development
projects continue to be disseminated and diffused after their completion
(Tacconi and Tisdell 1992). Based on his experience with development
projects in Latin America, Stockmann (1997) considers internal sustainability to be achieved if an NGO is able to develop problem-solving
structures that allow it to adapt successfully to the changing conditions
around it. In their strategy framework for promoting the sustainability of
development institutions, Brinkerhoff and Goldsmith (1992: 369) offer
more precise guidance for NGOs in developing internal sustainability.
They propose that 'institutional sustainability depends upon maintaining: responsive output flows (high quality and valued goods and
services); cost-effective goods and services delivery mechanisms (organization and management); and resource flows (recurrent costs, capital
investments, human resources)'.

This conception of NGO sustainability goes beyond the financial one
which is so often dominant in the field: that all it takes for an NGO to be

sustainable is steady funding arrangements. As we saw in the case study of Senegalese NGOs, even regular funding can be destabilising to an NGO, which means that NGO sustainability can never be just a question of financing. It is within Brinkerhoff and Goldsmith's framework for the sustainability of development institutions, which includes, but does not focus exclusively on the financial aspects of sustainability, that I will consider the internal sustainability of local African NGOs. Adapting it from the general context of development institutions to the specific NGO context, however, internal NGO sustainability becomes a composite of: i) the responsiveness, relevance and quality of an NGO's activities; ii) the efficiency and cost-effectiveness of an NGO's organisation and management structures; and iii) the security of an NGO's resource base.

While I have tended to portray NGO power as an absolute to this point in the book, arguing that none of the local African NGOs interviewed as part of this study have developed the kind of power demonstrated by local NGOs in Asia and Latin America in Chapter Two, NGO power is in fact a much more graded and relative term. While some groups will always fall into the absolute ends of the power scale, most can be found somewhere in the middle. Of the many local African NGOs that I met during my fieldwork in Zimbabwe, Tanzania and Senegal, several, while lacking any real power in an absolute sense, nonetheless enjoyed relatively high amounts of power *vis-à-vis* their fellow NGOs. When considering levels of sustainability it seems that power is a crucial factor: the more powerful local African NGOs are also the most sustainable, the less powerful tend to be less sustainable. As the example of individual NGOs in the case study countries will illustrate, this holds true both at the level of internal and external NGO sustainability.

The responsiveness, relevance and quality of the NGO's activities is the first factor contributing to an NGO's internal sustainability. A natural resources management NGO working in Zimbabwe and cited as a success story by the UNDP (NGO Z1), a Tanzanian gender issues NGO known across the country and throughout Eastern and Southern Africa (NGO T1) and a Senegalese human rights NGO with antennae offices in four other countries (NGO S1) are all regularly recognised for the responsiveness, the relevance or the quality of their projects. They are all also relatively powerful in their individual country contexts. These NGOs all started in response to demonstrated needs in their regions and have positioned themselves in empty development space, choosing to focus on sectors in which there is a large effective demand for services, but few, if any, other service providers. They are highly specialised and, as the recognised leaders in their field or sub-field, are regularly called on to participate in the committees and planning initiatives of government agencies and donor bodies. The services of these three organisations are also in demand from government and a variety of development agencies. NGO S1, for example, took part in creating and critiquing the new five-year strategic plan of one of its donors and has its services demanded by beneficiary groups in neighbouring countries. NGO T1 cannot keep up with the demand for its services from government, donors and the World Bank and is now referring its donors to other local partners. The high quality of the services of these NGOs and the demand for them from governments, donors and beneficiaries signal that these three relatively powerful NGOs have achieved a significant element of internal sustainability.

Brinkerhoff and Goldsmith sum up the significance of sustainability to these kinds of high-quality NGOs in this way: 'Performance is important for sustainability. Good performance can be the main 'sales pitch' for gaining support and marketing the output of institution-building efforts' (1992: 377). But they go on to say that, 'Failure to fulfil a function can have exactly the opposite effect, especially if expectations are high among stakeholders'. Unfortunately, relatively powerless local NGOs fall into this second category. In Senegal, a USAID representative spoke of how the lack of focus of certain local NGOs impaired the quality of their work, and in Tanzania, the 'poor standard among NGOs' saw local NGOs valued far behind INGOs by a donor searching for local partners (Interview with Representative, International Donor Agency, Dar es Salaam, 25 October 1999; Interview with Representative, USAID NGO Support Project, Dakar, 11 February 2000).

For local NGOs constantly living hand-to-mouth, responsiveness and relevance are often only secondary considerations to economic survival. Organisations like a Senegalese NGO created to train young people in marketable skills and help them to find employment (NGO S2) reinvent themselves biannually, as their donors choose new areas of focus. This NGO's director explained to me how this trend has affected his organisation throughout its fifteen-year history.

> Sometimes we can't follow, we deviate from the objectives that we have fixed. [...] Because we can't not do what certain donors want us to. When we know that it's not bad. And it's not bad to work on the environment, to empower women's groups. [...] I'm sure that if we were supported we could have contributed a lot to encourage the employment of youth in Senegal. But we are not funded for what we need, we are not helped, we are not supported. If we had been helped with funding we could have done a lot (Interview with President, Local NGO #55, Dakar, 6 March 2000).

NGO S2's adoption of a generalist strategy has made it difficult for it to remain relevant, and its responsiveness to the needs of its core beneficiaries will be impaired as long as it remains beholden to the priorities of its donors. The reluctance of some donors to get involved in highly charged political areas where conflict with government is possible has also meant that NGOs in some countries face a stark choice between fulfilling increased demand for advocacy and empowerment activities from their beneficiaries and losing funding because of the proclivities of their donors.

A women's business and credit NGO in Zimbabwe (NGO Z2) similarly finds its responsiveness constrained by a lack of funds in the over-crowded credit sector, and in Tanzania, another gender issues NGO (NGO T2) is held back by its lack of a full-time staff. Timeliness and compre-hensiveness in NGO activity, difficult to achieve at the best of times, are made all the more difficult when an organisation lacks a permanent infrastructure: office, communications networks and staff, or the funds required to achieve them. While the quality of the initiatives undertaken by these 'part-time' NGOs can be very high, the long periods of time involved in planning and in organising volunteers, and the limited amount of time that these groups are able to spend in the field with beneficiaries, impair their potential responsiveness and relevance to changing needs. These three relatively powerless local NGOs all lacked a full permanent staff and each expressed a desire to increase its full-time presence on the ground, and to institutionalise many of its internal organisational structures. I would expect their internal sustainability to increase if they are able to achieve these goals.

The second element that affects an NGO's internal sustainability is the efficiency and cost-effectiveness of its organisation and management structures. The part-time and volunteer-focussed adaptation of business and credit NGO Z2, gender issues NGO T2 and youth training NGO S2, however, highlight a conflict between NGO organisational practices that are cost-effective and ones that are efficient. To achieve internal sustain-ability, an NGO must be able to deliver its services at a price that donors are willing to pay for them, and a price consistent with that sought by government, international NGOs and the other development service providers in that environment. But no matter what the cost of the development services, these services must be delivered efficiently, with little waste or mismanagement, and with maximum accountability. The reliance on voluntarism and minimal organisational structures in these three relatively powerless African NGOs is a cost-effective strategy for running their organisations, but allows for little investment in capacity-building, and is hardly an efficient strategy for the long term. Responsi-bility for interaction with donors and government representatives regularly changes hands, staff policies are unwritten and inconsistent, roles, responsibilities and hierarchies are ill-defined, and executive boards rarely play a role in furthering the interests of these NGOs.

The relatively powerful NGO Z1 in natural resources management, NGO T1 in gender issues and NGO S1 in human rights advocacy, on the other hand, make use of their skilled and professional staff complements to build efficient and cost-effective organisational structures. These three NGOs have also developed innovative and cost-effective strategies that help them to overcome their particular shortcomings. Tanzanian NGO T1, which faced a large demand for its services but operated with only nine full-time staff members, relied on regular co-operation with other like-minded NGOs to mount large-scale campaigns. When lobbying its government for a new Sexual Offences Act, for example, it handled networking and central organisation for the campaign while other partner NGOs worked on developing legal challenges and liaising with parliamentarians and dealt with the publicity for the campaign. This strategy of sharing resources and mounting joint projects as an efficient and cost-effective way of working also extended to government. For all of these relatively powerful NGOs, relationships between family members, former school friends, university classmates and workplace colleagues on either side of the NGO–government divide facilitated contact and resource sharing between government and themselves, and proved to be an efficient means of buffering difficulties between them. This added considerably to the stability and, ultimately, to the long-term sustainability of these NGO organisational structures.

NGO sustainability is most often assessed based on the third factor of internal sustainability: the security of an NGO's resource base. Donors want to fund successful and high-quality NGOs and NGO projects, and relatively powerful local African NGOs, like NGO Z1, T1 and S1, all benefit from their strong reputations when it comes to accessing donor funding. Each has more funds, or the offer of more funds, than it can presently use in its projects. Donors also want to fund NGO projects which will eventually be able to pay for themselves, and are similarly keen to fund NGO structures which will be able to rely less and less on donor funds in the future. While few local NGOs anywhere in Africa have the financial security of a BRAC, which self-funds 75 per cent of its annual budget, an increasing number of the more powerful local NGOs in the case study countries are focussing on increasing their financial sustainability through alternative forms of income-generation. In Zimbabwe, NGO Z1 generates regular income from marketing the products of its sustainable forestry use projects and Tanzanian NGO T1 receives large amounts of rental income from its office complex and has set up a specific division to pursue other economic opportunities.

Less powerful NGOs seem to have far less secure resource bases. NGO Z2 is currently operating without donor funds and NGO T2 has only had two donors in its fifteen-year history. Their opportunities to generate revenue internally are weak and are limited to collecting annual fees from members – individuals who are already contributing large amounts of their time towards the activities of these NGOs. Senegalese NGO S2, on the other hand, is surprisingly able to raise an adequate level of donor financing with which to undertake a variety of projects. This is not necessarily indicative of a high degree of financial sustainability, however. This generalist NGO accepts whatever levels of funding it is offered, in whatever sectors they are offered, until these resources dry up and it has to search for new funding in new sectors.

If a key component of an NGO's sustainability is the security of its resource base, then despite the preoccupation of donors with financial resources, an NGO's human resources will also be critical. The relatively powerful NGOs in the case study countries have each succeeded in building a stable, well-qualified and professional staff and the sustainability of their projects has benefited accordingly. The relatively weak local NGOs I encountered are not so well off. Many of these NGOs have survived for several years with a skeletal permanent staff or no full-time staff at all, but their activities are constrained by the schedules and other commitments of their volunteers. Employing part-time or volunteer staff has proven to be a successful strategy for survival for organisations like NGOs Z2, T2 and S2, but it has not proven a successful strategy for sustainability.

This small sample of relatively powerful and powerless local African NGOs also illustrates that NGOs differ in terms of their levels of external sustainability, defined as the continuation of the lessons, impacts and benefits of development activities after their completion. One interpretation of the benefits produced by sustainable projects sees beneficiaries enjoying improved well-being, being empowered to act to promote their interests and having developed the capacity that allows them to do so (Fowler 2000c). Yet the beneficiaries of the relatively powerless NGOs in the case study countries enjoy few such benefits. NGOs Z2, T2 and S2, constrained by a lack of finances and full-time staff, have few resources to invest in project development, planning and research, especially when they are only able to afford very short projects. The activities of human and financial resource-poor NGOs Z2 and T2, for example, are also focussed around short-term endeavours such as weekend workshops and one-day training seminars – which while of value, are unlikely to catalyse long-term gains for participants. The external sustainability of NGO S2, which is diverted by the promise of donor funds into development activities in which it has no experience or expertise, is similarly constrained.

The long-term impact of an NGO also depends on its ability to involve beneficiary communities and to 'embed' its projects within existing community structures and processes (Fowler 2000c). The more involvement communities have in project development, implementation and decision-making, the more likely they will be either to refuse outright projects that do not meet their needs, or to maintain projects once the overseeing NGO has pulled out. Relatively powerful local NGOs Z1, T1 and S1 from Zimbabwe, Tanzania and Senegal respectively, all claim to focus their work on demonstrated community needs and to highlight beneficiary involvement in the design and implementation of their projects. Elizabeth Kleemeier (2000: 930) summarised some of the arguments for increasing community participation as a means of ensuring the sustainability of development projects: 'Getting beneficiaries involved would lower costs, better target people's needs, incorporate local knowledge […], and create grassroots capacity to undertake other development projects and to maintain benefits, particularly in the case of physical infrastructure.' As NGOs are increasingly accused of being upwardly accountable to their donors rather than to their beneficiaries, the power and freedom to increasingly involve beneficiary groups can only increase their legitimacy and sustainability. Project follow-up is another aspect of external sustainability on which the relatively powerful local NGOs focus. Yet a lack of financial and human resources has again constrained the ability of relatively weak NGOs Z2, T2 and S2 to achieve these key elements of external NGO sustainability.

I have defined internal NGO sustainability as dependent on: i) the responsiveness, relevance and quality of an NGO's activities; ii) the efficiency and cost-effectiveness of an NGO's organisation and management structures; and iii) the security of an NGO's resource base. External sustainability is the continued dissemination and diffusion of the benefits of an NGO's development activities after their completion. Based on these criteria it is apparent that the relatively powerful NGOs from Zimbabwe, Tanzania and Senegal are also more sustainable than their less powerful counterparts. It is also clear, however, that while we commonly think of NGO sustainability as primarily being about an NGO's survival, sustainability in fact demands not only the continued existence of an NGO, but also its continued relevance, efficiency, and benefit to local communities. NGOs Z2, T2 and S2, each relatively weak in its country context, have each survived for as long as, if not longer than their powerful counterparts. But none of them is truly sustainable.

While the elements of internal and external sustainability can be separated out and considered individually, it is important to note the extent to which they are all interrelated. Without secure resources, local NGOs will struggle to build strong organisational and management structures, to attract a high quality permanent staff and to focus their activities in fields where large, unmet demands for service exist. Yet financial sustainability is not the pivotal element of NGO sustainability either. A local NGO which has a secure enough funding base to offer beneficiaries cash or food incentives to participate in its programmes (as did several international NGOs in the fieldwork countries) may yet find its projects unsuitable and unsustainable in the long term.

This type of trade-off between achieving internal sustainability and achieving external sustainability affects many local African NGOs, whose pursuit of internal sustainability actually impairs their external sustainability. Pursuing a generalist strategy results in a degree of internal sustainability for several Senegalese NGOs, since their financial and organisational security are more assured; but at the same time, it impairs the level of external sustainability that they can achieve. With their short-term focus dictated by changing donor interests, these NGOs are rarely able to encourage meaningful stakeholder participation in project development and implementation, to install and train local field workers or to engage in follow-up and evaluation activities. Similarly, local NGOs unable to move beyond service delivery and welfare activities, despite beneficiary demand for advocacy or credit or democracy-building activities, are also less likely to mobilise community participation in their projects and to see these projects reach sustainability.

Sustainability is a complex concept and includes elements of both internal and external sustainability: elements that are not always achieved concurrently. As the case studies illustrated, local NGOs which are relatively powerful tend to be relatively sustainable, and local NGOs which are less powerful tend to be less sustainable. As such, could power be not only an end, but also the means to another end: that of sustainability? The notion that NGO power influences NGO sustainability is likely to be a controversial one. It calls into question the current belief that sustainability is all about planning and reporting, budgeting and financial management, that sustainability is learned, rather than acquired, that sustainability is all about survival. It also calls into question how sustainability is defined and measured, for power not only changes the perception of sustainability in the eye of the beholder, but also the identity of the beholder. With power, Southern development actors could exert their influence over concepts like sustainability, participation and partnership, which are globally applied, yet still defined in the North. The next section considers this idea in greater detail, exploring the ways in which NGO power actually influences NGO sustainability and can therefore help to alleviate underdevelopment sub-Saharan Africa.

The link between NGO power and NGO sustainability

I have defined power as the ability of an NGO to set its own priorities, define its own agenda and exert its influence on the international development community, even in the face of external opposition. This sort of organisational freedom from constraints provides an environment in which local NGOs can be more innovative and creative, take more risks and be willing to experiment, invest heavily in research and in building organisational capacity, and can spend more time closely and carefully developing projects with their intended beneficiaries. BRAC certainly believes that these characteristics have increasingly become features of its programmes as its power has grown. As they have improved the responsiveness of its projects, the efficiency of its organisational structures, the security of its resource base and the lasting impacts of its initiatives, these are also features that have improved BRAC's sustainability.

Would power similarly offer local African NGOs the chance to achieve sustainability? Certainly, the internal sustainability of African NGOs would be vastly improved by power. The quality, relevance and responsiveness of an NGO's work would increase when it developed the size, wealth and reputation to be able to ignore donor trends, government suasion and competition from international NGOs, and to focus its activities on its areas of strength. If 'sustainable institutions are ones whose strategies enable them to make the best of their capabilities and to capitalize on their surroundings' (Brinkerhoff and Goldsmith 1992: 375), then power, in allowing NGOs to focus on their capabilities and strengths irrespective of the development fashions of the day, helps NGOs to become sustainable institutions. With power, a local NGO run by educators, like NGO S2, would be able to focus on training and informal education for young people, without having its focus diverted from education to women's issues to the environment to AIDS over ten years. Power also allows local NGOs to survive, the most basic condition of sustainability, in so far as it keeps NGOs and their workers alive and unharmed while pursuing controversial projects in line with their capacities and the demands of their beneficiaries. The international ties and reputation that come with power make it difficult for government reprisals aimed at NGOs to go unnoticed. Democracy-building NGOs in Zimbabwe and environmental groups in Tanzania have both benefited from this type of protection merely by having powerful individuals associated with their causes.

The efficiency and cost-effectiveness of an NGO's organisation and management structure, the second key element of internal NGO sustainability, is also improved by power. Power enables local NGOs to invest more heavily in their internal structures and capacities without having to justify 'non-project related' expenses like training or publicity, or other elements of capacity building to donors. This serves to reinforce their sustainability, since they are now able to institutionalise procedures and policies that increase their efficiency, conduct research in their area of activity and invest in capital items that reduce their administrative burden. While many excellent rural development NGOs in Senegal ran their programmes without owning a single vehicle, and several well-known and well-subscribed Tanzanian NGOs managed without modern computers or internet access, these NGOs would be much more useful to their beneficiaries if they could invest in capital needs of strategic importance.

The most important capital request voiced by local NGOs I have met in Africa is for a permanent office that the NGO can own rather than rent; only a handful in the case study countries, like NGO Z1 in Zimbabwe and NGO T1 in Tanzania, have been able to buy their own premises. The obvious negative sustainability implications of paying rent month after month on office space, rather than paying off a mortgage, seems obvious to NGOs, though their donors fail to perceive the debate in the same way. Many of these donors object to contributing to NGO overheads, such as office space, for fear of what would happen to these investments once the NGO folded. Yet what will happen to their own buildings when their agency becomes obsolete? The irony of advocating unsustainable renting behaviours for fear that an NGO will indeed eventually prove unsustainable is lost on such donors. Having power would allow local NGOs to advocate for their needs without fearing a loss of vital income and support.

Links between short-term unsustainable NGO behaviours, such as relying heavily on donor funds, and long-term sustainability, have also been lost on donors. Without heavy donor support in their early years, the powerful local NGOs we saw in Chapter Two would never have been able to launch the many capital-intensive activities which now contribute significantly to their ability to generate large amounts of income internally. Power would also remove the paradox of cost-conscious or savings-minded NGOs losing all monies still unspent in their accounts at the end of the year, since donor organisations forbid NGO savings. BRAC's power has enabled it to force donors to fund a common expenditure pool, the administration of which rests solely with BRAC. This pool funding strategy further increases the efficiency and sustainability of BRAC's internal structures, as it reduces long negotiation periods with individual donors and eliminates the need for different reporting styles and schedules for each donor.

Lastly, power increases the internal sustainability of local NGOs by increasing the size and security of their resource flows, the third element of internal NGO sustainability. The reputation of powerful NGOs and the development space they occupy makes them the natural choice for donors interested in funding high-quality development initiatives in particular fields. This will become increasingly crucial to the survival of good NGOs, if donor agencies begin to rechannel their development resources to democratically elected and socially committed governments and away from NGOs – as DFID is currently doing (Wallace 2003). This not only increases an NGO's financial sustainability because of the sheer volume of funds it attracts to the NGO, but even more because it enables the NGO increasingly to dictate the terms of these donor funding relationships (Wallace 1997). Powerful NGOs can decide to accept only basket-funding, can insist on core funding being included in all project funding that they accept, can ask for longer-term commitments from donors, and can turn down potentially destabilising donor funds. Because of their reputation, the financial situation of powerful local NGOs is often even more dramatically improved by the amount that donors and international organisations are willing to pay for these NGOs' consulting, research and training skills. Power, reputation and wealth also add to the sustainability of an NGO's human resource base, as they enable it to compete with INGOs, government agencies and the private sector for high-quality staff.

In terms of the external sustainability of local NGOs, or the sustainability of NGO projects and programmes, NGO power could again produce positive results. Firstly, as power improves the quality of an NGO's activities, the efficiency of its structures and the stability of its resources, it would also improve the development, planning and implementation of NGO initiatives, and accordingly, their long-term impact. Power would similarly contribute to reducing an NGO's daily pressures for survival, a result which has been shown to be key to the development of innovative NGO projects and programmes (De Winter 1993). Thirdly, as NGO power develops from the acquisition of space and the minimising of competition and confrontation among NGOs and between NGOs and other development actors, NGO power would also be expected to have an impact on the receptiveness of the environment in which NGO projects take place. In her work on NGO health projects in Nepal, Peggy Henderson (1995) concluded that the actions of external actors were important determinants of NGO sustainability; in her case studies even the non-hostile behaviours of donors and government had negatively affected the sustainability of NGO health projects. Finally, by becoming more relevant and responsible to beneficiaries, and more accountable to their needs, NGOs will find that their activities meet with increased commitment and ownership by local communities, and are therefore more likely to be continued, improved and carried on into the future.

This influence of power over NGO sustainability at a practical, or operational level, is magnified by its impact at the conceptual level. The concept of sustainability that dominates development today is based on the definition of sustainability created by the WCED. It sought to reach a 'global agenda for change', to 'help define shared perceptions of long-term environmental issues', and to develop sustainability goals 'for the world community' (WCED 1987: ix). But in doing so, the Commission reflected predominant Western modes of thinking which assume that sustainability, like concepts of markets and needs and efficiency can, at once, resonate with all the cultures of the globe (Tijmes and Luijf 1995). Despite the increasingly 'transnational' nature of development, many of its concepts, like sustainability, remain culture-specific (Townsend 1999). As Meppem and Bourke (1999: 391–2) write, 'culture plays an active role in the construction of our perceived "reality" and therefore in our understanding and interpretation of sustainability.' In fact, since sustainability and development are value-laden concepts, definitions of sustainability and of its goals and measurement will depend on the perspectives of the development organisations involved and of their beneficiaries. And it is likely that 'those with the power to formulate and implement policy ... conceive sustainability differently from those affected by the policies' (Thomas 2001: 13).

But complex relations of domination and subordination between development actors: beneficiaries, local and international NGOs, governments and donors, make it likely that it will always be the powerful who define sustainability and evaluate who, and what, is sustainable (Yanarella and Levine 1992). It is because of this fact that NGO power additionally affects sustainability. As Foucault may well have predicted, powerful local NGOs not only achieve greater internal and external sustainability according to the prevailing definitions of sustainability in the field, but they are also able to exert influence over the definitions of sustainability by which they will be judged. As Fowler writes, 'The appropriation and control of language is key to exercising power' (1998: 140). Power gives local NGOs access and influence over national and regional decision-makers and gives them a seat at the tables of Rio and Beijing and New York and Geneva, where terms like sustainability are defined, and the definers, like the members of the Brundtland Commission, are chosen.

Power also gives local NGOs influence over how sustainability criteria will be applied to them and how the sustainability of their work will be measured. The decision of one of the largest foreign donor agencies in Bangladesh not to demand financial sustainability measures from NGOs working in advocacy and empowerment, for instance, demonstrated the power of this group of local NGOs. This donor organisation had recognised the pivotal role that these NGOs played in Bangladeshi society but also realised that these organisations:

> Don't want to be distracted by running around trying to increase their revenue generation and financial sustainability from five per cent to ten per cent because they're never going to be able to finance their activities, [...] unless there is a liberal, philanthropic middle class in Bangladesh who will support them. [... So they] will need donor support for five, ten, fifteen, twenty years' (Interview with Representative, International Donor Agency, Dhaka, 24 July 2000).

This donor's recognition that financial sustainability is not the sole measure by which an NGO's sustainability should be judged, and that sustainability is dependent not only on the quality of an NGO's work, but also on such specific environmental factors as the culture of giving in a country, illustrates the power of this small group of very successful advocacy NGOs in Bangladesh. For while this donor was willing to reconceive of its notion of sustainability, it was only in respect to this group of powerful local NGOs. The rhetoric of development is highly dependent on power relations among development actors, and when local NGOs achieve power, they are able to exert considerable influence in defining the terms of development debates. As Claude Alvares wrote, 'Knowledge is power, but power is also knowledge. Power decides what is knowledge and what is not knowledge' (1992: 230).

So powerful local NGOs are likely to be sustainable, firstly, because power reinforces an NGO's internal and external sustainability. Secondly, power allows local NGOs to participate in defining sustainability according to their cultural norms, and enables them to force donors who want to work with them to adapt their imported preconceptions of sustainability to the new environments in which they now find themselves. NGO power is, therefore, a key determinant of NGO sustainability and, as such, can make a substantial contribution to improving the quality of development services in Africa.

Conclusion

With power, local NGOs can meet many of the needs of their beneficiaries, offering them long-term support and projects with long-term benefits. With power NGOs can strive to undertake innovative and creative programming, to invest in research which can build their long-term organisational capacity and to take risks and experiment with new activities and approaches. With power NGOs can themselves define the terms on which their work will be judged and determine when their work is providing lasting benefits to their clients. This chapter has also argued that until local African NGOs are able to gain power, sustainability will elude them, and they will be yet another unsustainable element in the development of a continent already plagued by unsustainable ecosystems and environments, aid policies and government programmes.

8

Helping Local NGOs
in Africa
to Develop Power

No two development sectors in sub-Saharan Africa are the same. In each country, a different range of actors is at work in a distinct range of fields, enabling local NGOs to develop varying levels of power. In Zimbabwe, local NGOs are professional and experienced development actors. But they generally lack power – largely because of the extensive and often aggressive competition they face from government and international NGOs in the country. In Tanzania, NGOs are an active force for change and have strong links to academia, the media and northern NGOs, yet find strong competition for space and funds from INGOs and community-based organisations. Lastly, in Senegal, local NGOs, with their umbrella body CONGAD, have built a secure collective development space and reputation, while still beholden, as individual organisations, to the interests of their donors.

Empirical evidence from each of these countries illustrates that, irrespective of the particular country context, local NGOs across Africa have been unable to seize power. And that this absence of NGO power has undermined development across the continent. Yet there is nothing intrinsic to the character of NGO power – its evolution or enabling factors – or in the realities of African development space that would make it impossible for indigenous African NGOs to gain power. Now is a crucial time for local NGOs in Africa to focus on developing power. Extreme needs on the continent have created space for local NGOs and renewed global commitments and resource mobilisations present a window of opportunity for local NGOs to make themselves heard and develop a strong international following. So what lessons does this study have for local African NGOs trying to develop power? And what lessons does it have for both those actors which aim to support local NGOs in achieving this goal as well as those whose activities and policies have excluded local African NGOs from power?

What strategies should local African NGOs pursue in order to develop power?

The lot of local NGOs in sub-Saharan Africa is not an easy one when viewed from the inside. Telephones and internet connections are unreliable and expensive. People don't keep appointments and disappear upcountry for weeks. Equipment breaks down and takes months to fix. Seasonal rains wash out roads and bridges and isolate entire regions of a country. The working environment for these groups is not easy, and is a world away from the ones that development professionals are used to in New York and London and Geneva. Many African NGOs are overcome by the bloodiness of this environment and remain small, disorganised and unremarkable. The miracle is that some indigenous NGOs do overcome their environments to become high quality, relevant organisations capable of mounting effective projects, that some of them are so successful that their lack of power becomes significant.

Power is not a quality that local NGOs can passively develop; they must actively seek to create and defend it. In other words, power must be seized, not given. Local African NGOs themselves play a crucial role in determining whether or not they will gain power. NGO power is closely related to four elements: secure space, a high level of financial independence from donors, strong links to the international development community and links to the political aspects of development work. What can African NGOs themselves do to achieve these elements of power?

Within the context of social forces, Migdal (1994: 22) identified three dimensions along which groups can extend their existing power to increase their domination: (i) by dominating in a larger number of issue areas; (ii) by incorporating a larger number of people or territories into their fold and; (iii) by using the resources they have gained in one arena to dominate in others. Based on the case studies of local NGOs in Zimbabwe, Tanzania and Senegal in this book, I would argue there are a range of strategies that African NGOs have at their disposal to gain power – many of which follow the same avenues for increased domination identified by Migdal. These strategies are both internal: designed to increase an NGO's power by modifying its organisational and operational practices; and external: aimed at increasing an NGO's power by modifying or increasing its contact with other actors within development.

Internal Strategies

1. NGOs must seek to be active in sectors in which they have space
The first, and perhaps the most important, internal strategy that this research advocates for local African NGOs is the capturing of a niche in order to secure space. NGOs need to assess the sectors or regions in which their experience and expertise lie, and focus their activities within these fields, in order to outcompete the other actors that challenge them for

development space. Local NGOs in Senegal, which have benefited from the widespread availability of donor funding and the strong reputation of the NGO sector, have, so far, been able to thrive while remaining unspecialised and accepting grants which shift their focus away from the areas in which their capabilities lie. But the most powerful local NGOs in Senegal are those which have specialised, for example, in the fields of human rights and the environment. Should donor aid priorities change to favour funding development through government and should competition for donor funds become as acute as it is in other African countries, then those Senegalese NGOs recognised as the best in their fields will be the ones to survive and prosper.

Not all space in developing countries is equal, and some space will always be more crowded than others. Local NGOs need to position themselves, especially in their early days, in a sector in which their particular skills and experience allow them to maximise the space available to them. Several authors have specifically considered the sectors and range of activities in which the space for NGOs and social movements is greatest, noting that groups working on high visibility issues, as part of a large associational sector, in rural regions, in democratic countries or in countries with decentralised government, all enjoy greater space than their counterparts in other environments (Chazan 1992, Bratton 1994b, Magnusson 1996, Haynes 1997, Ngware 1997, Van Rooy 1997). NGOs must think strategically about these and the other sectors in which they can gain and protect space and contribute innovative ideas, whether because of their unique qualifications or because of the absence of competitor organisations. By doing so, they will be able to speak with authority in these issue areas.

In advocating that local NGOs stick to the fields they know best, and fields in which they have some competitive advantage, it may appear as though I am not saying anything terribly new or profound. Yet, as it happens, it cannot be taken for granted that all local NGOs adopt such a strategy. Many of the NGOs I encountered in the case study countries situated themselves in overcrowded space in which they were unable to distinguish themselves from other development organisations. Others, even when in possession of specialised skills and experience, moved from sector to sector so often that they were unable to develop an edge in any sector. In order to develop power, NGOs need to find what they are good at, build up their strengths and stick with it.

2. NGOs must pay attention to their own organisational and institutional development

In the current climate of aid, in which NGOs are encouraged to minimise overhead costs and maximise measurable outputs, local African NGOs have learned to prioritise project goals and project achievements over institutional goals and organisational achievements. Whether in terms of promoting staff development, undertaking organisational publicity or planning research projects, the majority of local NGOs in the case study countries are unable or reluctant to invest time and money in their own organisational development. Yet without undertaking these kinds of expenditures, local NGOs will find it difficult to develop power.

First-order necessities for any organisation include a clearly defined mandate and vision. Allan Kaplan (2000: 518) considers 'the development of a conceptual framework which reflects the organisation's understanding of the world' to be the foundation on which all other organisational development will be built. From this base, developing a clear vision for the NGO, setting goals for its work and targets for measuring progress towards these goals, and identifying the strategies and processes which can be used to meet goals will all aid NGOs in focussing on the issues they know best and around which they are able to innovate or hold some competitive advantage. In all of these 'capacity-building' endeavours, the input of lower-levels of staff and of beneficiaries, especially those from marginalised groups, must be encouraged and incorporated, inverting the normal top-down flow of ideas and information in organisations (Eade 1997, Beckwith *et al.* 2002).

From goal setting and strategic planning, local NGOs need to move to human resource development. With a smaller budget for salaries than INGOs or donor organisations, many local NGOs hire individuals interested and committed to development work, though inexperienced in its practice. Their employees learn by doing. But powerful local NGOs like BRAC, Proshika and SEWA prioritise the training and development of their employees. BRAC, for instance, which predominantly also hires recent university graduates, does not leave their training to chance and teaches its staff about all aspects of 'the business'. BRAC invests 7 per cent of its annual salary budget in staff development (Smillie and Hailey 2001). As Lovell (1992: 124) writes, 'the development of management skills, along with program-relevant technical skills, is an important part of the BRAC staff development program'. Proshika trains almost half a million staff and beneficiaries in its training programmes each calendar year, and SEWA's Academy is similarly busy, ambitious and well-known (Spodek 1994, Smillie and Hailey 2001).

While many NGO observers today use the term 'professional NGO' as an insult, equating professionalism with large overheads, fancy offices, vehicles and rigid, inflexible systems, a professional 'is one who is extremely competent in a job' (Smillie 1995: 147). It takes a substantial lack of imagination to believe that NGOs with a trained and experienced staff cannot be creative, sensitive and in touch with the needs and wishes of their clients. In fact, many of the most powerful local NGOs I encountered in the field-work countries were those which employed a dedicated, well-educated, experienced and well-trained staff. Others were quick to point to training for their staff as one of the elements of donor support that they most benefited from. To develop power, local African NGOs need to develop a professional, well trained and knowledgeable staff that has more to offer beneficiaries than just good intentions.

Publicity is also central to NGO power, especially as developing international links and an international reputation seem to be critical elements in expanding development space. Across Africa, where local NGOs face stiff competition from international NGOs, donors and governments, taking the time to share success stories can help local NGOs to capture the limited attention spans of national and international publics for development issues. Without it, local NGOs will always be overshadowed by their foreign counterparts, which have many more of the connections necessary to gain the attention of the international development community.

A strong reputation, built on publicity and high quality activities, has also helped certain local NGOs in the case study countries to increase their internally generated revenues and their financial independence. A strong reputation both at home and abroad spreads word of a local NGO's accomplishments and attracts additional donors, partners and clients. This gives an NGO greater freedom in deciding which donors to work with, increased revenues through contracts for research and consulting projects, and a stronger voice in national-level debates. Many local African NGOs are, however, loathe to become involved in publicising their work. Some want to maintain a low profile so as not to attract negative attention from government. Others want their results to speak for themselves, feel little need to impress anyone beyond their direct beneficiaries, or lack the financial and human resources to publicise their field and research activities. But power is often developed by investing in just such types of organisational growth and development expenditures.

Power is often also developed by undertaking and disseminating high-quality research. Through their many reports, books and journals, local NGOs like DESCO and IBASE have been able to generate international publicity and a world-wide reputation for their organisations. Additionally, the research and regular publications of these groups have contributed to their bank of information and knowledge. And information is power. As Wolfgang Sachs wrote, 'Knowledge … wields power by directing people's attention; it carves out and highlights a certain reality, casting into oblivion other ways of relating to the world around us' (1992: 5). And by developing knowledge, NGOs can shape the landscape of the possible for both themselves and their beneficiaries, as well as for groups throughout the wider international development community (Gaventa and Cornwall 2001, Mawdsley *et al.* 2002). Having the ability to 'direct people's attention', to their activities, their insights and their organisations has allowed such local NGOs to speak with authority in their issue areas of interest and has made them extremely powerful within international development.

By disseminating news of their projects and successes, publishing their research, and training their employees so that they are the most knowledgeable in the fields in which they work, African NGOs will be able to follow in the footsteps of other powerful local NGOs around the world, investing appropriate levels of time and money in their own organisational development. With a focus on developing both innovative projects and a high-quality organisation, these groups will find opportunities to assure themselves a share of development space in their countries, to integrate themselves into global development processes and to develop power.

3. NGOs must increase their focus on generating revenue

NGO power is the ability of a local NGO to set its own priorities and to influence the international development community, even in the face of opposition from other development groups. A key part of achieving this power, and the freedoms it brings, is gaining financial independence from donors and other funding bodies. Yet local NGOs in Africa have few of the opportunities for local fundraising that their northern and international counterparts enjoy. Small middle classes and young private sector corporations, combined with strong traditions of voluntarism within family, kin, ethnic and religious groups, and not third-party organisations, all mean that there are few local philanthropists able and willing to fund NGOs, and no large African donating public to which African NGOs can appeal for support (Fowler 1995a). One potentially untapped source of local financial support for African NGOs is funding from the African diaspora. In many countries, organised philanthropy from members of the diaspora funds education, health and other social programmes. Moreover, remittances to developing countries from its citizens and former citizens working abroad now total more than official development assistance (Ratha 2003). These sources of funding come from donors who have both a good understanding of local needs and priorities, and less call to control the terms of the funding than do more traditional aid donors. As such, diaspora philanthropy and remittances could play an important role in helping African NGOs to develop financial independence from their donors.

In the current climate of few opportunities for local fundraising, however, to be financially independent from donors, indigenous NGOs in Africa must be able to generate funds themselves. Only a minority of local NGOs in the case study countries have been able to locate and invest in sustainable ways to generate income for their organisation. Many need to modify their work to respond to each successive fad in development in order to sustain themselves financially. By adapting their focus to donor sectoral or geographic priorities, these local NGOs ensure that they will not be casualties of the competition for funding in their environment. In doing so, however, they spread themselves across a vast number of areas of activity and geographic regions, often losing their organisational focus and sacrificing the value of the specific technical skills of their employees along the way. In securing the survival of their organisations, most of these NGOs sacrifice the long-term impact of their programmes, which are modified with the cycling of donor priorities, and restrict their potential to develop power. Yet with their own secure sources of funding, few, if any of these NGOs, would continue to play musical chairs with donors, adapting their work to donor trends.

Even those local African NGOs which hold tightly to a focussed mandate have seen their power constrained by their lack of financial independence from donors and the resulting feast and famine cycles of funding that they endure. For example, credit-based local NGOs have recently lost favour with Zimbabwean donors after enjoying preferential status for many years, as their counterparts working in HIV/AIDS educa-tion and advocacy may well do in the future. This trend of changing donor priorities is one which affects a wide range of local NGOs across the continent. Almost all of the local NGOs I interviewed across the case studies professed increased financial security as one of their main goals for the future, but they must also work to develop the financial indepen-dence from donors which is crucial to power.

How should local NGOs go about developing such financial inde-pendence? Unfortunately, it is much easier to recognise that local NGOs need to develop financial independence in order to gain power than to prescribe precisely how they should go about gaining it. Alan Fowler (2000c) suggests a whole range of strategies available to NGOs to generate income, from subsidisation to enterprise creation. African NGOs will need to recognise, however, that while different strategies carry with them different benefits, in terms of regularity and amounts of income streams, for instance, each also has its own drawbacks. As but one example, commercialisation 'invites problems in the areas of political intolerance, government suspicion, policy dilemmas, public confusion and poten-tially serious management difficulty' (Fowler 2000c: 98).

Equally, income generation through the provision of credit will not be suitable for all local NGOs and many have already suffered by adopting, wholesale, the microcredit programmes which have so benefited organ-isations like SEWA and the Grameen Bank. The handful of NGOs in the case-study countries which had successfully capitalised on opportunities for internal income generation were all doing so in fields intimately connected to their expertise, whether by marketing locally produced foodstuffs abroad, selling NGO consulting and research services, or developing productive enterprises such as rental properties. Their example suggests that in order to generate meaningful and sustainable streams of income, local African NGOs must pursue enterprises and opportunities to which their knowledge, capabilities and body of contacts are suited, which directly benefit the NGO and its beneficiaries where possible, and in which they possess a competitive advantage. Local African NGOs must also work towards a goal of diversifying their income-generating opportunities in order to achieve a true sense of long-term financial independence from donors.

To this point, I have considered it crucial for local NGOs to develop their own sources of revenue in order to decrease their dependence on donors, and increase their ability to set their own priorities independently of donor interests. But it is also of key importance that African NGOs be able to withstand the decline of aid monies and scaling-back of donor agencies which has already begun in many countries and is likely to continue over the next few decades (Fowler 2000b). The UK Department for International Development, for example, is currently shifting its aid monies away from NGOs and back towards governments, in a reversal of the dominant donor trend in Africa during the 1980s and 1990s (Wallace 2003). Capitalizing on opportunities to capture government and business enterprise surpluses through partnerships will help local NGOs to diversify their income in the 'beyond aid scenario' in which local NGOs in certain regions around the world now find themselves (Aldaba *et al.* 2000). The Prime Minister of Tanzania once confidently told NGOs in his country that ' "*hela za nje hazina mwisho*" – money from outside is without end' (Igoe 2003: 871). Yet while NGOs have long enjoyed preferential access to donor aid in sub-Saharan Africa, the continuing trend of decreasing aid from the North to the South will not leave these NGOs unaffected for long.

4. NGOs must build a strong and well-connected leadership
Leadership has often been cited as one of the most important criteria of NGO success. To gain power, local African NGOs need to be run by an experienced, well-connected and committed leadership. Clark (1991) identifies two categories of NGO leaders, charismatic and collegial, both based on their structure of decision-making. The majority of powerful local NGO leaders in South Asia and Latin America tend to fall into the first category.

   BRAC, for example, is in many ways indistinguishable from its chairperson, F.H. Abed. Abed, as BRAC's founder and director until recently, set the vision and tone of the organisation, whether in terms of its programme direction, human resources policy or organisational management. Internally, Abed's presence and influence is felt at every level of the organisation. Externally, for many donors and governments it is not BRAC that they deal with, but Abed. It is Abed, as the spokesperson and figurehead for BRAC, who instils confidence in donors, who assuages their fears and inspires their trust. BRAC's donors have remarked on the remarkable success that Abed has had as BRAC's spokesperson and in the words of one of BRAC's largest donors, 'Donors wouldn't have the same confidence in the organisation in the absence of Abed' (Interview with Representative, International Donor Agency, Dhaka, 19 July 2000). In many ways it is difficult for anyone, whether in a donor agency, a government department or a northern donating public, to relate personally to a large NGO like BRAC: a mammoth organisation with thousands of staff, millions of beneficiaries and hundreds of millions of dollars. It is much easier to relate to a single intelligent, charismatic person. Babar Sobhan reinforces this point, 'In the absence of a charismatic leader such as an F.H. Abed or a Mohammed Yunus [Director, Grameen Bank], the donor is almost always in a dominant position in its dealings with [partner] NGOs' (1997: 23). The leadership of F.H. Abed has inspired BRAC and provided it with the necessary vision and strategy to see it grow, something that is true of any good leader. Moreover, his charisma has put a human face on BRAC as an organisation, and allowed for highly personal connections to be developed with a variety of important development actors. This example suggests that to gain power, local African NGOs need to invest more time in strategically choosing their leadership. The leadership of the majority of the local African NGOs I interviewed differed considerably from the highly charismatic and personalistic forms of leadership generally ascribed to powerful NGOs in other parts of the developing world, and tended more towards Clark's vision of collegial leadership. This was especially so in Tanzania, where leadership positions within many NGO were rotated equally among its members every several years.

While the 'leadership' of an NGO is often taken to refer to its individual director or chairperson, the influence of an NGO's executive board, middle management and senior staff can be equally important to local African NGOs in developing power (Roberts 2000). Local NGOs which are able to assemble a leadership whose members, between them, have good foreign contacts, high-level local connections, marketable names and reputations which evoke admiration and trust, and experience with social, political and economic systems, will be able to translate these resources into secure space and links to the wider development community. The financial experience of the board members of a local Zimbabwean NGO working in environmental management, for example, led this organisation to prioritise the development of sustainable forms of income generation and to start a campaign to create an endowment of almost one million UK pounds for the NGO. And the contacts of board members, especially in the private sector, helped to get this campaign off to a strong start. For other local NGOs, the contacts and reputations of board members and directors attract opportunities to partner with, or undertake contracts for, a variety of international development actors. As these various opportunities help local NGOs to achieve financial independence from donors, thrive outside of the aid system and build solid links to the international development community, they also help them to increase their power.

As the case studies illustrated, many local African NGO directors value their connections to government officials, which help to protect NGOs in difficult situations; these connections at the level of executive boards are also crucial to creating space. Not only do strong relationships to government allow local NGOs to gain preferential access to government development contracts, but they also provide an opportunity for local NGOs to expand into political development issues which have traditionally been within the purview of government. In his research in Kenya, for example, Ndegwa found that the decision of local NGOs to be involved in 'political actions' is 'ignited by the organisation's leadership' (Ndegwa 1996: 81). In other cases, local NGOs specifically design their boards to help them build working relationships with the whole range of actors relevant to their work – a strategy which has given them a considerable edge over the other development actors with which they compete for space and financing. One NGO director described how the composition of his NGO's board had helped his organisation to develop this sort of comparative advantage:

> I think one of the most important things that has happened so far for me is that, if you see the board, [it] represents diverse interests – the commercial farmers, the farm workers, people in government, human rights activists – who might at one time or another have [had] divergent views on what was happening. [...] But I think so far we have managed to negotiate or to act as a broker between these diverse interests that are represented on the board and to try to get them to have a common view of what's happening. [... They can] now understand and appreciate and they will be in a position themselves to go back and defend, you know, our decisions to their constituents, the people who put them there. [...] Which is, I think, a source of our strength' (Interview with Director, Local NGO #11, Harare, 30 August 1999).

Yet despite the importance of leadership, a remarkably small number of the local African NGOs I encountered in the field work countries had chosen an executive board which could play an instrumental role in helping them to gain power. The majority tend to think of an executive board as a body which they have to create and call together once a year in order to satisfy government legislation governing the operation of NGOs. But the set of external conjunctures that provide a local NGO with a ready and viable development space at its inception and thus help it to achieve power are rare, and few new local NGOs in Africa are able to slide immediately into vacant development space in their country. As such, they have to create their own space: by jockeying for existing space with other NGOs and civil society organisations; by choosing to collaborate with government to gain preferential access to their space; by working to expand the existing boundaries of development space in their countries or sectors. The implementation of these strategies and the very choice of which strategy a local NGO should pursue to gain space, require critical leadership decisions to be made. It is the leadership of an individual NGO which sets the tone of the organisation, whether in terms of its programme direction, human resources policy, organisational management, financial strategy or long-term vision and it is a strong and well-connected leadership which is required by local African NGOs to capture power.

5. NGOs must increase their engagement with political aspects of development work

The first power-enhancing strategy suggested by this research was for local African NGOs to specialise in the sectors in which they have expertise, in order to create or capture maximum space and to develop their own competitive advantage. But within whatever field they choose to be active, local NGOs must also be ready to confront the underlying social and political forces that perpetuate underdevelopment, whether in terms of poor health, gender inequalities or environmental degradation. Now is a time of tremendous opportunity for NGOs to adopt such a stance – as multilateral institutions and governments around the globe commit to achieving the Millennium Development Goals and politicised issues like women's empowerment, health as a human right and access to essential medicines become critical to their achievement. Without confronting these political elements within development, local NGOs will never truly be able to change the lives of the poor and marginalised in their regions and to effect the kinds of changes on which their reputations have been based.

The political aspects of development are not only as important as direct service delivery, but are also the one aspect of development to which local NGOs are better suited than any of their competitors. Advocacy, lobbying and empowerment activities all require the kind of respect and legitimacy in the eyes of beneficiaries that international NGOs and government agencies often lack. A recent survey of over fifty INGOs working in advocacy, for example, revealed that only two had consulted with southern partners in selecting the topic for their advocacy work, and questioned the 'legitimacy [of INGOs] to claim to speak as advocates for the Southern poor' (Anderson 2000: 448). Moreover, to succeed at these activities, an organisation must not only have strong local knowledge and experience, but also the higher-level national linkages that CBOs rarely develop.

INGOs are reluctant, and CBOs ill-equipped, to undertake politicised development activities such as voter education, lobbying government for policy change, or building consumer advocacy groups to hold government accountable for high-quality social service provision. This provides an opportunity for local NGOs to create their own space no matter how small or crowded the sector or region in which they operate. Despite declining levels of aid to Central America, NGOs have been able to carve themselves a niche in countries like Guatemala and El Salvador by playing an active role in peace processes and political consensus building (Aldaba *et al.* 2000). Peter Van Tuijl has also identified two ways in which the human rights sector, as one avenue of politically engaged development, offers space to local African NGOs. Firstly, it offers NGOs space in the international development community, or, as Van Tuijl writes, 'the possibility to strategically position themselves at the crossroads of emerging transnational relationships between different actors in the state, market and civil sector' (2000: 617). Secondly, human rights offer NGOs space even in a post-aid world, for even 'in a world without aid there will still be human rights' (ibid.: 618). Many of the local African NGOs I interviewed were reluctant to increase their involvement with political aspects of development work, such as human rights advocacy or lobbying for democratisation, because few donors explicitly funded such activity. But as the example of local NGOs in Zimbabwe illustrates, donors do not necessarily shy away from funding politicised development activities, and the more 'political' NGOs in that country rarely want for donor funds. Local NGOs working on political issues within development can also find strong support from like-minded northern NGOs, whose international contacts are capable of buffering the relationship between local NGOs and their governments.

Local NGOs will encounter a range of difficulties in increasing their engagement with the relevant political issues that affect their bene-ficiaries and will have varying degrees of success in such endeavours (Mercer 2002). But building strong links, especially at a personal level, to government officials can be of considerable help in overcoming these difficulties. This is a vital lesson for local NGOs to learn. Many assume that to oppose government in a constructive way, they must abandon all links to government and talk at them from a distance. But the government is not a homogenous entity. Different levels and layers of government will respond to NGOs and civil society organisations in different and, often, contrasting ways, depending on their individual histories and experiences, as well as on the pressures they face from state and nonstate actors (Migdal 1994, Clayton 1998, Fisher 1998). The local NGOs in the case study countries which have been most successful in tackling political development issues, have recognised this reality and have worked to develop close, though never uncritical, relationships with the govern-ment bodies in their fields. To gain power, both locally and inter-nationally, more African NGOs will have to work to build strong links to their governments and to other relevant international development actors.

External strategies

6. NGOs must increase their focus on networking with other African development actors

Networking, especially with other civil society organisations, is an important strategy for acquiring power on which local African NGOs need to focus considerably more of their time and resources. Networking with other local groups in the same region or country can assist NGOs to develop a stronger voice in debates at national level, thereby helping them to gain space and security and to engage with political issues in development. CBOs in particular, highlighted as the 'most important institutions in poor people's daily lives' in a recent global survey of poor communities, will be a crucial partner for local NGOs, helping them to gain roots in remote and rural areas and adding the legitimacy of genuine grass-roots participation to their initiatives (Narayan *et al.* 2001: 219). Networking internationally, within sub-Saharan Africa or with NGOs in other parts of the developing world, can raise the profile of Southern development movements and help African NGOs to gain a larger following and build the kinds of international links to the wider development community which are critical to finding power.

Throughout the case study chapters, I have attempted to highlight the importance of networking to local African NGOs. The close horizontal ties these groups have built to like-minded organisations allow them to pool their labour to undertake large-scale initiatives and create a network of support for the lobbying and advocacy efforts of individual organisations. As networking encourages greater inter-NGO communication and division of labour, it reduces inter-NGO competition for space and financing. In addition, networking also actually creates new development space. By increasing the visibility of local NGOs, and allowing them to tackle as a group issues that would have been dangerous for them to broach as individual organisations, networking helps to change national perceptions of the realms in which development organisations and developmental approaches are relevant. As such, networking changes both the composition and the frontiers of development space in favour of local NGOs.

Increasingly, the local African NGOs that I encountered were seeking to reconceive the traditional boundaries of development space: to erase the line between the development issue and the social issue, the economic issue or the political issue. They are no longer content to accept the definition of development offered to them by the North, or by their national or regional power structures in the South. Where northern development agencies want to see local NGOs primarily concerned with grass-roots empowerment, local NGOs are increasingly pushing to have a voice in international debates over environmental policy, trade agreements and structural adjustment. And where many African governments would like to see the role of local NGOs confined to complementing, or supplementing, government provision of social services, local NGOs are fighting for their place in debates on land reform, constitutional change and human rights.

By working together, these are goals that local African NGOs can achieve. The gender budget initiative discussed in Chapter Four is one significant example of how networking can expand NGO development space. Working together, local Tanzanian NGOs convinced the government to consider the gender implications of the national accounts and in doing so, changed the government's perception of its budgeting process as lying outside of the development space of local NGOs. Henceforth, the government's creation of a national budget will be one process in which local NGOs are invited to take part and are assumed to have a substantial contribution to make. A study of the policy influence of environmental

NGOs in Botswana, Nigeria and Zimbabwe showed collaboration and networking to be equally important to groups in this sector, concluding that most successful environmental policy campaigns involved the presence of 'several NGOs playing complementary roles' (Thomas *et al.* 2001: 183). While the space doesn't exist here to detail the potential contribution of NGO networking to building social capital in African countries, these examples illustrate that by building strong networks, NGOs will be able to translate their social capital into political capital.

The importance of networking to NGO power highlights why NGO umbrella or co-ordinating bodies are so significant to their members. As the primary means of facilitating regular communication between NGOs, these groups play a key role in encouraging networking. The case study on Senegal highlighted CONGAD's success in facilitating networking and in providing direct services to its member organisations. In the context of the present discussion, however, an even greater benefit of NGO co-ordinating bodies could be their ability to unite individual NGO voices to challenge the accepted boundaries of NGO space and, in so doing, to help these groups to seize power. Many of the other roles of NGO umbrellas, such as running training sessions and administering resource centres, can be played by multilateral institutions, international NGOs, and other development actors. Co-ordinating local NGO activity in sectors not traditionally considered part of their development space and drumming up public support for these moves, however, are essential roles that few development actors are better placed to play than NGO umbrella bodies.

One final way I would like to suggest for strong NGO or civil society networks to help African NGOs to gain power is through the development of a branding or 'seal of approval' programme. At the national or regional level, networks could highlight and elevate especially effective and well managed NGOs by issuing them with a network seal of approval, much like earning a fair-trade designation or Michelin star. Such a system would bring worthy local NGOs to the attention of operational partners, funding sources and media organisations, both local and international, and help such chosen NGOs to develop their international profile. At present, donors are often more likely to fund INGOs as project partners because of the difficulty of vetting local NGO alternatives. But such a system, independently run, could function as a minimum guarantee of successful programming and sound organisational practices, thereby reducing the informational asymmetries that a donor might currently face. Such a programme could later be expanded to the whole continent, so that all NGOs could strive towards the achievement of seals of approval on both national and Africa-wide bases.

7. NGOs must pursue stronger links with Northern NGOs
While much is currently written of the increasing support given to local NGOs in developing countries by international NGOs, the experiences of NGOs in the African case study countries provide little evidence of this

trend. For many local NGOs, collaboration with their operational INGO counterparts is as rare as ever, while competition with them for funds, space and opportunities is on the rise. In this context, local NGOs are increasingly turning to non-operational northern NGOs for funding, institutional support and contacts in the North. According to the local NGOs I interviewed, these relationships often come closest to being true partnerships, as many NNGOs treat local NGOs as equals in a reciprocal relationship. Unlike INGOs, these groups do not have operational programmes of their own in Africa, and must depend on the expertise of their local NGO partners to be involved in development on the continent.

Building strong horizontal partnerships with like-minded northern NGOs abroad provides three main benefits to indigenous African NGOs. The first is funding. By building funding relationships with northern bodies that lack a local presence, local NGOs do not have to compete with the other actors in their immediate environment for funding. These NNGO funders are unlikely to have more than one local partner in a particular country, or to spend much time considering the option of funding an NGO's competitor organisations, as most donor agencies would do. Moreover, they are often also willing to fund an NGO's core, or organisational costs. Local NGOs in Tanzania receive such funding from their northern partners, as well as assistance in making capital purchases for their organisations. This significantly improves their potential to generate their own revenue in the future.

The second benefit of receiving financial support from NNGOs abroad is that they offer local NGOs the opportunity for publicity, especially in international circles. This publicity is difficult to gain on the local scene because of the number of other development actors present and the limited number of local opportunities for publicity. Foreign NGOs, on the other hand, can act as a mouthpiece in the North for their local partners in Africa and, because of their small number of partners world-wide, can devote considerable time to acting as an advocate for each of the local partners they do have. Looking to NNGOs for publicity was a strategy commonly employed by local NGOs in Tanzania and Senegal, especially in sectors such as environmental protection, where mass international support was critical to the success of individual projects. The publicity that their northern partners generate can also help African NGOs to expand their operations northwards, and create offices focussed on fundraising and development education in the North. Strong international African groups, like AMREF and ENDA, have reversed the trend of northern organisations working in the South by creating their own offices in North America and Europe. Northern NGOs can help to facilitate such a trend among local African NGOs.

Like-minded, non-resident NNGOs also offer their local partners non-financial support, including opportunities for further education or training in their home country, support to attend international conferences and workshops, vehicles for local NGOs to publish the results of their work and the chance to participate in international fora and campaigns on issues which affect their beneficiaries. Most critically perhaps, these links help local NGOs to gain rapid international support for their initiatives and to shield themselves from government reprisals during situations of conflict. Many local NGOs, especially in Zimbabwe and Tanzania, described to me how their northern contacts had benefited them in such situations. As access to the internet and to computer technology increases in sub-Saharan Africa, the ability of local African NGOs to build power-enhancing links to northern NGO partners should improve, as they become able to establish regular contact with a wide range of development actors throughout the world.

8. NGOs must pursue stronger links with private-sector organisations
Several international NGOs have long enjoyed strong partnerships with the private sector. Many of the world's largest and wealthiest corporations are involved in philanthropy, and many even have their own branded foundations. While their charitable aims are diverse, many of the giving programmes of these businesses, whether international financial corporations, automobile manufacturers or soft-drink giants, target international development in some way and, accordingly, have benefited many NGOs in the North (Heap 1998, Heap 2000, Henderson 2000). But while corporate donations to INGOs in their home countries are tax-deductible and impress northern consumers, their support of little-known foreign groups does not necessarily provide similar benefits. The impact of private sector philanthropy on local African NGOs has been minimal, and only a handful of the indigenous NGOs I encountered had received support from such international organisations. In the majority of cases, this support was limited to one-time, in-kind product donations.

Links between local African NGOs and local private sector enterprises have been similarly weak. In countries like Tanzania, where economic liberalisation is little more than a decade old and the majority of local businesses are still relatively small and fragile, this trend is easy to understand and is likely to change as the private sector gains strength. In other countries like Zimbabwe, for instance, embryonic NGO–private sector partnerships are already in place. Whether with goods manufacturers or service providers, these partnerships have been crucial to the NGOs involved, and have helped them to gain several of the elements of power. First, NGOs can learn a tremendous amount about organisational and human resource development from their private sector partners – who invest considerable attention and resources in these areas. Businesses often have expertise in everything from financial management to leadership training to strategies for innovation and risk-taking – all of which can be useful to local NGOs in creating and maintaining space.

Second, the funding offered by private sector businesses has helped local NGOs to develop greater financial independence from their donors. Funding from corporate sources tends to be targeted at NGOs' existing areas of expertise; unlike much donor financing, it helps local NGOs to develop an increased competitive advantage within their particular field. In many instances, such partnerships have also offered local NGOs opportunities to generate revenue internally, by doing research or consulting contracts for their partners in banking, agriculture and heavy industry. As the processes of globalisation have increased the political space available to local African NGOs from that contained within a single sovereign state to opportunity 'whose only limit is the globe', partnerships with private sector enterprises have also become important in helping local NGOs to increase their links to the wider international business and development communities (Jarvis and Paolini 1995: 15). To the present, organisations across sub-Saharan Africa have tended to 'remain on the periphery' of these integrated global networks (Alonso 2000: 349). Yet private sector companies are quick to publicise the public service work that they do, and as they publicise their programme of giving, the partners they support also get free publicity. Multinational corporations often have powerful voices across the global marketplace and their support for local NGOs in Africa can considerably improve the international reputation and standing of their local-NGO partners.

While many NGOs and observers might fear that collaborating with private sector interests will compromise their developmental and anti-poverty agenda, carefully chosen partnerships – in which both the business and the NGOs bring something to the table – do not have to compromise either partner. Simon Heap, who has written extensively on the business–NGO relationships and the conditions under which they are most successful, writes: 'NGOs should not be endorsing companies, but engaging with them critically … some of the most successful partnerships will be formed by partners who constructively disagree with each other' (2000: 11).

Building strong ties to national and international private sector groups and convincing them to participate in the funding of development activities will not be easy for all African NGOs. For many groups it will be difficult to find private enterprises with which they feel an ideological connection, and whose business practices and profit-making strategies they are able to respect. While NGOs working in fields like agriculture, health care and environmental management may be able to find natural partnerships with businesses in their fields, their counterparts working in education or human rights, for example, will have fewer such opportunities (Puplampu and Tettey 2000). Similarly, NGOs in countries with a strong socialist history might find few current opportunities to work in collaboration with the small and relatively modest business sector in their country. But as the strength and numbers of these local businesses increase, as greater numbers of international corporations begin operations in Africa and as the northern ethos of 'trade, not aid' gathers steam, local NGOs will need to create opportunities to work with such organisations. IBASE in Brazil, for example, has cultivated a strong partnership with American Express, and counts both the Brazilian oil company and energy company as among its financial supporters (IBASE 1999).

9. NGOs must participate in international development conferences and international development forums

As creating strong links to the international development community is one of the key elements of NGO power, more local NGOs in Africa need to invest in becoming a part of that wider development community. Building relationships to their operational NGO counterparts in other developing countries as well as to the range of important development actors in the North can be difficult for many African NGOs, which have no budget for international travel and limited access to the communications infrastructure that organisations in the North take for granted. But as many of the local NGOs I met across the case study countries have discovered, the circuit of international development conferences, such as those run under the auspices of the United Nations, have been important global events which have created development space and expanded it proportionally towards local NGOs.

For example, in 1992 and 1995 respectively, the Rio UN World Conference on the Environment and Development and the Beijing UN World Conference on Women redefined the issues in those sectors which would henceforth be considered a part of development space (Howard and Allen 1996, Van Rooy 1997, Tandon 2000). Both of these conferences are widely recognised as having provided a major impetus to local NGO activity in Africa, a belief that was shared by the local African NGOs in my survey (TGNP 1997, Abdallah and Kasse 1999). To many NGOs, the recommendations coming out of the conferences had increased development space in their countries, and their very inclusion at the international table had helped them to gain an increasing proportion of that space (Mathews 1997). The networking, international links and experience gained during such conferences have also been invaluable to African NGOs, which were able to parlay these links into greater international support and publicity for their work and to consulting and research opportunities with international development groups eager to learn more about their countries. Moreover, while few local NGOs can afford to attend meetings abroad, opportunities are created and funding is set aside specifically to facilitate the attendance of southern NGOs at these meetings. So while international development conferences are often considered as little more than a holiday by northern development actors, they can play a critical role in helping local NGOs in Africa to gain power. Accordingly, the local NGOs I encountered had two pieces of advice for their counterparts in other African countries: find out about these conferences and find a way to attend them.

This analysis has offered several policy prescriptions for local African NGOs to develop power:

- specialise in the fields in which you have the greatest experience and expertise, and do not deviate from them
- invest in your own organisational development
- work to develop not only financial security, but also financial independence from donors
- choose your leadership strategically
- engage wherever possible with the political development issues within your field
- focus on networking with other like-minded local NGOs
- explore the potential benefits of creating partnerships with northern NGOs and private sector organisations
- start building local and international contacts right away, as they will be instrumental in helping you to develop an international reputation.

While all of these recommendations are based on the strategies which have helped local NGOs in the case study countries to develop elements of power, many of them are not revolutionary. Many local African NGOs are working to increase their financial self-sufficiency, for example, and to incorporate political aspects of development into their work. Pursued together, however, this set of internal and external strategies should help improve the access of local African NGOs to power and to improve the sustainability of development activities across Africa.

What strategies should donors, governments and other interested actors pursue in order to support the development of powerful African NGOs?

While local African NGOs must rethink many of their current strategies in order to become powerful, their power is also dependent on the practices and activities of a number of external actors. The policies and practices of many of the international NGOs, governments and donor agencies at work in sub-Saharan Africa have been responsible for hindering local African development NGOs in their search for power. They, therefore, have a major role to play in supporting the development of powerful African NGOs. And, as NGO power aids NGO sustainability and service to beneficiary groups, the emergence of powerful African NGOs is a good that a number of other external actors will want to work towards. Based on the experiences of local African NGOs in the case study countries, governments, donors, international NGOs and the media all have a role to play in assisting NGOs in Africa to gain power.

Government

10. African governments should investigate ways to influence local NGOs constructively
It is clear that certain African governments do not currently want to help

local NGOs in their countries to gain power. Afraid of relinquishing political space or political power to civil society, they have actively worked to hinder the operations of certain NGOs in their countries and to destroy others. This is not true of all governments on the continent, however. Many have moved from repressing NGO activity to contracting development work to NGOs, or co-operating with them on isolated initiatives. Still others, like the government of Senegal, now regularly work in collaboration with NGOs. Aided by close ties between their personnel and NGO workers, these governments hire NGOs to undertake small development projects, provide them with seats on government committees, meet regularly with the national NGO-co-ordinating body and allow them to participate in registering new NGOs (van Klinken 1998). But while this relationship has not been wholly negative, for many Senegalese NGOs, government has not been a very positive influence on their work either. This NGO director highlighted the distinction as he saw it:

> Here in Senegal, [government support] will be the next battle for NGOs. Because the state here doesn't subsidise NGOs in a direct manner, but in an indirect manner. [...] If we want to buy computers or a vehicle, then there is a concession. But that's it. (Interview with President, Local NGO #47, Dakar, 15 February 2000)

Other NGOs I encountered in Senegal pointed to the government's tendency to ignore local NGOs when choosing partners for its national development programmes, preferring, within the field of youth training for example, to subsidise sporting associations over NGOs. Still others found it difficult to be called in by government to 'participate' in planning and implementing government projects, without receiving any financial recompense for that time and effort. So while the attitude of national government in Senegal towards its local NGOs is hardly hostile, these examples illustrate that neither is it as supportive or enabling as NGOs themselves would like.

Many African governments are experiencing a financial crisis and lack the money with which to fund local NGOs directly in their countries. But there are still resources and opportunities that they can offer local NGOs, if they have an interest in seeing the best among them develop power, sustainability and an increased ability to serve the needs of the poor and marginalised in the country. One such opportunity is providing local NGOs with access to rural government workers. These associations have been invaluable to a handful of local NGOs in Zimbabwe, who looked to knowledgeable and experienced government extension workers for input on the local context when planning their projects. Once projects were running, many NGOs relied on these government workers to make regular reports on progress, and to conduct follow-up visits whenever necessary. This reduced the need for local NGO staff to travel to remote project areas and reduced the cost of running projects, both in terms of financial and human resources.

A second way in which African governments can help their local

NGOs to gain power, is by helping them to gain space and links to the international development community through publicity. Government ministries, departments and agencies have contacts on the continent and across the globe, and opportunities to publicise the work that they do in the local media, official reports and parliament; as such, they have many occasions to vocalise their support for outstanding local NGOs. Endorsing local NGOs in this way is not difficult for government to do; it costs them nothing financially to voice their appreciation of NGOs which have made a considerable impact in national development or have assisted the government in some way. Yet such endorsements can do wonders for the power of individual NGOs and for the relationship between government and the NGO sector overall.

Lastly, local NGOs are among the most highly skilled and experienced development actors within their fields in Africa. In order to help them to gain power, their governments must begin to treat them like the experts that they are. Governments often require external expertise to train government employees, undertake research contracts and oversee, monitor or evaluate government development projects. Yet many prefer to hire consultants from abroad, rather than engage qualified local NGOs which can offer the same services, usually at a lower price. By patronising local NGOs, where they offer the same standards of service as foreign consultants, African governments will contribute to the financial independence of these NGOs and, in the process, promote a more harmonious relationship between state and civil society actors within development. The home governments of international NGOs have long offered a whole range of incentives to the NGOs in their countries, whether in terms of direct financial subsidies, tax concessions or work opportunities. Governments in Africa interested in helping local NGOs in their countries to develop power, must now learn from this example, and investigate the many ways in which they can be a positive influence on their home-grown NGOs.

Donor agencies

11. Donors should create pools of funding exclusively for local NGOs
Throughout the case studies we saw that many donors consider local NGOs and their operational INGO counterparts as roughly substitutable, and fund both groups out of the same pool of financing. The USAID NGO Support Project discussed in Chapter 5, for example, did not discriminate in its grants between Senegalese and American NGOs. And while foreign NGOs might be expected to amass their funding from their home governments or from donating publics in their home countries, many apply for funds from local donor agencies in direct competition with local NGOs (Wallace 2003). For a long time, development practitioners have accepted that operational international NGOs attract personnel away from their local counterparts. But as the examples of local NGOs in the case study countries illustrate, since many donors do not earmark funds for local

NGOs in particular, INGOs also attract funds away from African NGOs. The experiences of several local NGOs in Tanzania will illustrate this point. Here, local NGOs are continually compared to INGOs, and despite the ready availability of donor funds, lose out on funding because of the way they compare. Many of the donors I interviewed in Tanzania thought of local NGOs as lower-skilled and lower-capacity versions of their international counterparts. As such, these donors choose to channel the bulk of their funding and contract opportunities into INGOs and largely ignore the majority of local NGOs.

Should donors be forced to fund local NGOs in which they have little or no confidence? Surely not. But what the current situation illustrates is that few local NGOs will ever achieve donor confidence if donors fail to take a chance on them or to provide them with exclusive channels of funding. The ultimate value of local NGOs lies not only in the immediate development services that they provide, but also in their long-term contribution to civil society growth and development. International NGOs may be sustainable in the short term, where they do not require core funding from donors, but in the long run they are unlikely to be as culturally sustainable as their local counterparts. By creating special channels of funding for local African NGOs, donors can help local NGOs to access regular funding and to benefit from the other important aspects of donor support: close and regular contact, opportunities to meet other development actors, and long-term commitment. As many of the NGO directors interviewed in the case study chapters suggested, these resources can often be as important as financial support.

12. Donors should widen the range of support that they offer local NGOs
While no two donor agencies working in Africa conduct their business in the same way and certain donor agencies enjoy better relationships and reputations with local NGOs, donor approaches to funding NGOs are nonetheless fairly consistent. These approaches tend to be fixed and based on foreign procedures and norms of accountability. To encourage power among their local NGOs partners, donor agencies have to make an effort to modify their approaches, expanding their notions of what they will and will not fund, and how this funding should be dispensed. They must also begin to accept 'mutual responsibility' for the performance of the local NGOs they support and recognise that their policies and procedures can have as great an impact on NGO success as the efforts of local NGOs themselves (Fowler 2000a: 3). As Howell and Pearce write: 'Donors need to recognize their own role as actors in the drama of civil society. They are not neutral players' (2001: 234). Based on the positive and negative experiences of local NGOs in the case study countries with their donors, I believe that there are several ways in which donors need to reconceive of NGO funding, NGO funding contracts and 'partnership' in order to help the local NGOs they work with to develop power.

The greatest financial difficulty that local NGOs in the case study countries described to me was that of finding donor funding for their core or overhead expenses. In Rick James' (1994) survey of over a hundred northern NGOs and development agencies from North America and Europe, 85 per cent of respondents claimed to provide core funding support to local partners. This professed commitment of northern groups to fund the institutional development of their local partners is at odds with the practices of the international NGOs and donors agencies I met in Zimbabwe, Tanzania and Senegal, and with the experience of local African NGOs in those countries. Whether in terms of salaries, rents or investments, donor agencies working in Africa are reluctant to fund core NGO expenses.

This has had serious repercussions for the power that local NGOs are able to wield. Unable to pay the salaries required to attract qualified, full-time staff, many African NGOs must make do with part-time volunteers. International NGOs, multilateral institutions like the UN and World Bank, and donor agencies, meanwhile, attract the best qualified and most experienced individuals, often making little use of their skills and placing them in support positions which require little expertise (Mukasa 1999). Without an ability to develop a cadre of well-trained and experienced staff members, capable of being groomed for leadership positions, local NGOs have little chance of gaining power.

Without support for their overhead expenditures, local NGOs will also continue to find it difficult to expand and improve their programming. They will be unable to invest heavily in undertaking research and building organisational capacity, elements that fall outside of the purview of pure project expenses, to take risks and experiment with their projects, and to spend more time closely and carefully developing projects with their intended beneficiaries. Unfortunately, as Fowler writes, 'because overheads must be kept low, learning is the easiest budget line to cut – no one will miss it anyway' (2000c: 136).

In the absence of core funds, local NGOs will also have a difficult time finding the capital necessary to invest in opportunities for internal revenue generation. As we saw in the last chapter, many donors are more than happy to provide monies for NGOs to rent office space from which to run their projects, but are unwilling to provide a lump-sum payment which would allow the same NGOs to buy, or save for the purchase of, property that could provide office space as well as rental income. Local African NGOs have devised a range of ways to generate their own income, but the majority of these initiatives, whether based on marketing beneficiary products, undertaking short-term contracts for training, research or other consultancies, or renting out office space or facilities, all require some initial injection of funds in order to be successful. The majority of donor organisations generate overhead expenditures of their own, and seek to recoup these expenses in their contracts with their own funders.[1]

---

[1] In Canada, for instance, registered charities, including those which fund local development organisations in the South, are allowed to spend up to 20 per cent of the funding they receive for their overhead expenditures.

If these same donor agencies could agree to pay a set percentage for over-head on the projects they support – thereby funding not just the minimum number of expenses associated with running projects, but also the core expenses which help organisations to grow and flourish – they would play a major role in helping their partners to improve their power.

The second way in which donor organisations need to expand the support they offer local NGOs is by extending the length of their funding contracts. In other words, donor agencies must diverge from conventional wisdom and begin to consider local NGO funding a long-term investment. Many donors seem to want to wait until a local NGO can prove that it is sustainable before they will fund it. But as this research has shown, the more power an African NGO has, the more sustainable it is likely to be. So donors who want to work with sustainable local NGOs must first help these local NGOs to achieve space, financial independence, international links and a political profile. This means channelling a significant propor-tion of their funds to local NGOs even where well-resourced INGOs seem more efficient in the short term, and continuing to provide this support over five or ten years, as the NGOs grow and evolve. For as discussed in the last chapter, many NGOs which seem financially secure in the short-term, and therefore the most likely to receive funding by current donor reasoning, are in fact, the least likely to achieve internal sustainability and to provide long-term benefits to the individuals and communities with which they work. Reconceiving of funding as a long-term commit-ment, to a smaller number of groups than at present if necessary is, therefore, a second way in which donor agencies can help African NGOs to develop power.

In order to help their local partners gain power, donor agencies can also increase the non-financial capacity-building support that they offer to African NGOs. While donor support to local NGOs is often conceived of solely in terms of funding, the preferred partners of the majority of the local NGOs I interviewed in Zimbabwe, Tanzania and Senegal were not necessarily the ones which gave them the most money. Often they were the ones who offered their partners the most flexible funding or the best opportunities for NGO development and capacity building. NGOs I encountered had benefited from a range of capacity-building oppor-tunities, from management skills courses to further training in their field to chances to learn about new approaches to working with beneficiaries. Helping local NGOs to develop power is not solely about giving them more funds; by helping local NGOs to sharpen their skills, organisational vision and strategic planning, donor agencies can contribute to improving the power which local African NGOs are able to capture. Mutual capacity building, which prioritises a two-way exchange of skills and capacities between local NGOs and donors can be especially important in this regard (Roland and Omar 2001).

However, within the realm of 'capacity building' donors must be careful to investigate fully the needs of their partner NGOs. Experience illustrates that successful capacity-building interventions are driven by the needs of the recipient organisation (James 2001). No single approach to capacity building or organisational development will suffice for all NGOs or local partners; experienced and well-established NGOs are unlikely to require the same amount of skills training and structural support that one of their newer counterparts would benefit from (Kaplan 2000). Moreover, donors must recognise that they are often not the most appropriate provider of capacity-building services for their partners, whether because of their lack of local experience, their lack of neutrality or their influence – and that playing such a role can actually undermine the power of the partner organisations they are seeking to help (James 1998).

Donors must also offer local NGOs the training, networking and development opportunities that they require and that will benefit their beneficiaries – and not just provide them with opportunities to learn the skills, practices, and discourse that donors deem relevant or that would make the lives of donor officials easier (Sahley 1995, Eade 1997, Lewis 1998, James 2001, Townsend *et al.* 2002). The capacity-building opportunities currently offered by donors tend to fall into this second category and Wallace writes, 'most training in capacity building provided at present is logframe or financially-based – a very narrow definition of capacity building' (2002: 237–8). Moreover, with nine out of ten INGO respondents to a recent survey currently involved in capacity-building with their local partners, inappropriately designed and targeted capacity-building interventions will quickly lead to capacity-building fatigue within local NGOs (James 2001).

Finally, donors need to expand the support that they offer to NGOs in Africa to include funding to encourage NGO networking, whether as part of their capacity-building support or as a separate area of focus. Throughout the case study chapters, networking played a crucial role in helping local NGOs to create space, strong links to the international community, and support for the political elements of their work. Yet regular networking with organisations outside of urban centres can be a costly venture in many African countries where travel and communications infrastructures are poor across much of the nation; without the extra funds to invest in such activities, most local NGOs restrict their networking activities to other organisations within their immediate vicinity. This can limit the voice of NGOs in national-level debates and contributes to the image of local NGOs as unable to organise themselves into an established network able to react quickly and in co-ordination to development issues.

To encourage increased networking among African NGOs and strong and viable NGO networks, donor agencies will also have to address the needs of NGO co-ordinating bodies across the continent. Co-ordinating bodies can play a key role in organising NGO networks and in ensuring the development of these important resources. CONGAD's success in playing this role in Senegal is unusual, however; neither its counterparts in Zimbabwe and Tanzania, nor in countries like Malawi and Ghana, have made similar achievements (Simukonda 1992, Oquaye 1996, Lawson 2000). This pattern seems to predominate throughout the continent. With increased funds from donors, however, NGO co-ordinating bodies across Africa can seek to redress this imbalance, supporting increased networking among their member organisations, working with them to develop a strong and united national-level voice in lobbying and advocacy work and helping local NGOs to translate this into increased power.

To be powerful, sustainable, and even just successful at what they do, local NGOs in Africa need to be able to generate their own income, conduct relevant research, build an experienced cadre of staff and work in concert with other development actors. Donor agencies working with local African NGOs will, therefore, have to reconsider the ways in which they currently support these local groups, beginning, instead, to offer funding for overheads, to provide longer-term funding contracts and to provide funding for both capacity building and networking. Increased co-ordination among donors as they adopt these changes will add to the efficiency of funding transfers and reduce the toll of donor-specific planning, reporting and evaluating demands on NGOs (Lewis and Sobhan 1999). Finally, and perhaps most importantly, donors will need to determine and commit to their own individual notion of partnership, based on the principles of common goals, mutual resource exchange and power sharing.

13. Donors should work to help local NGOs gain space *vis-à-vis* government
In addition to the ways in which donor agencies can use their direct financial and institutional support to help local African NGOs to gain power, they can also use their influence to assist NGOs in gaining space in development. Space is a key element of NGO power, and one that many African NGOs have had difficulty attaining as the governments in their countries have attempted to monopolise it. But as the Zimbabwean case study illustrated, donors have the ability to change the existing division of space between government bodies and civil society organisations.

The impact of donor agencies on the space available to local African NGOs has increased in recent years. As the financial health of many African countries has worsened and foreign aid has become more significant to them, the fates of African states have become increasingly tied to their donors. As the old adage goes, he who pays the piper calls the tune, and in many countries, it is donor governments and international financial institutions choosing the music to which African governments will dance. While this trend may rightfully cause concern for the national development paths of many African states, with donor interest in democratisation and pluralism it has, nonetheless, increased the development space available to local African NGOs in their countries (Hearn

2000, Goldsmith 2001). Donors now have the influence to 'encourage' governments to include local NGOs in donor-financed projects and to collaborate with a range of civil society groups when planning and executing larger development programmes. This is an increasingly common phenomenon across Africa and one which has seen the distribution of space between local NGOs and government change in favour of the NGOs.

Moreover, the decentralisation of government and scaling back of social spending advocated by the international financial institutions and large aid-donor organisations has created additional space for local NGOs, and made them key figures in a wide range of local development activities. They have now, for instance, become major providers of social and natural resource management services in local communities in Senegal, and the focal point for community development activities within these areas (CONGAD 1997, Ndiaye 1999, Roberts 2000). Donor agencies also have the ability to encourage local NGOs to branch into new areas of development. In Zimbabwe, for example, donor mistrust and lack of confidence in national government resulted in a widening of development space in that country. As local NGOs received both moral and financial support from donors, they were able to extend their work to include political development activity. Not long ago, or in other countries, issues such as constitutional reform and land redistribution would rarely have fallen within NGO space. But with the support of donors interested in good governance and democratisation, local NGOs have gained access to development space that was once the sole province of the state and its development programmes.

International NGOs (INGOs)

14. International NGOs in Africa should reconsider their operational mandates
International NGOs have provided regular, and in many cases, serious, competition to local NGOs in Africa. As a result of this competition, many local NGOs have been unable to find the space, financial support, and links to the international development community that could help them to develop power. International NGOs have been a consistent and valued presence on the continent and have been responsible for much of the relief and development work that takes place today. Yet, as the numbers of local organisations created to deal with these same development issues are rising, perhaps it is time for international NGOs to reconsider the operational roles that the majority of them currently play and to investigate the alternative roles in development to which they are best suited and from which beneficiaries will derive the greatest value. The previous UK Minister responsible for international development echoed this sentiment in a 1999 speech:

> [The] most pressing challenge for international NGOs is to give greater focus in their work within developing countries to ways of genuinely

empowering the poor – and to acknowledge, as must governments – that the role of external players should be a transitional one. The ultimate aim of all of us – development departments and international development NGOs – should be to make ourselves redundant and success should be measured by how soon we leave, not how long we stay. (Speech by the Rt. Hon. Clare Short MP, 13 January 1999)

Providing support to local NGOs is the role that the African NGOs I interviewed would most like to see their international counterparts play. It is a role that is in considerable demand across the continent. As Fowler *et al.* (1992: 27) wrote, 'There is a recognised gap in the market for support services that operate at the strategic and institutional levels of African NGO need.' In Senegal, I encountered several INGOs that existed solely to support local NGOs. One of the more remarkable, within the field of HIV/AIDS issues, worked to create networks of AIDS organisations across the country, to train people working in the field about the latest developments in AIDS research, treatment and awareness, to develop teaching materials which local NGOs could use to educate people about AIDS, and to distribute teaching aids with the technology required by NGOs to use them in the field. It was a strong and well-respected organisation, able to fill a real need within the local NGO sector and able to find steady donor funding for its activities despite its non-operational mandate. In other countries, like Tanzania, however, few such INGOs exist.

Other local NGO directors I met wanted to see their international counterparts act as more aggressive advocates for African development in the parliaments, media and universities of their home countries. This is a redefinition of their role that would provide INGOs with many new occupations, and their local counterparts with many new opportunities. Decreasing their immediate operations on the ground in the South, for example, would allow INGOs to increase their commitment to development education in the North and to 'facilitate and enable much more direct advocacy and lobbying by SNGOs in Washington DC, Brussels and other traditional Northern centres of power' (Malhotra 2000: 663).

Even if, in evaluating the future of their work, INGOs in Africa decide that they do possess a considerable competitive advantage over their local counterparts, and, as such, should continue to pursue operational mandates, they must nonetheless consider the ways in which they work. Where possible, they should work in partnership with local NGOs in their fields to help develop their capacity, to ensure that a local group will be able to continue to support INGO projects once the international groups move on, and to fulfil the commitment to 'partnership' with local African groups on which they raise considerable amounts of funds in the North. Moreover, in localities in which local NGOs are already at work, INGOs must refrain from offering financial and other incentives in order to secure the participation of these communities on INGO projects and initiatives. Building trust between local and international NGOs will be a first step to healthy dialogue on the division of labour between them, and to helping local NGOs to gain greater space and funds for their work in Africa.

The media

15. Media organisations should increase their coverage of NGO activities
The power of the media in Africa is well-recognised, and it is the media which in many ways controls general perceptions of how large the development space in a country should be (Alexander and McGregor 1999, Tettey 2001). By covering development issues and the activities of local NGOs, the media helps to increase citizens' exposure to local NGOs, helping these organisations to raise their profile locally, and to gain a greater proportion of the space available for development. In Tanzania, for example, the strong partnership between the media and local NGOs has helped local NGOs to extend their reach to communities they cannot reach in conventional ways and to address developmental issues, such as women's legal rights, which they might never have been invited into communities to tackle. In other contexts, it is the media itself which defines the limits of development space, deciding the appropriate level of NGO involvement in various issues and the appropriate issues for NGO involvement in the first place. The media also plays a crucial role in exposing the corruption and unethical practices which can influence government's relationships with NGOs (Makumbe 2000). Local African media support for NGO involvement in key political issues in development can therefore be critical to NGOs gaining approval for such ventures.

Northern media organisations have a similarly significant role to play in helping African NGOs to expand their development space. They have helped local NGOs to make connections with like-minded groups around the globe and to survive the potentially serious consequences of involvement in political debates. Their support for the campaign by Tanzanian NGOs against the creation of a prawn processing plant in the Rufiji delta was critical in attracting northern environmental groups and government agencies to the cause, and in halting the planned project. In Zimbabwe, the support that local NGOs and other civil society actors have received from the international media has brought them support in their clashes with government and a measure of security in these conflicts. Knowing that powerful international groups are interested in local NGOs, has almost certainly encouraged the government of Zimbabwe to refrain from openly retaliating against local NGOs that speak out against them. Northern media groups can also help local African NGOs to gain space by using their expertise to propose new conceptions of where the boundaries of development space should fall and to encourage their governments and other development actors in their countries to respect those new boundaries. As strong historic supporters of NGO movements, international media organisations and their local counterparts in Africa should now embrace the potential they have to assist indigenous African NGOs in gaining the elements of power which have eluded them for so long.

A number of external actors have key roles to play in helping African NGOs to gain power. Donor agencies, among the strongest supporters of local NGOs on the continent, need to devote resources exclusively to local NGOs, widen the breadth of the funding that they currently provide to these groups and use their influence where necessary to encourage governments to include local NGOs in their development programmes. Governments themselves also need to investigate the policies they can adopt in order to turn their largely neutral attitude towards local NGOs in their countries into a positive one. The competition that international NGOs provide to their local NGO counterparts suggests that these groups need to begin to refocus their attention on the local NGO support roles that they can play and that many observers see as their future niche in the developing world. Finally, media organisations, already such valued partners for local NGOs in the case study countries, can continue to exert their influence in the international development community to help African NGOs gain additional space, partners and attention. If, as local NGOs are working on strategies to increase their power, committed groups within these categories of development actors can also adopt the strategies suggested to them here, many of the best and brightest local NGOs in Africa should begin to achieve the power that their fellow NGOs in Asia and Latin America now wield.

Implications for African development

This is not an exhaustive list of either the strategies that local NGOs can pursue in order to gain power, or of the ways in which interested observers can encourage such a trend. Rather, it is a small collection of policies and practices, general enough to be of use to NGOs throughout sub-Saharan Africa, which can help local NGOs to develop elements of power. The primary lesson for local NGOs to be taken from this research and from the strategies it suggests is that power is not something that all hard-working, experienced and relevant groups will achieve by keeping their noses to the grindstone and getting on with their work. To gain power, an NGO must actively seek space, financial independence from donors, links to the international development community and an engagement with the political aspects of development work. Power is not granted by some external actor, and the only way to gain power is to create it and preserve it yourself. NGOs do not have to undertake this struggle alone, however, and their supporters, whether other local development groups, donor agencies, governments, international and northern NGOs, private sector businesses and the media, can all play significant roles in helping them to achieve power.

Not all of the strategies recommended here are easy to adopt or to implement. Many local African NGOs, for example, are financially unable to undertake research programmes or to attend international colloquia and conferences. For others, undertaking publicity and drawing attention to their work goes against the spirit of voluntarism and charity that lies at the heart of their enterprise. And these are understandable hurdles. But if these groups recognise the ways in which their lack of power is currently undermining development in Africa, and the extent to which their ability to wield power could improve their relevance and sustainability, then they will need to re-evaluate their priorities. I am not suggesting here that local NGOs forsake their development programming in order to spend time and money building up their organisations; rather, I want indigenous NGOs to be aware of the trade-offs that exist in each programming, allocative or organisational decision they make, and the externalities that different options carry with them.

For example, an awareness of the importance of international links and an international reputation – as demonstrated by SEWA, Proshika and DESCO, as well as by local African NGOs in all three case study countries – should encourage local NGOs to overcome the reservations they have over increasing their international ties, and to identify the increasing accessibility of internet technology on the continent as one means of making this increased level of contact with international development actors possible. An appreciation for how making similar efforts – to create space for increased development activity, financial opportunities, and ways to engage with political issues within development – can improve an NGO's power should also encourage local African NGOs to consider, perhaps for the first time, how to address these considerations strategically in their day-to-day activities. For with power, local African NGOs will be able to be more innovative and creative, take more risks and experiments in their programming, invest heavily in research and in building organisational capacity, and spend more time closely and carefully developing projects with their intended beneficiaries. With power, local NGOs can advance a longer-term and more sustainable approach to development across Africa.

Donors, governments and the other groups who work with local African NGOs must also rethink their role in supporting indigenous NGOs in Africa. This study has suggested that a fundamental challenge facing these NGOs is gaining power. In identifying the factors that have prevented the emergence of powerful NGOs across the continent, it will help development agencies to target their institutional and capacity-building support to NGOs and to focus their policy-level lobbying and advocacy on behalf of local NGOs. Implicit in the suggestions made here is the notion that the achievement of power and sustainability by African NGOs stands to make a positive contribution to development initiatives in Africa. Another book could certainly be written on the influence, both positive and negative, of NGOs, their effectiveness as agents of development in the field, and their level of impact on beneficiaries and on the social, economic and political systems in which they work. But for now their power is considered to be crucial to development in Africa as they 'contribute to the general interest society has or ought to have in pluralism, tolerance, the protection of human rights, the alleviation of poverty and suffering, the advancement of science and thought, the preservation and advancement of culture and art, the protection of the environment – and all of the multifarious activities and concerns that go to make up a vibrant civil society' (World Bank 1997: 5).

While this research has focussed on the experiences of NGOs in three African countries it has much wider implications. Firstly, it provides an opportunity for local NGOs across African to learn from their counterparts in other countries. This is an opportunity that local African NGOs are rarely offered, given the high cost and difficulty of travel and communication, whether by mail, telephone, or the internet, on the continent. Secondly, given the importance that is often placed on African civil society in ensuring democracy and political stability on the continent, this research into the power of local NGOs should help to better understand the power of other civil society organisations on the continent: labour unions, student movements, church groups, cultural societies; and their ability to play a transforming role in African societies. NGOs are often considered representative of African civil society at large; the reasons for their weakness may also be representative of the difficulties that their fellow civil society movements face in gaining power. Finally, in calling attention to the varying climates in which, and paths by which, NGOs originate and grow, this work offers some universal lessons which are applicable to local NGOs throughout the developing world. The strategies available to local African NGOs to increase their power and to development agencies to support NGOs in this pursuit, could prove equally valuable to indigenous NGOs in Asia and South America, as well as to the host of local development NGOs currently emerging across parts of Eastern Europe.

Some concluding remarks

Local NGOs in sub-Saharan Africa are one of the most visible elements of African civil society, and are growing in number, scope, and importance. Yet substantial gaps still exist in our knowledge and understanding of these organisations. This book has sought to fill in some of these information gaps in one of the most dynamic and important areas of development research. Within the African context it asked why the growth in size and responsibility of the NGO sector has not been accompanied by a growth in the power that NGOs wield. Moreover, it sought to illustrate how the absence of power among local African NGOs has undermined development on the continent.

NGO power is the ability of a local NGO to set its own priorities, define its own agenda, and exert its influence on the international development community, even in the face of opposition from government, donors, international NGOs and other development actors. The rise of the local NGO sector in Bangladesh, and of BRAC, in particular, illustrated that several factors seem to help a local NGO to gain power. These elements are: space, financial independence from donors, solid links to the international development community, and a willingness to engage with the political aspects of development work; all of which have been key in BRAC's progression to power. Meanwhile, the inability of local African NGOs in Zimbabwe, Tanzania and Senegal to achieve these factors has impaired their ability to develop power.

Power is not only an end in itself, but is also a means of helping local NGOs to achieve sustainability. NGO sustainability is not merely a reflection of an NGO's survival or financial viability; to be sustainable, an NGO must develop a responsive, efficient and secure organisational structure as well as projects which have lasting impact and value to its beneficiaries. Powerful local NGOs are likely to be sustainable, both because power reinforces an NGO's internal and external sustainability and, because power gives local NGOs greater say in determining the definitions of sustainability by which they will be judged. It is in terms of this influence of power on sustainability that helping local NGOs to develop power is of ultimate benefit to the individuals and communities with which an NGO works. Helping local African NGOs to develop power should therefore be an immediate priority for development actors working to improve the lives of the poor and the marginalised, and to promote development in Africa.

Abdallah, Taoufik Ben and Nabou Kasse, 1999. 'Nouveaux défis pour l'Afrique: lutte contre la pauvreté, démocratie et mondialisation', *Les Cahiers du Congad*, 1: 45–76.

Abdillahi, Mohamed Sheikh, 1998. 'The Emergence of Local NGOs in the Recovery and Development Process of Somaliland (Northwest Somalia)', *Voices From Africa*, 8: 73–83.

Acharya, Shrawan and Leo Thomas, 1999. *Finding a Pathway: Understanding the Work and Performance of NGOs in Ahmedabad, India*, Oxford: INTRAC, Occasional Papers Series, 22.

Adedeji, Adebayo, 1997. 'Looking Back to the Journey Forward: Renewal from the Roots?' in *Nigeria: Renewal from the Roots?* Adebayo Adedeji and Onigu Otite (eds), London: Zed Books: 195–207.

Africa Rights, 1999. *Zimbabwe: In the Party's Interest?* Africa Rights Discussion Paper, 8.

African Development Bank, 2001. *African Development Report 2001*, New York: Oxford University Press.

Ahmad, Mohiuddin, 1999. *Bottom Up: NGO Sector in Bangladesh*, Dhaka: Community Development Library.

Aldaba, Fernando, Paula Antezana, Mariano Valderrama and Alan Fowler, 2000. 'NGO Strategies Beyond Aid: Perspectives from Central and South America and the Phillippines', *Third World Quarterly*, 21(4): 669–83.

Alexander, Jocelyn, and JoAnn McGregor, 1999. 'Representing Violence in Matabeleland, Zimbabwe: Press and Internet Debates', in *The Media of Conflict*, Tim Allen and Jean Seaton (eds), London: Zed Books, 244–67.

Alonso, José Antonio, 2000. 'Globalisation, Civil Society, and the Multilateral System', *Development in Practice*, 10, (3 & 4): 348–60.

Alvares, Claude, 1992. 'Science', in *The Development Dictionary: A Guide to Knowledge as Power*, Wolfgang Sachs (ed.), London: Zed Books, 219–32.

Alvord, Sarah H., L. David Brown and Christine W. Letts, 2002. *Social Entrepreneurship and Social Transformation: An Exploratory Study*, Hauser Center for Non-Profit Organizations, Harvard: Harvard

University Working Paper, 15.

Amnesty International, 2001. *Amnesty International Report 2001*, London: Amnesty International Publications.

Anang, Frederick T, 1994. 'Evaluating the Role and Impact of Foreign NGOs in Ghana', in *The Changing Politics of Non-Governmental Organizations and African States*, Eve Sandberg (ed.), Westport, CT: Praeger Publishers, 101–20.

ANC, 1994. *The Reconstruction and Development Programme: A Policy Framework*, Johannesburg: Umanyano Publications.

Anderson, Ian, 2000. 'Northern NGO Advocacy: Perceptions, Reality, and the Challenge', *Development in Practice*, 10 (3 & 4): 445–52.

Angwazi, Joseph, 1993. 'Resolving Conflicts and Building Coalitions: The Case of TANGO and its Constituent NGOs', in *Empowering People: Building Community, Civil Associations and Legality in Africa,* Richard Sandbrook and Mohamed Halfani (eds), Toronto: Centre for Urban and Community Studies, University of Toronto, 180–2.

Anheier, Helmut, Marlies Glasius and Mary Kaldor (eds), 2001. *Global Civil Society 2001*. Oxford: Oxford University Press.

Atack, Iain, 1999. 'Four Criteria of Development NGO Legitimacy', *World Development*, 27 (5): 855–64.

Auret, M.T.H, 1993. 'The Contribution of NGOs to Democratic Transitions: Zimbabwe', in *Empowering People: Building Community, Civil Associations and Legality in Africa,* Richard Sandbrook and Mohamed Halfani (eds), Toronto: Centre for Urban and Community Studies, University of Toronto: 184–8.

Ayoade, John A.A, 1988. 'States Without Citizens: An Emerging African Phenomenon', in *The Precarious Balance: State and Society in Africa*, Donald Rothchild and Naomi Chazan (eds), Boulder, CO: Westview Press, 100–18.

Azarya, Victor, 1988. 'Reordering State-Society Relations: Incorporation and Disengagement', in *The Precarious Balance: State and Society in Africa*, Donald Rothchild and Naomi Chazan (eds), Boulder, CO: Westview Press: 3–21.

Bâ, Moussa, 1999. 'Le mouvement ONG au Sénégal, outil de développement participatif', *Les Cahiers du Congad*, 1: 11–28.

Bachrach, Peter and Morton S. Baratz, 1962. 'Two Faces of Power', *American Political Science Review*, 56 (4): 947–52.

Bailey, Michael, 1999. 'Fundraising in Brazil: The Major Implications for Civil Society Organisations and International NGOs', *Development in Practice*, 9 (1&2): 103–16.

Bayart, Jean-François, 1986. 'Civil Society in Africa', in *Political Domination in Africa: Reflections on the Limits of Power*, Patrick Chabal (ed.), Cambridge: Cambridge University Press, 109–25.

Beckwith, Colin, Kent Glenzer and Alan Fowler, 2002. 'Leading Learning and Change from the Middle: Reconceptualising Strategy's Purpose, Content and Measures', *Development in Practice*, 12 (3&4): 409–23.

Behrman, Lucy C, 1970. *Muslim Brotherhoods and Politics in Senegal*, Cambridge, MA: Harvard University Press.

Bhatt, Ela R, 1998. 'Empowering the Poor Through Micro-Finance: The SEWA Bank', in *Social Change Through Voluntary Action*, M.L. Dantwala, Harsh Sethi and Pravin Visaria (eds), New Delhi: SAGE Publications, 146–61.

Blair, David, 2002. *Degrees in Violence: Robert Mugabe and the Struggle for Power in Zimbabwe*, New York: Continuum Publishing.

Bornstein, Lisa, 2000. 'Institutional Context', in *Poverty and Inequality in South Africa*, Julian May (ed.), London: Zed Books, 173–204.

Bosch, Margarita, 1997. 'NGOs and Development in Brazil: Roles and Responsibilities in a "New World Order"', in *NGOs, States and Donors: Too Close for Comfort?*, David Hulme and Michael Edwards (eds), London: Macmillan Press and The Save the Children Fund, 232–42.

Bouvard, Marguerite Guzman, 1994. *Revolutionizing Motherhood: The Mothers of the Plaza de Mayo*, Wilmington, DE: Scholarly Resources Inc.

Bowyer-Bower, T.A.S. and Colin Stoneman, 2000. *Land Reform in Zimbabwe: Constraints and Prospects*, Aldershot: Ashgate.

BRAC, 1992. 'Bangladesh Rural Advancement Committee', in *Non-Governmental Organizations of Developing Countries: And the South Smiles*, Sjef Theunis (ed.), Dordrecht: Kluwer Academic Publishers, 53–63.

BRAC, 2000. *BRAC Annual Report 1999*.

Bratton, Michael, 1989. 'The Politics of Government-NGO Relations in Africa', *World Development*, 17 (4): 569–87.

—— 1994a. 'Civil Society and Political Transitions in Africa', in *Civil Society and the State in Africa*, John W. Harbeson, Donald Rothchild and Naomi Chazan (eds), Boulder, CO: Lynne Rienner Publishers, 51–81.

—— 1994b. 'Non-Governmental Organizations in Africa: Can they Influence Public Policy?', in *The Changing Politics of Non-Governmental Organizations and African States*, Eve Sandberg (ed.), Westport, CT: Praeger Publishers, 33–58.

Brinkerhoff, Derick W. and Arthur A. Goldsmith, 1992. 'Promoting the Sustainability of Development Institutions: A Framework for Strategy', *World Development*, 20 (3): 369–83.

Brown, L. David, 1988. 'Organizational Barriers to Strategic Action by NGOs', *IDR Reports*, 5 (2): 1–11.

Calderón, Fernando, Alejandro Piscitelli and José Luis Reyna, 1992. 'Social Movements: Actors, Theories, Expectations', in *The Making of Social Movements in Latin America*, Arturo Escobar and Sonia E. Alvarez (eds), Boulder, CO: Westview Press, 19–36.

Callaghy, Thomas, 1986. 'Politics and Vision in Africa: The Interplay of Domination, Equality and Liberty', in *Political Domination in Africa: Reflections on the Limits of Power*, Patrick Chabal (ed.), Cambridge:

Cambridge University Press, 30–51.

Campfens, Hubert, 1996. 'Partnerships in International Social Development: Evolution in Practice and Concept', *International Social Work*, 39 (2): 201–23.

Cawthra, Helle Christiansen, Andrea Helman-Smith and Dudley Moloi, 2001. 'Annual Review: The Voluntary Sector and Development in South Africa 1999/2000', *Development Update*, 3 (3).

Chabal, Patrick, 1992. *Power in Africa: An Essay in Political Interpretation*, London: Macmillan Press.

Chabal, Patrick and Jean-Pascal Daloz, 1999. *Africa Works: Disorder as a Political Instrument,* Oxford: James Currey, Bloomington: Indiana University Press.

Charlton, Roger, Tony Clearberry, and Roy May, 1994. *NGOs, Development and Civil Society in Africa: From Bingo to Tango*, Caledonian Papers in the Social Sciences, International Political Economy Series, 1.

Chaudhury, Iftekhar A, 1999. *A Study on Membership Overlap Among Different NGOs in Selected Villages: Its Impact on Micro-credit Programmes and the Rural Poor*, A BRAC-commissioned study.

Chazan, Naomi, 1988. 'Patterns of State-Society Incorporation and Disengagement in Africa', in *The Precarious Balance: State and Society in Africa*, Donald Rothchild and Naomi Chazan (eds), Boulder, CO: Westview Press: 121–48.

Chazan, Naomi, 1992. 'Liberalization, Governance and Political Space in Ghana', in *Governance and Politics in Africa*, Goran Hyden and Michael Bratton (eds), Boulder, CO: Lynne Rienner Publishers, 121–41.

Chazan, Naomi, 1994. 'Engaging the State: Associational Life in Sub-Saharan Africa', in *State Power and Social Forces: Domination and Transformation in the Third World*, Joel. S. Migdal, Atul Kohli and Vivienne Shue (eds), Cambridge: Cambridge University Press, 255–89.

Chege, Sam, 1999. 'Donors shift more aid to NGOs', *Africa Recovery*, 13 (1).

Chinchilla, Norma Stoltz, 1992. 'Marxism, Feminism, and the Struggle for Democracy in Latin America', in *The Making of Social Movements in Latin America*. Arturo Escobar and Sonia E. Alvarez (eds), Boulder, CO: Westview Press: 37–51.

Clark, John, 1991. *Democratizing Development: The Role of Voluntary Organizations,* London: Earthscan Publications Ltd.

Clark, Andrew F, 1999. 'Imperialism, Independence, and Islam in Senegal and Mali', *Africa Today*, 46 (3/4): 149–67.

Clarke, Gerard, 1998. 'Non-Governmental Organizations (NGOs) and Politics in the Developing World', *Political Studies*, XLVI: 36–52.

Clayton, Andrew, 1998. *NGOs and Decentralised Government in Africa*, INTRAC Occasional Papers Series, 18, Oxford: INTRAC.

Club of Rome, 1972. *The Limits to Growth*. London: Earth Island Limited.

CONGAD, 1995. 'Le combat du CONGAD', *CONGAD Infos* (The CONGAD

Newsletter), 18 (3): 15–16.

CONGAD, 1997. *Rapport genéral: symposium sur l'identité des ONG.*

CONGAD, 1999. *Code d'éthique et de déontologie des ONG membres du CONGAD.*

Cooksey, Brian, 1997. 'How Much Corruption is Acceptable?' *Africa Analysis*, 267: 4.

Concept, 1997. *Municipalités et ONG: quelles synergies pour le développement local.*

Copestake, James G, 1993. 'Zambia: Country Overview', in *Non-Governmental Organizations and the State in Africa*, Kate Wellard and James G. Copestake (eds), London: Routledge, 161–73.

Coulon, Christian, 1981. *Le marabout et le prince*, Paris: Editions A. Pedone.

Craske, Nikki, 1999. *Women and Politics in Latin America*, Cambridge: Polity Press.

Creevey, Lucy E, 1985. 'Muslim Brotherhoods and Politics in Senegal in 1985', *The Journal of Modern African Studies*, 23 (4): 715–21.

Dahl, Robert, 1957. 'The Concept of Power', *Behavioral Science*, 2 (July): 201–15.

Daily News (Tanzania). 8 April 1998. 'State Axe to Fall on 24 NGOs'.

(The) *Daily News* (Zimbabwe). 29 July 1999. 'No Misuse and Abuse of Funds'.

Danielson, Anders and Gun Eriksson Skoog, 2001. 'From Stagnation to Growth in Tanzania: Breaking the Vicious Circle of High Aid and Bad Governance?', in *From Crisis to Growth in Africa?* Mats Lundahl (ed.), London: Routledge, 147–68.

Datta, Rekha, 2000. 'On Their Own: Development Strategies of the Self-Employed Women's Association (SEWA) in India', *Development*, 43 (4): 51–5.

de Graaf, Martin, 1987. 'Context, Constraint or Control? Zimbabwean NGOs and their Environment', *Development Policy Review*, 5 (3): 277–301.

De Winter, Eric R. 'Which Way to Sustainability? External Support to Health Projects in Developing Countries', *Health Policy and Planning*, 8 (2): 150–6.

DESCO, 2002. DESCO Website. Available online at: http://www.desco.org.pe

Devey, Muriel, 2000. *Le Sénégal*, Paris: Éditions KARTHALA.

DFID, 1999. *Zimbabwe Country Strategy Paper*, London: DFID.

DFID Bangladesh, 2000. *Partners in Development: A Review of Big NGOs in Bangladesh*, A DFID-commissioned study. (Unpublished).

Dia, Mamadou, 1964. 'African Socialism', in *African Socialism*, William H. Friedland and Carl G. Rosberg Jr. (eds), Stanford: Stanford University Press, 248–9.

Diop, Momar Coumba, 1981. 'Fonctions et activités des *dahira* mourides urbains (Sénégal)', *Cahiers d'Études Africaines*, XXI (81–3): 79–91.

Duffy, Rosaleen, 2000. *Killing for Conservation: Wildlife Policy in Zimbabwe*, Oxford: James Currey, Bloomington: Indiana University Press.

Dunn, John, 1986. 'The Politics of Representation and Good Government in Post-Colonial Africa', in *Political Domination in Africa: Reflections on the Limits of Power*, Patrick Chabal (ed.), Cambridge: Cambridge University Press: 158–74.

Eade, Deborah, 1997. *Capacity-Building: An Approach to People-Centred Development*, Oxford: Oxfam.

ECOSOC, 2003. ECOSOC Website. Available online at: http://www.un.org/esa/coordination/ngo

Edwards, Michael and David Hulme, 1995. 'NGO Performance and Accountability: Introduction and Overview', in *Non-Governmental Organisations – Performance and Accountability: Beyond the Magic Bullet*, Michael Edwards and David Hulme (eds), London: Earthscan Publications and The Save the Children Fund, 3–16.

—— 1996. 'Too Close for Comfort? The Impact of Official Aid on Non-Governmental Organizations', *World Development*, 24 (6): 961–73.

Edwards, Michael and John Gaventa (eds), 2001. *Global Citizen Action*, Boulder, CO: Lynne Rienner Publishers.

Elliott, Charles, 1987. 'Some Aspects of Relations between the North and the South in the NGO Sector', *World Development*, 15 (supplement): 57–68.

Elshtain, Jean Bethke, 1995. 'Exporting Feminism', *Journal of International Affairs*, 48 (2): 541–58.

Embassy of Sweden in Tanzania, 1999. Internal Memorandum. 12 October 1999. (Unpublished).

Engberg-Pedersen, Lars and Neil Webster, 2002. 'Introduction to Political Space', in *In the Name of the Poor: Contesting Political Space for Poverty Reduction*, Neil Webster and Lars Engberg-Pedersen, London: Zed Books, 1–29.

Farrington, John, Anthony Bebbington, Kate Wellard, David J. Lewis, 1993. *Reluctant Partners? Non-Governmental Organizations, the State and Sustainable Agricultural Development*, London: Routledge.

FASE, 2002. FASE Website. Available online at: http://www.fase.org.br

Fatton, Robert Jr, 1995. 'Africa in the Age of Democratization: The Civic Limitations of Civil Society', *African Studies Review*, 38 (2): 67–99.

Feijoo, Maria del Carmen and Monica Gogna, 1990. 'Women in the Transition to Democracy', in *Women and Social Change in Latin America*, Elizabeth Jelin (ed.), London: Zed Books, 79–114.

Financial Gazette (Zimbabwe). 19 November 1998. 'Stayaway Signals Mugabe's Hold on Power Slipping Fast'.

Fisher, William F, 1997. 'Doing Good? The Politics and Antipolitics of NGO Practices' *Annual Review of Anthropology*, 26: 439–64.

Fisher, Julie, 1998. *Nongovernments: NGOs and the Political Development of the Third World*, West Hartford, CT: Kumarian Press.

Ford-Smith, Honor, 1989. 'Ring Ding in a Tight Corner: a Case Study in

Funding and Organizational Democracy in Sistren, 1977–88', Toronto: International Council for Adult Education. As referenced in: Ian Smillie, 1995, *The Alms Bazaar*, London: Intermediate Technology Publications.

Foucault, Michel, 2000. *Power*, New York: The New Press.

Fowler, Alan, 1988. *Non-Governmental Organisations in Africa: Achieving Comparative Advantage in Relief and Micro-Development*, IDS Discussion Paper, 249.

—— 1991. 'Building Partnerships Between Northern and Southern Developmental NGOs: Issues for the Nineties', *Development in Practice*, 1 (1): 5–18.

—— 1995a. 'NGOs and the Globalization of Social Welfare: Perspectives from East Africa', in *Service Provision Under Stress in East Africa: The State, NGOs and People's Organizations in Kenya, Tanzania and Uganda*, Joseph Semboja and Ole Therkildsen (eds), Copenhagen: Centre for Development Research; London: James Currey, 51–69.

—— 1995b. 'Assessing NGO Performance: Difficulties, Dilemmas and a Way Ahead', in *Non-Governmental Organisations – Performance and Accountability: Beyond the Magic Bullet*, Michael Edwards and David Hulme (eds), London: Earthscan Publications and Save the Children Fund, UK, 143–56.

—— 1997. *Striking a Balance*, London: Earthscan Publications.

—— 1998. 'Authentic NGDO Partnerships in the New Policy Agenda for International Aid: Dead End or Light Ahead?' *Development and Change*, 29 (1): 137–59.

—— 2000a. *Partnerships: Negotiating Relationships – a Resource for Nongovernmental Organisations*, INTRAC Occasional Papers Series 32, Oxford: INTRAC.

—— 2000b. 'NGDO Values and the Fourth Position', *Third World Quarterly*, 21 (4): 589–603.

Fowler, Alan, 2000c. *The Virtuous Spiral: A Guide to Sustainability for NGOs in International Development*, London: Earthscan.

Fowler, Alan, Piers Campbell and Brian Pratt, 1992. *Institutional Development and NGOs in Africa: Policy Perspectives for European Development Agencies*, INTRAC NGO Management Series, 1.

Galbraith, John Kenneth, 1983. *The Anatomy of Power*, Boston: Houghton Mifflin.

Garilao, Ernesto D, 1987. 'Indigenous NGOs as Strategic Institutions: Managing the Relationship with Government and Resource Agencies', *World Development*, 15 (supplement): 113–20.

Gary, Ian, 1996. 'Confrontation, Co-operation or Co-optation: NGOs and the Ghanaian State during Structural Adjustment', *Review of African Political Economy*, 68 (23): 149–68.

Gaventa, John and Andrea Cornwall, 2001. 'Power and Knowledge', in *Handbook of Action Research: Participative Inquiry and Practice*, Peter Reason and Hilary Bradbury (eds), London: Sage, 70–80.

Gellar, Sheldon, 1995. *Senegal: An African Nation Between Islam and the West*, Boulder, CO: Westview Press.

Geiger, Susan, 1997. *TANU Women*, Portsmouth, NH: Heinemann, Oxford: James Currey.

Gibbon, Peter, 1995. 'Merchantisation of Production and Privatisation of Development in Post-Ujamaa Tanzania: An Introduction', in *Liberalised Development in Tanzania: Studies on Accumulation Processes and Local Institutions*, Peter Gibbon (ed.), Uppsala: Nordiska Afrikainstitutet, 9–36.

Gibbs, Christopher, Claudia Fumo and Thomas Kuby, 1999. *Non-Governmental Organizations in World Bank-Supported Projects: A Review*, Washington, DC: World Bank Operations Evaluation Department.

Goldsmith, Arthur A, 2001. 'Donors, Dictators and Democrats in Africa', *Journal of Modern African Studies*, 39 (3): 411–36.

Government of Zimbabwe, 1996. *Private Voluntary Organizations Act*. Revised Edition.

Gueye, Cheikh, 2001. 'Touba: The New *Dairas* and the Urban Dream', in *Associational Life in African Cities*, Arne Tostensen, Inge Tvedten and Mariken Vaa (eds), Stockholm: Nordiska Afrikainstitutet, 107–23.

Gueye, Mamadou Bara, Richard Ketley, and John Nelson, 1993. 'Senegal: Country Overview', in *Non-Governmental Organizations and the State in Africa*, Kate Wellard and James G. Copestake (eds), London: Routledge, 253–63.

Gueye-Tall, Seynabou, 1989. 'Femmes, agents et bénéficiares de l'action des ONG', in *Femmes, agents et bénéficiares de l'assistance au développement*. A report of the Association of African Women for Research and Development: 67–118.

Gulati, Anita, David Everatt and Ann Kushlick, 1996. *Tango in the dark: Government and Voluntary Sector Partnerships in the New South Africa*. Johannesburg: INTERFUND.

Gyimah-Boadi, E, 1996. 'Civil Society in Africa', *Journal of Democracy*, 7 (2): 118–32.

Hanashiro, Olaya, 2000. 'Democratizing State and Civil Society in Brazil', *Development*, 43 (3): 103–5.

Hann, Chris and Elizabeth Dunn, 1996. *Civil Society: Challenging Western Models*, London: Routledge.

Harbeson, John W., Donald Rothchild and Naomi Chazan (eds), 1994. *Civil Society and the State in Africa*, Boulder, CO: Lynne Rienner Publishers.

Hashemi, Syed, 1995. 'NGO Accountability in Bangladesh: Beneficiaries, Donors and the State', in *Non-Governmental Organisations – Performance and Accountability: Beyond the Magic Bullet*, Michael Edwards and David Hulme (eds), London: Earthscan Publications and The Save the Children Fund, 103–10.

Havnevik, Kjell J, 1993. 'The Emergence, Development and Breakdown of the Post-Colonial Model in Tanzania', in *Tanzania: The Limits to Development from Above*, Uppsala: Nordiska Afrikainstitutet, 29–62.

Haynes, Jeff, 1997. *Democracy and Civil Society in the Third World*, Cambridge: Polity Press.

Hayward, Clarissa Rile, 1998. 'De-Facing Power', *Polity*, 31 (1): 1–22.

—— 2000. *De-Facing Power*. Cambridge: Cambridge University Press.

Heap, Simon, 1998. *NGOs and the Private Sector: Potential for Partnerships?* INTRAC Occasional Papers Series, 27, Oxford: INTRAC.

—— 2000. *NGOs Engaging with Business: A World of Difference and a Difference to the World*, Oxford: INTRAC.

Hearn, Julie, 2000. 'Aiding Democracy? Donors and Civil Society in South Africa', *Third World Quarterly*, 21 (5): 815–30.

Henderson, Peggy L, 1995. 'Donor and Government Constraints to Sustainability in Nepal', *Health Policy and Planning*, 10 (supplement): 17–27.

Henderson, Judy, 2000. 'Dissonance or Dialogue: Changing Relations with the Corporate', *Development in Practice*, 10 (3 & 4): 371–76.

Herbst, Jeffrey, 1992. 'The Dilemmas of Land Policy in Zimbabwe', in *Zimbabwe in Transition*, Simon Baynham (ed.), Stockholm: Almqvist & Wiksell International, 129–48.

—— 2000. *States and Power in Africa: Comparative Lessons in Authority and Control*, Princeton, NJ: Princeton University Press.

Hindess, Barry, 1996. *Discourses of Power: From Hobbes to Foucault*, Oxford: Blackwell Publishers.

Hobbes, Thomas, [1651] 1985. *Leviathan*, London: Penguin Classics.

Holloway, Richard, 1998. *Supporting Citizens' Initiatives: Bangladesh's NGOs and Society*, Dhaka: University Press Limited.

Houtzager, Peter P, 2000. 'Social Movements amidst Democratic Transitions: Lessons from the Brazilian Countryside', *The Journal of Development Studies*, 36 (5): 59–88.

Howard, Judith A. and Carolyn Allen, 1996. 'Reflections on the Fourth World Conference on Women and NGO Forum '95', *Signs*, 22 (1): 181–5.

Howe, Charles, W, 1997. 'Dimensions of Sustainability: Geographical, Temporal, Institutional and Psychological', *Land Economics*, 73 (4): 597–607.

Howell, Jude, 2000. 'Making Civil Society from the Outside – Challenges for Donors', *The European Journal of Development Research*, 12 (1): 3–22.

Howell, Jude and Jenny Pearce, 2001. *Civil Society and Development: A Critical Exploration*, Boulder, CO: Lynne Rienner Publishers.

Howes, Mick and M.G. Sattar, 1992. 'Bigger and Better? Scaling-up Strategies pursued by BRAC 1972–1991', in *Making a Difference: NGOs and Development in a Changing World*, Michael Edwards and David Hulme (eds), London: Earthscan, 99–110.

Hulme, David and Michael Edwards, 1997. 'NGOs, States and Donors: An Overview', in *NGOs, States and Donors: Too Close for Comfort?* David

Hulme and Michael Edwards (eds), London: Macmillan Press and The Save the Children Fund, 3–22.

Hutchful, Eboe, 1995. 'The Civil Society Debate in Africa', *International Journal*, 51 (1): 54–77.

Hyden, Goran, 1980. *Beyond Ujamaa in Tanzania: Underdevelopment and an Uncaptured Peasantry*, London: Heinemann.

—— 1995. 'Bringing Voluntarism Back In: Eastern Africa in Comparative Perspective', in *Service Provision Under Stress in East Africa: The State, NGOs and People's Organizations in Kenya, Tanzania and Uganda*, Joseph Semboja and Ole Therkildsen (eds), Copenhagen: Centre for Development Research; London: James Currey, 35–50.

IBASE, 1992. 'Instituto Brasileiro de Análises Sociais e Econômicas (IBASE)', in *Non-Governmental Organizations of Developing Countries: And the South Smiles*. Sjef Theunis (ed.), Dordrecht: Kluwer Academic Publishers, 211–21.

IBASE, 1999. *Relatório 1999*, Rio de Janeiro: Insituto Brasiliero de Análises Sociais e Econômicas.

Igoe, Jim, 2003. 'Scaling up Civil Society: Donor Money, NGOs and the Pastoralist Land Rights Movement in Tanzania', *Development and Change*, 34 (5): 863–85.

Ikelegbe, Augustine, 2001a. 'The Perverse Manifestation of Civil Society: Evidence from Nigeria', *The Journal of Modern African Studies*, 39 (1): 1–24.

—— 2001b. 'Civil Society, Oil and Conflict in the Niger Delta Region of Nigeria: Ramifications of Civil Society for a Regional Resource Struggle', *The Journal of Modern African Studies*, 39 (3): 437–69.

(The) *Independent* (Zimbabwe). 1 April 1999. 'Embattled President Mugabe Lashes Out at his Critics'.

Institute of Development Studies, 1999. *Participatory Assessment on Civic Participation in Municipal Governance in Tanzania*. Dar es Salaam: University of Dar es Salaam (Unpublished).

InterAction, 2003a. *Synopses of Forum 2003 Panels*, Overview of Forum 2003 – The Challenge of Global Commitments: Advancing Relief and Development Goals through Advocacy and Action. Available online at: <http://www.interaction.org/ forum2003/panels.html#Natsios>

—— 2003b. *Foreign Assistance in Focus: Emerging Trends*, InterAction Policy Paper, Washington, DC: InterAction.

Ishumi, Abel G.M, 1995. 'Provision of Secondary Education in Tanzania: Historical Background and Current Trends', in *Service Provision Under Stress in East Africa: The State, NGOs and People's Organizations in Kenya, Tanzania and Uganda,* Joseph Semboja and Ole Therkildsen (eds), Copenhagen: Centre for Development Research; London: James Currey, 153–65.

Islam, Nurul, 1981. 'The Debate', in *Aid and Influence: The Case of Bangladesh*, Just Faaland (ed.), Bergen, Norway: The Chr. Michelsen Institute, 14–24.

James, Deborah, 2000. '"After Years in the Wilderness": The Discourse of Land Claims in the New South Africa', *The Journal of Peasant Studies*, 27 (3): 142–61.

James, Rick, 1994. *Strengthening the Capacity of Southern NGO Partners*. INTRAC Occasional Papers Series (5), Oxford: INTRAC.

James, Rick, 1998. *Demystifying Organisation Development: Practical Capacity-Building Experiences of African NGOs*, Oxford: INTRAC.

James, Rick (ed.), 2001. *Power and Partnership? Experiences of NGO Capacity-Building*, INTRAC NGO Management and Policy Series (12), Oxford: INTRAC.

Jamil, Ishtiaq, 2000. 'NGOs and the Administration of Development Aid in Bangladesh: Does There Exist a Development Regime?', in *Learning NGOs and the Dynamics of Development Partnerships*, Farhad Hossain, Marko Uvila and Ware Newaz (eds), Dhaka: Ahsania Books, 143–70.

Jarvis, Anthony P. and Albert J. Paolini, 1995. 'Locating the State', in *The State in Transition: Reimagining Political Space*, Joseph A. Camilleri, Anthony P. Jarvis and Albert J. Paolini (eds), Boulder, CO: Lynne Rienner Publishers, 3–19.

Jenkins, Karen, 1994. 'The Christian Church as an NGO in Africa: Supporting Post-Independence Era State Legitimacy or Promoting Change?', in *The Changing Politics of Non-Governmental Organizations and African States*, Eve Sandberg (ed.), Westport, CT: Praeger Publishers, 83–99.

Juma, Monica Kathina, 2003. 'The Political Economy of Building Local Relief Capacity in Africa', in *Eroding Local Capacity: International Humanitarian Action in Africa*, Monica Kathina Juma and Astri Suhrke (eds), Uppsala: Nordiska Afrikainstitutet, 159–82.

Kagwanja, Peter Mwangi, 2003. 'Strengthening Local Relief Capacity in Kenya', in *Eroding Local Capacity: International Humanitarian Action in Africa*, Monica Kathina Juma and Astri Suhrke (eds), Uppsala: Nordiska Afrikainstitutet, 94–115.

Kaplan, Allan, 2000. 'Capacity Building: Shifting the Paradigms of Practice', *Development in Practice*, 10 (3 & 4): 517–26.

Kasfir, Nelson, 1998. 'Civil Society, the State and Democracy in Africa', in *Civil Society and Democracy in Africa: Critical Perspectives*, Nelson Kasfir (ed.), London: Frank Cass, 123–49.

Keck, Margaret E. and Kathryn Sikkink, 1998. *Activists beyond Borders: Advocacy Networks in International Politics*, Ithaca: Cornell University Press.

Kelsall, Tim, 2001. 'Donors, NGOs and the State: Governance and "Civil Society" in Tanzania', in *The Charitable Impulse: NGOs and Development in East and North-East Africa,* Ondine Barrow and Michael Jennings (eds), Oxford: James Currey, 133–48.

Khagram, Sanjeev, James V. Riker and Kathryn Sikkink (eds), 2002. *Restructuring World Politics: Transnational Social Movements, Net-*

works, and Norms, Minneapolis: University of Minnesota Press.

Khan, Mafruza, David J. Lewis, Asgar Ali Sabri and Md Shahabuddin, 1993. 'Proshika's Livestock and Social Forestry Programmes', in *Non-Governmental Organizations and the State in Asia*, John Farrington and David J. Lewis (eds), London: Routledge, 59–65.

Kiondo, Andrew S. Z, 1995. 'When the State Withdraws: Local Development, Politics and Liberalisation in Tanzania', in *Liberalised Development in Tanzania: Studies on Accumulation Processes and Local Institutions*, Peter Gibbon (ed.), Uppsala: Nordiska Afrikainstitutet, 109–76.

Kleemeier, Elizabeth, 2000. 'The Impact of Participation on Sustainability: An Analysis of the Malawi Rural Piped Scheme Project', *World Development*, 28 (5): 929–44.

Korten, David C, 1987. 'Third Generation NGO Strategies: A Key to People-Centered Development', *World Development*, 15 (supplement): 145–59.

Krieger, Norma, 2000. 'Zimbabwe Today: Hope against Grim Realities', *Review of African Political Economy*, 27 (85): 443–50.

Kukah, Matthew Hassan, 1999. *Democracy and Civil Society in Nigeria*, Ibadan: Spectrum Books Limited.

Lange, Siri, Hege Wallevik and Andrew Kiondo, 2000. *Civil Society in Tanzania*, Bergen, Norway: Chr. Michelsen Institute.

Lawson, Max, 2000. *The Current Context of the Malawian NGO Sector*, a report prepared to inform the strategic assessment of CABUNGO.

Lewis, David, 1998. 'Development NGOs and the Challenge of Partnership: Changing Relations between North and South', *Social Policy and Administration*, 32 (5): 501–12.

Lewis, David and Babar Sobhan, 1999. 'Routes of Funding, Roots of Trust? Northern NGOs, Southern NGOs, Donors, and the Rise of Direct Funding', *Development in Practice*, 9 (1 & 2): 117–29.

Lindenberg, Marc and Coralie Bryant, 2001. *Going Global: Transforming Relief and Development NGOs*, Bloomfield, CT: Kumarian Press.

Lipton, Michael, 1989. *New Seeds and Poor People*, London: Unwin Hyman Ltd.

Lister, Sarah, 2000. 'Power in Partnership? An Analysis of an NGO's Relationships with its Partners', *Journal of International Development*, 12 (2): 227–39.

Locke, John, [1690] 1967. *Two Treatises of Government*, Cambridge: Cambridge University Press.

Lovell, Catherine, 1992. *Breaking the Cycle of Poverty: the BRAC Strategy*, West Hartford, Conn: Kumarian Press.

Lukes, Steven, 1974. *Power: A Radical View*, London: MacMillan Press.

Luz, Juan Miguel, 1991. 'Managing a Professional NGO: Bangladesh Rural Advancement Committee', in *The Management of NGOs: Case Studies of Asian Non-Governmental Organizations*, Jose Ibarra A. Angeles (ed.), Manila: Approtech Asia, 115–31.

Maathai, Wangarĩ, 1988. *The Green Belt Movement: Sharing the Approach and the Experience*, Nairobi: Environment Liaison Centre International.

Machiavelli, Niccolò, [1513] 1997. *The Prince*, Ware: Wordsworth Editions.

Magnusson, Warren, 1996. *The Search for Political Space: Globalization, Social Movements and the Urban Political Experience*, Toronto: University of Toronto Press.

Maina, Wachira, 1998. 'Kenya: The State, Donors and the Politics of Democratization', in *Civil Society and the Aid Industry*, Alison Van Rooy (ed.), London: Earthscan, 134–67.

Makumbe, John, 2000. 'NGOs' Transparency and Accountability', in *NGOs, the State and Politics in Zimbabwe*, Sam Moyo, John Makumbe and Brian Raftopoulos (eds), Harare: SAPES Books, 80–6.

Malena, Carmen, 2000. 'Beneficiaries, Mercenaries, Missionaries and Revolutionaries: "Unpacking" NGO Involvement in World Bank-Financed Projects', *IDS Bulletin*, 31 (3): 19–34.

Malhotra, Kamal, 2000. 'NGOs Without Aid: Beyond the Global Soup Kitchen', *Third World Quarterly*, 21 (4): 655–68.

Mancuso Brehm, Vicky, 2001. *Promoting Effective North-South NGO Partnerships*, INTRAC Occasional Papers Series (35), Oxford: INTRAC.

Manji, Firoze, 1997. 'Collaboration with the South: Agents of Aid or Solidarity?', in *Development and Patronage*, Deborah Eade (ed.), Oxford: OXFAM, 72–4.

Marcussen, Henrik Secher, 1996. 'NGOs, the State and Civil Society', *Review of African Political Economy*, 69 (23): 405–23.

Marongwe, Nelson, 1999. *Civil Society's Perspective on Land Reforms in Zimbabwe*, ZERO Discussion Paper Series 2.

Matanga, Frank Khachina, 2000. *Non-Governmental Organizations, the State and the Politics of Rural Development in Kenya, with particular reference to Western Province*, PhD Thesis, Rhodes University.

Mathews, Jessica, 1997. 'Power Shift', *Foreign Affairs*, 76 (1): 50–66.

Mawdsley, Emma, Janet Townsend, Gina Porter and Peter Oakley, 2002. *Knowledge, Power and Development Agendas: NGOs North and South*, INTRAC NGO Management and Policy Series (14), Oxford: INTRAC.

Mbithi, Philip M and Rasmus Rasmusson, 1977. *Self Reliance in Kenya: The Case of Harambee*, Uppsala: Scandinavian Institute of African Studies.

Meena, Ruth, 1997. 'The State and the Civil Society in Tanzania: The State of the Art', in *Political Culture and Popular Participation in Tanzania*, A Report of the Research and Education for Democracy in Tanzania Project, Dar es Salaam: University of Dar es Salaam, 33–47 (Unpublished).

Meppem, Tony and Simon Bourke, 1999. 'Different Ways of Knowing: A Communicative Turn Toward Sustainability', *Ecological Economics*, 30 (3): 389–404.

Mercer, Claire, 1999. 'Reconceptualizing State–Society Relations in Tanzania: Are NGOs "Making a Difference"?', *Area*, 31 (3): 247–58.
—— 2002. 'NGOs, Civil Society and Democratisation: a Critical Review of the Literature', *Progress in Development Studies*, 2 (1): 5–22.
Meyer, Carrie A, 1999. *The Economics and Politics of NGOs in Latin America*, Westport, CT: Praeger.
Microcredit Summit Campaign (The), 2002. The Microcredit Summit Campaign Website. Available online at: http://www.microcreditsummit.org/press/wwf2.htm
Migdal, Joel S, 1988. *Strong Societies and Weak States: State-Society Relations and State Capabilities in the Third World*, Princeton: Princeton University Press.
—— 1994. 'The State in Society: An Approach to Struggles for Domination', in *State Power and Social Forces: Domination and Transformation in the Third World*, Joel. S. Migdal, Atul Kohli and Vivienne Shue (eds), Cambridge: Cambridge University Press, 7–34.
Mohammed, Abdul, 1992. 'The Role of Non-Governmental Organizations in Situations of Civil Conflict', in *A Research and Advocacy Agenda for African NGOs in Eastern and Southern Africa*, Background Papers for the PIP-Funded Mwengo Seminar, Washington, DC: DATEX INC, 30–46. (Unpublished).
Monga, Célestin, 1996. *The Anthropology of Anger: Civil Society and Democracy in Africa*, Boulder, CO: Lynne Rienner Publishers.
Moyo, Ambrose, 1996. *Zimbabwe: The Risk of Incarnation,* Geneva: WCC.
Moyo, Sam, 1992a. *Institutional Issues for Appropriate Technology Development: Rural NGOs in Zimbabwe*, ZERO Working Paper, 7.
—— 1992b. *NGO Advocacy in Zimbabwe: Systematising an Old Function or Inventing a New Role?* ZERO Working Paper, 1.
—— 2000a. 'The Structure and Characteristics of NGOs', in *NGOs, the State and Politics in Zimbabwe*, Sam Moyo, John Makumbe and Brian Raftopoulos (eds), Harare: SAPES Books, 47–61.
—— 2000b. 'Financial and Institutional Sustainability of NGOs', in *NGOs, the State and Politics in Zimbabwe*, Sam Moyo, John Makumbe and Brian Raftopoulos (eds), Harare: SAPES Books, 62–79.
Moyo, Sam and Yemi Katerere, 1992. *NGOs in Transition: An Assessment of Regional NGOs in the Development Process*, ZERO Working Paper, 6.
Mtatifikolo, Fidelis P, 1997. *Establishing, Developing and Sustaining NGOs in Tanzania: Legal, Institutional and Regulatory Framework Challenges*, Dar es Salaam: University of Dar es Salaam. (Unpublished).
Mukasa, Sarah, 1999. *Are Expatriate Staff Necessary in International Development NGOs? A Case Study of an International NGO in Uganda*, CVO International Working Paper 4.
Mushauri, Joshua, 1997. 'Civil Society and Forms of Political Participation in Zimbabwe', in *Traditional and Contemporary Forms of Local Participation and Self-Government in Africa*, William Hofmeister and

Ingo Scholz (eds), Johannesburg: Konrad Adenauer-Stiftung, 249–74.

Mutepfa, Fannie, Shereen Essof, and Joseph Matowanyika, 1998. *Setting the Basis for Dialogue on Land in Zimbabwe: Report of the NGO Consultative Land Conference, Harare, Zimbabwe, 27–28 May 1997*, Harare: ZERO.

NANGO, 1999. *Report on the Strategic Planning Workshop held on 5–6 August 1999*. (Unpublished).

NANGO. Undated. Pamphlet entitled, *NANGO*.

Narayan, Deepa, Robert Chambers, Meera K. Shah and Patti Petesch, 2001. *Voices of the Poor: Crying out for Change*, New York: Oxford University Press, for the World Bank.

Navarro, Marysa, 1989. 'The Personal is Political: Las Madres de Plaza de Mayo', in *Power and Popular Protest: Latin American Social Movements*, Susan Eckstein (ed.), Berkeley, CA: University of California Press, 241–58.

Nchama, C.M. Eya, 1991. *Développement et droits de l'homme en Afrique*, Paris: Editions Publisud.

Ndaro, Japheth M.M, 1992. 'Local Coping Strategies in Dodoma District, Tanzania', in *Development From Within: Survival in Rural Africa*, D.R.F. Taylor and Fiona Mackenzie (eds), London: Routledge, 170–96.

Ndegwa, Stephen N, 1996. *The Two Faces of Civil Society: NGOs and Politics in Africa*, West Hartford, CT: Kumarian Press.

Ndiaye, Birame Owens, 1999. 'Rôle des ONG dans la décentralisation pour un développement local', *Les Cahiers du Congad*, 1: 29–44.

Ngware, Suleiman S. A, 1997. 'Civil Society and Forms of Political Participation in Tanzania', in *Traditional and Contemporary Forms of Local Participation and Self-Government in Africa,* Wilhelm Hofmeister and Ingo Scholz (eds), Johannesburg: Konrad Adenauer-Stiftung, 237–48.

Nkrumah, Kwame, 1964a. 'Some Aspects of Socialism in Africa', in *African Socialism*, William H. Friedland and Carl G. Rosberg Jr. (eds), Stanford: Stanford University Press, 259–63.

—— 1964b. *Consciencism*, London: Heinemann.

Norton, Bryan G. and Michael A. Toman, 1997. 'Sustainability: Ecological and Economic Perspectives', *Land Economics*, 73 (4): 553–68.

Nyerere, Julius K, 1964. 'Ujamaa: The Basis of African Socialism', in *African Socialism*, William H. Friedland and Carl G. Rosberg Jr. (eds), Stanford: Stanford University Press, 238–47.

Nyerere, Julius K, 1968. *Freedom and Socialism: A Selection from Writings and Speeches 1965–1967*, Dar es Salaam: Oxford University Press.

Nzouankeu, Jacque M, 1997. 'Stakes and Perspectives of Decentralisation as a Means of Achieving Democracy in Senegal', in *Traditional and Contemporary Forms of Local Participation and Self-Government in Africa,* Wilhelm Hofmeister and Ingo Scholz (eds), Johannesburg: Konrad Adenauer-Stiftung, 305–30.

O'Brien, Donal B. Cruise, 1971. *The Mourides of Senegal: The Political and Economic Organization of an Islamic Brotherhood*, Oxford: Oxford University Press.

OECD 1998 Development Co-operation Report, Statistical Annex (Tables 2, 25).

OECD 2002 Development Co-operation Report, Statistical Annex (Tables 2, 25).

Office of the Vice President, 1999. *The National Policy on Non-Governmental Organizations (NGOs) in Tanzania.* Draft. Dar es Salaam: Republic of Tanzania. (Unpublished).

Olorunsola, Victor A. with Dan Muhwezi, 1988. 'State Responses to Disintegration and Withdrawal: Adjustments in the Political Economy', in *The Precarious Balance: State and Society in Africa*, Donald Rothchild and Naomi Chazan (eds), Boulder, CO: Westview Press, 189–207.

Onuoha, Father Bede, 1965. *The Elements of African Socialism*, London: Andre Deutsch.

Oquaye, Mike, 1996. 'Government/Non Governmental Organisations Relations in Ghana: a Framework for Policy Formulation', in *Government and NGO Relations in Ghana*, Bridget Katsriku and Mike Oquaye (eds), Accra: Friedrich Ebert Foundation Accra, 1–37.

Padron, Mario, 1987. 'Non-Governmental Development Organizations: From Development Aid to Development Cooperation', *World Development*, 15 (supplement): 69–77.

Patterson, Amy S, 1999. 'The Dynamic Nature of Citizenship and Participation: Lessons from Three Rural Senegalese Case Studies', *Africa Today*, 46 (1): 3–27.

Perera, Jehan, 1997. 'In Unequal Dialogue with Donors: The Experience of the Sarvodaya Shramadana Movement', in *NGOs, States and Donors: Too Close for Comfort?* David Hulme and Michael Edwards (eds), London: Macmillan Press and The Save the Children Fund, 156–67.

Pérez, Carlos A, 1998. 'NGOs and Development: The Space for Social Science Intervention', in *Development Anthropologist*, 16 (1–2): 11–21.

Peter, Chris Maina, 1997. *Human Rights in Tanzania: Selected Cases and Materials*, Dar es Salaam: University of Dar es Salaam. (Unpublished).

——— 1999. *The State and Independent Civil Organisations: The Case of Tanzania Women's Council (BAWATA).* A Case Study prepared for the Civil Society and Governance in East Asia Project. (Unpublished).

Pfeffer, Jeffrey, 1981. *Power in Organizations*, New York: Harper Business.

——— 1992. *Managing with Power: Politics and Influence in Organizations*, Boston: Harvard Business School Press.

Pieterse, Edgar, 1997. 'South African NGOs and the Trials of Transition', *Development in Practice*, 7 (2): 157–66.

PROSHIKA, 1999. *Towards A Poverty-Free Society: PROSHIKA Five-Year*

Plan 1999–2004, Dhaka: Information and Documentation Resource Cell (IDRC).

PROSHIKA, 2001. *Semi-Annual Progress Report, Phase VI: No. 4*, Dhaka: Information and Documentation Resource Cell (IDRC).

PROSHIKA, 2002. Proshika Website. Available online at: http://www.proshika.org

Puplampu, Korbla P. and Wisdom J. Tettey, 2000. 'State-NGO Relations in an Era of Globalisation: The Implications for Agricultural Development in Africa', *Review of African Political Economy*, 27 (84): 251–72.

Qorro, Patrick S, 1993. 'Self-Help Organizations in the Sub-District of Karatu, Tanzania', in *Empowering People: Building Community, Civil Associations and Legality in Africa*, Richard Sandbrook and Mohamed Halfani (eds), Toronto: Centre for Urban and Community Studies, University of Toronto, 111–15.

Rafi, Mohammad and A.M.R. Chowdhury, 2000. 'Human Rights and Religious Backlash: The Experience of a Bangladeshi NGO', *Development in Practice*, 10 (1): 19–30.

Raftopoulos, Brian, 1996. *Zimbabwe: Race and Nationalism in a Post-Colonial State*, Harare: SAPES Books, Seminar Paper 10.

—— 2000. 'The State, NGOs and Democratisation', in *NGOs, the State and Politics in Zimbabwe*, Sam Moyo, John Makumbe and Brian Raftopoulos (eds), Harare: SAPES Books, 21–46.

Raftopoulos, Brian and Ian Phimister (eds), 1997. *Keep on Knocking: A History of the Labour Movement in Zimbabwe 1900–1997*, Harare: Baobab Books.

Ramesh, Janaki, 1995. 'Strategies for Monitoring and Accountability: the Working Women's Forum', in *Non-Governmental Organisations – Performance and Accountability: Beyond the Magic Bullet*, Michael Edwards and David Hulme (eds), London: Earthscan Publications and The Save the Children Fund, 95–102.

Ratha, Dilip, 2003. 'Workers' Remittances: An Important and Stable Source of External Development Finance', in *Global Development Finance 2003 – Striving for Stability in Development Finance*, The World Bank, Washington, DC: The International Bank for Reconstruction and Development/ The World Bank.

Ribeiro, Gustavo Lins, 1998. 'Cybercultural Politics: Political Activism at a Distance in a Transnational World', in *Cultures of Politics/Politics of Cultures: Re-Visioning Latin American Social Movements*, Sonia E. Alvarez, Evelina Dagnino and Arturo Escobar (eds), Boulder, CO: Westview Press, 325–52.

Rich Dorman, Sara, 2000. 'NGOs in Zimbabwe', *Britain Zimbabwe Society Review*, Issue 00/2.

—— 2001. *Inclusion and Exclusion: NGOs and Politics in Zimbabwe*, PhD Thesis, Oxford University.

Riddell, Roger C, 1987. *Foreign Aid Reconsidered*, London: James Currey.

Riddell, Roger C. and Mark Robinson, 1995. *Non-Governmental*

Organizations and Rural Poverty Alleviation, Oxford: Clarendon Press.

Roberts, Bill, 2000. 'NGO Leadership, Success and Growth in Senegal: Lessons from Ground Level', *Urban Anthropology*, 29 (2): 143–80.

Roland, Rachel J. and Rasha Omar, 2001. 'Case Study of a North-South Partnership: An Analysis of the Capacity-Building Process Between CDS, Cairo and CRDT, UK', in *Power and Partnership? Experiences of NGO Capacity-Building*, Rick James (ed.), INTRAC NGO Management and Policy Series (12), Oxford: INTRAC, 66–79.

Rose, Kalima, 1992. *Where Women Are Leaders: The SEWA Movement in India*, London: Zed Books.

Rothchild, Donald and Letitia Lawson, 1994. 'The Interactions between State and Civil Society in Africa: From Deadlock to New Routines', in *Civil Society and the State in Africa*, John W. Harbeson, Donald Rothchild, and Naomi Chazan (eds), Boulder, CO: Lynne Rienner Publishers, 255–81.

Sachs, Wolfgang, 1992. 'Introduction', in *The Development Dictionary: A Guide to Knowledge as Power*, Wolfgang Sachs (ed.), London: Zed Books, 1–5.

Sahley, Caroline, 1995. *Strengthening the Capacity of NGOs: Cases of Small Enterprise Development Agencies in Africa*, Oxford: INTRAC.

Sandberg, Eve, 1994. 'The Changing Politics of Non-Governmental Organizations and the African State', in *The Changing Politics of Non-Governmental Organizations and African States*, Eve Sandberg (ed.), Westport, CT: Praeger Publishers, 1–31.

Sandbrook, Richard, 1993. 'Introduction', in *Empowering People: Building Community, Civil Associations and Legality in Africa*, Richard Sandbrook and Mohamed Halfani (eds), Toronto: Centre for Urban and Community Studies, University of Toronto, 1–12.

Sanyal, Bishwapriya, 1991. 'Antagonistic Cooperation: A Case Study of Nongovernmental Organizations, Government and Donors' Relationships in Income-Generating Projects in Bangladesh', *World Development*, 19 (10): 1367–79.

Scruton, Roger, 1996. *A Dictionary of Political Thought*, London: Macmillan.

Senghor, Leopold, 1964. *On African Socialism*, London: The Pall Mall Press.

Shailo, Iqbal, 1994. 'Genesis and Growth of NGOs: Their Achievements and Successes in National Development', *Grassroots*, IV, Issue XIII–XIV: 9–30.

Short, Clare. *NGOs in a Global Future*. Speech at Birmingham University. 13 January 1999. Available online at: http://www.dfid.gov.uk

Simukonda, H.P.M, 1992. 'Creating a National NGO Council for Strengthening Social Welfare Services in Africa: Some Organizational and Technical Problems Experienced in Malawi', *Public Administration and Development*, 12 (5): 417–31.

Sithole, Masipula, 1997. 'Zimbabwe's Eroding Authoritarianism', *Journal of Democracy*, 8 (1): 127–41.

Skaar, Elin, 1994. *Human Rights Violations and the Paradox of Democratic Transition. A Study of Chile and Argentina*, Bergen, Norway: Chr. Michelsen Institute.

Sklar, Richard, 1986. 'Democracy in Africa', in *Political Domination in Africa: Reflections on the Limits of Power*, Patrick Chabal (ed.), Cambridge: Cambridge University Press, 17–29.

Smillie, Ian, 1995. *The Alms Bazaar*, London: Intermediate Technology Publications.

Smillie, Ian and John Hailey, 2001. *Managing for Change*, London: Earthscan.

Smit, Warren, 2001. 'The Changing Role of Community Based Organisations in South Africa in the 1990s, with Emphasis on Their Role in Development Projects', in *Associational Life in African Cities*, Arne Tostensen, Inge Tvedten and Mariken Vaa (eds), Stockholm: Nordiska Afrikainstitutet, 234–49.

Sobhan, Rehman, 1982. *The Crisis of External Dependence: The Political Economy of Foreign Aid to Bangladesh*, Dhaka: University Press Limited.

Sobhan, Babar, 1997. *Partners or Contractors? The Relationship Between Official Agencies and NGOs: Bangladesh*, INTRAC Occasional Paper Series 14.

Spodek, Howard, 1994. 'The Self-Employed Women's Association (SEWA) in India: Feminist, Gandhian Power in Development', *Economic Development and Cultural Change*, 43 (1): 193–202.

Stewart, Sheelagh, 1997. 'Happily Ever After in the Marketplace: Non-Government Organisations and Uncivil Society', *Review of African Political Economy*, 24 (71): 11–34.

Stockmann, Reinhard, 1997. 'The Sustainability of Development Projects: An Impact Assessment of German Vocational Training Projects in Latin America', *World Development*, 25 (11): 1767–84.

Strange, Susan, 1996. *The Retreat of the State: The Diffusion of Power in the World Economy*, Cambridge: Cambridge University Press.

Stremlau, Carolyn, 1987. 'NGO Coordinating Bodies in Africa, Asia and Latin America', *World Development*, 15 (supplement): 213–25.

Suhrke, Astri, 2003. 'From Relief to Social Services: An International Humanitarian Regime Takes Form', in *Eroding Local Capacity: International Humanitarian Action in Africa*, Monica Kathina Juma and Astri Suhrke (eds), Uppsala: Nordiska Afrikainstitutet, 19–34.

(The) *Sunday Mail*. 11 April 1999. 'UK, US Conspire to Oust Mugabe?', Harare, Zimbabwe.

(The) *Sunday Mail*. 18 July 1999. 'Misuse of Funds Alleged at ZimRights', Harare, Zimbabwe.

Sunday News. 5 January 1997. 'Bawata Told to Submit Constitution, Accounts'. Dar es Salaam, Tanzania.

Tacconi, Luca and Clem Tisdell, 1992. 'Rural Development Projects in LDCs: Appraisal, Participation and Sustainability', *Public Administration and Development*, 12 (3): 267–78.

Tandon, Yash, 1991. 'Foreign NGOs, Uses and Abuses: An African Perspective', *IFDA Dossier*, 81: 68–78.

Tandon, Rajesh, 2000. 'Riding High or Nosediving: Development NGOs in the New Millenium', *Development in Practice*, 10 (3 & 4): 319–29.

TANGO, 1994. *Needs and Opportunities of NGOs in Tanzania*. (Unpublished).

TANGO, 1999. 'The Making of a Policy for NGOs by the Government: Civil Society not Happy', *Semezana* (The TANGO Newsletter), 6 (2): 1.

Taylor, Lucy, 1998. *Citizenship, Participation and Democracy: Changing Dynamics in Chile and Argentina*, Basingstoke: Macmillan Press.

Tettey, Wisdom J, 2001. 'The Media and Democratization in Africa: Contributions, Constraints and Concerns of the Private Press', *Media Culture and Society*, 23 (1): 5–31.

TGNP, 1997. *Beyond Inequalities: Women in Tanzania*, Harare: Southern African Research and Documentation Centre (SARDC).

Therkildsen, Ole and Joseph Semboja, 1995. 'A New Look at Service Provision in East Africa', in *Service Provision Under Stress in East Africa: The State, NGOs and People's Organizations in Kenya, Tanzania and Uganda,* Joseph Semboja and Ole Therkildsen (eds), Copenhagen: Centre for Development Research; London: James Currey, 1–34.

Thomas, Alan, 1996. 'NGO Advocacy, Democracy and Policy Development: Some Examples Relating to Environmental Policies in Zimbabwe and Botswana', *The Journal of Commonwealth and Comparative Politics*, 34 (1): 38–65.

Thomas, Alan, 2001. 'NGOs and their Influence on Environmental Policies in Africa: a Framework', in *Environmental Policies and NGO Influence: Land Degradation and Sustainable Resource Management in Sub-Saharan Africa'*, Alan Thomas, Susan Carr and David Humphreys (eds), London: Routledge, 1–22.

Thomas, Alan, David Humphreys and Susan Carr, 2001. 'Influence Thrust Upon Them? NGOs' Role in Public Action on the Environment in Africa', in *Environmental Policies and NGO Influence: Land Degradation and Sustainable Resource Management in Sub-Saharan Africa'*, Alan Thomas, Susan Carr and David Humphreys (eds), London: Routledge, 171–91.

Tijmes, Peter and Reginald Luijf, 1995. 'The Sustainability of Our Common Future: An Inquiry into the Foundations of an Ideology', *Technology in Society*, 17 (3): 327–36.

Townsend, Janet Gabriel, 1999. 'Are Non-Governmental Organizations Working in Development a Transnational Community?', *Journal of International Development*, 11 (4): 613–23.

Townsend, Janet G., Gina Porter and Emma Mawdsley, 2002. 'The Role of the Transnational Community of Non-Governmental Organizations:

Governance or Poverty Reduction?', *Journal of International Develop-ment*, 14 (6): 829–39.

Tripp, Aili Mari, 1992. 'Local Organizations, Participation and the State in Urban Tanzania', in *Governance and Politics in Africa*, Goran Hyden and Michael Bratton (eds), Boulder, CO: Lynne Rienner Publishers, 221–42.

—— 2000. 'Political Reform in Tanzania: The Struggle for Associational Autonomy', *Comparative Politics*, 32 (2): 191–214.

—— 2001. 'The Politics of Autonomy and Cooptation in Africa: The Case of the Ugandan Women's Movement', *The Journal of Modern African Studies*, 39 (1): 101–28.

Tvedt, Terje, 1998. *Angels of Mercy or Development Diplomats?: NGOs and Foreign Aid*, Oxford: James Currey.

UNDP, 2002. *Human Development Report 2002*, New York: Oxford University Press.

UNDP, 2003. *Human Development Report 2003*, New York: Oxford University Press.

UNDP. Undated. *UNDP and Civil Society Organizations: Building Alliances for Development*, New York: UNDP.

UNDP Zimbabwe, 1999. *UNDP Zimbabwe Key Documents*, Harare: UNDP.

United Nations General Assembly, 2001. *Road Map Towards the Imple-mentation of the United Nations Millennium Declaration: Report of the Secretary-General*. Document A/56/326, 6 September 2001.

Urban and Rural Planning Department, 1999. *An Investigation of CBOs and NGOs Characteristics and Roles in Managing Urbanization*, Dar es Salaam: University College of Lands and Architectural Studies. Unpublished.

van Klinken, Marinus K, 1998. 'Beyond the NGO-Government Divide: Network NGOs in East Africa', *Development in Practice*, 8 (3): 349–53.

Van Pelt, Michiel J.F, 1993. *Ecological Sustainability and Project Appraisal*, Aldershot: Avebury.

Van Rooy, Alison, 1997. 'The Frontiers of Influence: NGO Lobbying at the 1974 World Food Conference, the 1992 Earth Summit and Beyond', *World Development*, 25 (1): 93–114.

—— 1998. 'Civil Society as Idea: An Analytical Hatstand?' in *Civil Society and the Aid Industry*, Alison Van Rooy (ed.), London: Earthscan, 6-30.

—— 2000. 'Good News! You May be Out of a Job: Reflections on the Past and Future 50 Years for Northern NGOs', *Development in Practice*, 10 (3 & 4): 300–18.

Van Tuijl, Peter, 2000. 'Entering the Global Dealing Room: Reflections on a Rights-Based Framework for NGOs in International Development', *Third World Quarterly*, 21 (4): 617–26.

Vener, Jessica I, 2000. 'Prompting Democratic Transitions from Abroad: International Donors and Multi-partyism in Tanzania', *Democratiza-tion*, 7 (4): 133– 62.

Villalón, Leonardo A, 1995. *Islamic Society and State Power in Senegal: Disciples and Citizens in Fatick*, Cambridge: Cambridge University Press.

—— 1999. 'Generational Changes, Political Stagnation, and the Evolving Dynamics of Religion and Politics in Senegal', *Africa Today*, 46 (3/4): 129–47.

Vivian, Jessica, 1994. 'NGOs and Sustainable Development in Zimbabwe: No Magic Bullets', *Development and Change*, 25 (1): 167–93.

Vudzijena, Vimbai, 1998. 'Land Reform and Community Based Natural Resource Management in Zimbabwe', in *Enhancing Land Reforms in Southern Africa*, F. Mutefpa, E. Dengu and M. Chenje, Harare: ZERO, 76–103.

Wade, Robert, 1990. *Governing the Market: Economic Theory and the Role of Government in East Asian Industrialization*, Princeton: Princeton University Press.

Wallace, Tina, 1997. 'New Development Agendas: Changes in UK NGO Policies and Procedures', *Review of African Political Economy* (71): 35–55.

—— 2002. 'The Role of Non-Governmental Organisations in African Development', in *Renewing Development in Sub-Saharan Africa*, Deryke Belshaw and Ian Livingstone (eds), London: Routledge, 230–47.

—— 2003. 'Trends in UK NGOs: A Research Note', *Development in Practice*, 13 (5): 564–69.

Wallace, Tina, Sarah Crowther and Andrew Shepherd, 1997. *Standardising Development: Influences on UK NGOs' Policies and Procedures*, Oxford: WorldView Publishing.

Wangoola, Paul, 1991. *De la crise africaine: la pleine participation des populations et des ONG indigènes au redressement et au développement de l'Afrique*. A Report of the African Association for Literacy and Adult Education.

WCED, 1987. *Our Common Future*, Oxford: Oxford University Press.

Wellard, Kate and James G. Copestake, 1993. 'Introduction', in *Non-Governmental Organizations and the State in Africa*, Kate Wellard and James G. Copestake (eds), London: Routledge,1–12.

Westergaard, Kirsten and Abul Hossain, 2002. 'Local Institutions in Bangladesh: An Analysis of Civil Society and Local Elections', in *In the Name of the Poor: Contesting Political Space for Poverty Reduction*, Neil Webster and Lars Engberg-Pedersen, London: Zed Books, 208–32.

White, Sarah C, 1999. 'NGOs, Civil Society, and the State in Bangladesh: The Politics of Representing the Poor', *Development and Change*, 30: 307–26.

Wils, Frits, 1995. 'Scaling-up, Mainstreaming and Accountability: the Challenge for NGOs', in *Non-Governmental Organisations – Performance and Accountability: Beyond the Magic Bullet*, Michael Edwards and David Hulme (eds), London: Earthscan Publications and The Save the Children Fund, 53–62.

Working Women's Forum, 2002. Working Women's Forum Website. Available online at: http://www.workingwomensforum.org

World Bank, 1996. *Pursuing Common Goals: Strengthening Relations Between Government and Development NGOs in Bangladesh*, Dhaka: University Press Limited.

World Bank, 1997. *Handbook on Good Practices for Laws Relating to Non-Governmental Organizations.* Discussion draft. Washington, DC: Environment Department.

World Bank, 2002. *World Development Report 2003*, New York: Oxford University Press.

Wunsch, James S, 1990. 'Foundations of Centralization: The Colonial Experience and the African Context', in *The Failure of the Centralized State: Institutions and Self-Governance in Africa*, James S. Wunsch and Dele Olowu (eds), Boulder, CO: Westview Press, 23–42.

Wunsch, James S and Dele Olowu, 1990. 'The Failure of the Centralized African State', in *The Failure of the Centralized State: Institutions and Self-Governance in Africa*, James S. Wunsch and Dele Olowu (eds), Boulder, CO: Westview Press, 1–22.

Yanarella, Ernest J. and Richard S. Levine, 1992. 'Does Sustainable Development Lead to Sustainability?', *Futures*, 24 (8): 759–74.

Young, Crawford, 1988. 'The African Colonial State and its Political Legacy', in *The Precarious Balance: State and Society in Africa*, Donald Rothchild and Naomi Chazan (eds), Boulder, CO: Westview Press, 25-66.

Young, Crawford, 1994. 'In Search of Civil Society', in *Civil Society and the State in Africa,* John W. Harbeson, Donald Rothchild and Naomi Chazan (eds), Boulder, CO: Lynne Rienner Publishers, 33–50.

Young, Crawford and Babacar Kante, 1992. 'Governance, Democracy and the 1998 Senegalese Elections', in *Governance and Politics in Africa*, Goran Hyden and Michael Bratton (eds), Boulder, CO: Lynne Rienner Publishers, 57–74.

(The) *Zimbabwe Independent.* 23 January 2002. 'Unemployment Rate to Reach 70%'. Harare.

ZWRCN, 1998. *Beyond Inequalities: Women in Zimbabwe*, Harare: Southern African Research and Documentation Centre (SARDC).